Inside a Juvenile Court

R

INSIDE A JUVENILE COURT:

The Tarnished Ideal of Individualized Justice

M. A. BORTNER

New York University Press
New York *and* London

Copyright © 1982 by New York University

Library of Congress Cataloging in Publication Data

Bortner, M. A., 1948–
Inside a juvenile court.
Bibliography: p.
Includes index.
1. Juvenile courts—United States. 2. Juvenile
delinquency—United States. I. Title.
KF9794.B67   345.73′081   82-6478
347.30581   AACR2
ISBN 0-8147-1041-7
ISBN 0-8147-1062-X   pbk.

Clothbound editions of New York University Press books are Smythe-sewn and printed
on permanent and durable acid-free paper.
p 10 9 8 7 6 5 4 3 2
c 10 9 8 7 6 5 4 3 2 1
Manufactured in the United States of America

Contents

1. **The Juvenile Court: Philosophy, Orientation, Controversy**   *1*

   The Emergence of an Experiment   *2*

   Innocence and Individualized Justice   *3*

   Positivistic Criminology and Social Reform   *4*

   An Age of Controversy and Transition   *5*

   The Tarnished Ideal   *8*

   The Dilemmas   *9*

2. **Going Inside: The Examination of an Ideal**   *15*

3. **The Beginning of the Process: Court Personnel and the Detention and Screening Decisions**   *21*

   The Research Setting   *22*

   The Decision-makers   *23*

   Statutory Guidelines   *26*

   The Referral Process   *27*

   The Detention Decision   *28*

   The Screening Decision   *33*

   Informal and Formal Processing   *35*

4. **Guilt and Punishment: Adjudication and Disposition**   *38*

   The Initial Hearing   *39*

Contested Hearings and Pretrial
Conferences   44

Disposition   46

Courtroom Sessions   57

Alternative Dispositions   58

5. External Considerations and Pressures   63

Police Involvement in Court Action   63

School Decisions   71

Parental Referrals   72

Treatment Facilities and Outside Agencies   82

6. The Basis for Decision-making   93

The Social Investigation and File   97

7. Legal Variables: The Offense   102

**8. Additional Legal Factors: Past Referrals; Degree
of Involvement; Legal Representation; Presiding
Officer**   123

Number and Nature of Past Referrals   123

"Number of Referrals": An Ambiguous
Variable   131

Degree of Involvement   132

Legal Representation   136

The Impact on Decisions   139

The Lack of Commitment   142

The Presiding Officer   143

**9. The Influence of Social Characteristics: The
Issue of Race**   148

Race and Discretion   149

The Black Dialect   160

CHAPTER 1

The Juvenile Court: Philosophy, Orientation, Controversy

A focal point of controversy since its inception in 1899, the juvenile justice system has been simultaneously heralded as a symbol of enlightenment and humanism as well as condemned as a bastion of discrimination and oppression. The court's most distinctive yet most controversial characteristics are its ideological emphasis on individualized justice and the unique organizational structure through which this philosophy is pursued.

Traditional juvenile justice philosophy depicts the court as nonpunitive and therapeutic, a legal institution whose espoused goals are the protection and guidance of children. It is praised as a socialized court offering individualized consideration and treatment on the basis of juvenile needs and characteristics. In order to implement the ideal of individualized justice, court personnel have been granted vast discretionary power. The nature and extent of that decision-making power as well as the procedures established to facilitate it are paramount issues in the controversy that presently engulfs the juvenile court.

Although not without detractors, the juvenile court has enjoyed an extended period of widespread acceptance and support within American society.[1] For over 80 years the prevailing interpretation of the court has depicted it as an expression of humanitarian sentiments in which children are not truly capable of criminal intent and the state, embodying the principle of *parens patriae,* is their benevolent protector.

Traditionally, court personnel have envisioned themselves as providing the protection necessitated by juveniles' inexperience and age: protection from adult exploitation and abuse and protection from their own youthful indiscretion. Not only has the juvenile court been portrayed as providing guidance and protection, but it has purported to do so in a manner tailored to the needs of each individual child. Few would deny that children need and have a right to be shielded from abuse and exploitation by adults and to receive reasoned counsel from mature, experienced advisors. Nevertheless, increasingly vocal critics have accused the court not only of failing to meet the needs of juveniles, but, equally damning, failing to protect society.

The juvenile justice system is an institution in crisis, one which can no longer rest on the rhetoric proclaiming individualized justice. Rather, it must face close scrutiny of the manner in which it has implemented that ideal. This book is about individualized justice, not the ideal, but the embodiment of that ideal within the context of a contemporary metropolitan juvenile court.

The Emergence of an Experiment

Created at the end of the nineteenth century, the juvenile justice system may be viewed as the culmination of several major historical elements: an era of vast social change; positivistic explanations of delinquency; a belief in scientific social work as a vehicle for rehabilitation; and the proliferation of social reform movements (Mennel, 1973; Schlossman, 1977; Ryerson, 1978).

The historical era in which the juvenile court emerged was foremostly a time of widesweeping social change and unrest. Immigration, industrialization, and urbanization combined to create a society of turmoil, one in which former values and institutions seemed incapable of supporting a new developing social structure. The plethora of reform movements designed to quell social unrest and restore the status quo encompassed many activities viewed as "social problems," including youthful misbehavior (Rothman, 1980; Dahl, 1977).

There are divergent interpretations of the juvenile court origins. One portrays the juvenile justice system as a thinly disguised system of oppression, dedicated to controlling the indigent and powerless (Platt, 1978; Krisberg, 1978). The founders of the juvenile system are viewed as representatives of the entrenched interests within society, actors engaged in a power struggle between the status quo and emergent challenges to that order. But the most pervasive image of the system's beginnings portrays it as a benign and child-oriented institution. In this interpretation founders of the juvenile system were well-intentioned reformers who sought to create an institution permitting a unique status for juveniles and providing the nurturance and guidance necessitated by a changing society. In this image, the court was a symbol of society's concern for its young, an expression of humanitarian sentiment and enlightened legal philosophy. This is the image that has dominated within American society, an image that presently is being challenged severely.

Innocence and Individualized Justice

The concept of criminal responsibility is central to traditional Anglo-American criminal law. Inherent in this concept is the assumption that criminal behavior is voluntaristic, that is, that crime is a willful breach of legal codes. Accordingly, criminal behavior is portrayed as freely chosen by the individual; the perpetrator is responsible and, most importantly, punishable for such behavior (Faust, 1974; Wales, 1976; Faust and Brantingham, 1977).

Despite this stance regarding free will and individual responsibility, the legal codes have traditionally acknowledged excusing conditions. Certain situations have been accepted as evidence demonstrating a lack of criminal intent, therefore absolving the individual of criminal responsibility. The conditions in which criminal behavior might be excused have included necessity (self-defense), insanity, and infancy.[2]

The legal tradition of depicting "infancy" as a mitigating circumstance and as a basis for excusing a child from full culpability necessitates specification of criteria for defining infancy. Historically, divergent images of adolescence and childhood have emerged; even so, infancy as an excusing factor has been defined disparately.[3] In the eighteenth and nineteenth centuries children were legally as responsible and punishable as adults, but, as Sanders (1945:58–70) and Platt (1977:193–212) have suggested, the judiciary was reticent to execute the harsher sentences meted out to children. Nevertheless, concern regarding the lack of care and special treatment for children has been viewed as a contributing factor to the creation of the juvenile court.

Reformers asserted that children must be afforded a unique status, one in which criminal responsibility is mitigated and the state acts as benevolent protector rather than vengeful punisher. But even though children were not to be punished, their unlawful behavior was of great concern to the society. Under the principle of *parens patriae,* the state was to assume the position of a substitute parent and intervene in the lives of wayward children. Thus, although they were relieved of full criminal responsibility, juveniles were given a unique status that facilitated extensive state involvement in their activities and development.

Positivistic Criminology and Social Reform

In addition to the creation of a unique status for children, the development of positivistic criminology and its promulgation by social reform movements were extremely influential in the creation of a unique juvenile justice system. In contrast to classical criminology's emphasis on crime as voluntaristic behavior, positivistic criminology stressed the influence of forces outside the individual's control, such as biological, psychological, and sociological conditions.

In what Faust and Brantingham term "a practical and optimistic slant," (1974:3) American reformers interpreted these theories as indication that criminal behavior might be curtailed through manipulation of such forces. For, indeed, if asocial behavior is beyond the will and control of the individual, the challenge to society is to identify and change criminogenic conditions.

Inherent in the concept of criminal behavior as treatable was the crucial idea that such behavior could be prevented through early diagnosis and intervention. This assumption was particularly attractive to moral entrepreneurs and social reformers concerned with the criminal tendencies and behavior of juveniles. Children were the "natural" beneficiaries of these theories: They were not truly responsible for unlawful acts, their lives were yet malleable, and their behavior patterns were susceptible to influence. Thus, the positivistic image of crime and the Americanized medical analogy of diagnosis and treatment were extremely influential in the formation of the juvenile justice system (Hawes, 1971:191–222; Jeffrey, 1971:24–36).

Coupled with the belief that criminal behavior could be prevented and treated was the emergent faith that science would provide the techniques necessary for such treatment. Positivistic criminology provided the vision, and scientific social work was to provide the vehicle for the prevention and treatment of delinquency. Thus, the juvenile justice system emerged as a separate and unique system, an experiment in socialized justice.

The theoretical distinctions between the juvenile court and the adult criminal court are many. The juvenile court is civil, not criminal; juveniles are "taken into custody," never arrested; a petition is filed "on behalf of" juveniles, not against them; allegations are made, but no criminal charges are filed; a hearing is held, but juveniles are not on trial; juveniles may be adjudicated "delinquent," but never convicted; juveniles may be found "in violation of the juvenile code," but they are never found guilty; and if allegations are ruled true, juveniles are supervised and treated, never punished (Johnson, 1974:1–17; Ellis, 1976:697–700; Caldwell, 1976:399–400; Blumberg, 1970:170–1).

All of the distinctions between the adult and juvenile system purportedly are made on behalf of juveniles and designed to provide a cloistered, confidential atmosphere in which juvenile life circumstances may be reviewed, problems diagnosed, and individualized treatment prescribed. Noting the theoretical distinctions, a major question becomes the extent to which they are reflected in present day realities. Numerous critics have charged that they are more rhetorical than real, and equally disparaging, that the advantages of such a structure are dubious.

An Age of Controversy and Transition

Few would deny the uniqueness of the juvenile court, but many question whether its unique structure and procedures do, in fact, benefit juveniles and society. The court is beset with criticism from people who hold vastly divergent perspectives: Some critics indict it as failing to meet the needs of the general community, while equally adamant opponents indict it for failing to meet the needs of juveniles. Retributionists and advocates of deterrence argue that the court's emphasis on treatment rather than punishment has thwarted the effectiveness of criminal law. Accordingly, a sense of moral unity should be created by punishing law violators, but the juvenile court's lenient treatment of adolescents undermines the moral structure of society. Lawbreakers must be punished in order to deter others from committing criminal acts (Platt, 1977:152–8; Faust and Brantingham, 1974:570–1).

Closely related to this critique is the assertion that the juvenile court is failing to protect the larger community from the unlawful acts of juvenile offenders. The involvement of juveniles in major property crimes and violent offenses has generated widespread criticism of the juvenile justice system as exceedingly permissive in their handling of adolescents. These critics suggest that such youngsters *do* have criminal intent and should be made accountable for their actions. According to this view, the juvenile court coddles criminals and fails to protect the interests and safety of the larger society adequately.

The court has simutaneously been indicted for its failure to meet the needs of juveniles. Increasing numbers of observers suggest that the distinctions between the juvenile and criminal courts are merely rhetorical homage to an ideal which has never been realized. More serious still, they suggest that the "uniqueness" of the juvenile court has not only failed to provide effective treatment but has served as a rationale for the denial of legal and human rights. This argument, often called the constitutionalist argument, challenges the informality of the court as well as its lack of concern for juvenile procedural rights. This critique argues that, under the guise of a benevolent protector, the traditional juvenile justice system not only fails to guide and treat, but equally important, it violates the basic tenets of fairness and due process. Accordingly, juveniles could be deprived of their freedom of choice and movement, but they are denied constitutional protection of their rights because the juvenile system is viewed as acting in "their best interests." The constitutionalist critique demands that the coercive and punitive potential of the system be acknowledged and that juveniles be afforded equal protection under the law.

In a series of decisions during the sixties and early seventies (*Kent v. United States, In re Gault, In re Winship, McKeiver v. Pennsylvania, Breed v. Jones*) the Supreme Court changed the complexion of American juvenile justice, granting some procedural rights during the adjudicatory ("guilt-finding") portion of delinquency proceedings and in cases involving decisions regarding the transfer of juveniles to the adult court. In delinquency proceedings that might result in commitment to a state institution juveniles were granted the right to timely notification of the specific charges against them, access to counsel, privilege against self-incrimination, and the right to confront and cross-examine witnesses. Equally important, proof beyond a reasonable doubt was established as the level of proof necessary for a juvenile to be adjudicated guilty. In cases dealing with transfer to the adult court, juveniles were granted access to counsel and all relevant juvenile court records, a judicial statement regarding the reasons for transfer, and protection against double jeopardy, that is, being prosecuted in adult court after having been found guilty in juvenile court.

Although decisions of the Supreme Court affecting juvenile offenders have been heralded as an indication of the ascendance of procedural rights, they cannot be construed as a mandate for the juvenile court to alter its basic orientation. Despite these decisions, the Supreme Court did not grant juveniles all the rights afforded adults. Juveniles do not have the right to release on bail when awaiting trial, the right to grand jury indictment before being charged with a serious crime, the right to a public trial, or the right to be tried before a jury rather than before a judge.

Thus, although the Supreme Court has ordered that juveniles be granted certain rights, it has also instructed the juvenile justice system to maintain informality, flexibility, and expediency in processing youthful offenders.[4] Equally important, all of the rulings pertain to the transfer of juveniles to adult court or to the adjudicatory portion of juvenile proceedings. No new guidelines have been established for preadjudication or disposition, that is, the sentencing or treatment phase.

In addition to facing controversy regarding juvenile procedural rights, the juvenile court presently confronts diverse challenges regarding its purpose and proceedings. Chief among these controversies are those pertaining to the potential stigmatizing of juveniles processed through the court, accusations that court personnel have used their discretionary powers in a discriminatory manner, and the contention that the court has failed to provide

nent. Essentially, the experiment in individualized
scrutinized, and, in the eyes of many, it has been

The Tarnished Ideal

The overriding issue within American juvenile justice and the
major concern of this analysis is whether or not the juvenile court
has realized its espoused mission of individualized treatment and
justice, and whether or not the actions of the court are, indeed,
beneficial to individual juveniles and the larger society. The grand
experiment must be evaluated and decision-makers, their procedures, and results challenged.

The controversies regarding the ideal of individualized justice
are myriad. They encompass both the basic concept as well as
the manner in which it has been given life within the juvenile
court. The very concept of individualized justice is equivocable,
for, by definition, it is in conflict with the principles basic to the
American philosophy of justice and the underlying tenets of the
legal system (Blumberg, 1970:169–177). Equity before the law
and due process as prerequisite for fairness form the keystone of
that rational-legal structure (Gerth and Mills, 1946:147–150).

But individualized justice abandons such principles and promises to provide justice within an individual context. Accordingly,
the concept of fairness and measures by which it is assessed are
obscured (Matza 1964:115–120). Rather than viewing justice as
a social relationship, the ideal of individualized justice envisions
justice as a personal experience and phenomenon. The quality
of justice can be assessed only by exclusive reference to the individual case.

The ideal of individualized justice is powerfully seductive, both
in its seemingly humanitarian concern with the individual and its
promise of mercy tailored to each person and each life circumstance.[5] It portends a vision of transcendent justice, one not confined to the average or established, but a superior justice finely
tuned to restore harmony between the individual and the collective.

Enticing as the ideal may be, its realization is the paramount
issue. The implementation of that ideal has been impeded, if not

rendered impossible, within the present social context. Paradoxically, the neglect of social context condemns that ideal to failure: The ideal is tarnished by harsh realities. Essentially, the ideal may provide a cloak for discrimination and injustice. Organizational expediency, structural inequities, professional ideologies, and the idiosyncracies of decision-makers all may take precedence over individual juvenile needs. And far superseding these concerns, the economic and political relations within society as a whole may relegate individualized justice to a meaningless, bureaucratized, and impersonal pursuit. The very institution premised upon the needs of juveniles may indeed cripple the human spirit rather than liberate it.

The Dilemmas

Many observers suggest that a child's experience with the juvenile justice system produces not rehabilitative treatment, but a far-reaching, irrevocable stigma. Accordingly, any beneficial influence exerted by the court is negated by its pejorative consequences: contact with the court may severely damage both the child's self-concept and social identity.

Critics argue that, although the intended function of the juvenile court may be benevolent, or the motivation of individual decision-makers admirable, the actual impact is often the converse of that ideal. They further assert that, in reality, the court's involvement in the lives of juveniles may burden them with a discredited social identity, as well as potentially initiating a life-long criminal career. Accordingly, even when the label "criminal" or "immoral" is not stated explicitly, the juvenile may perceive and internalize such condemnations as well as view the proceedings as punitive and vengeful in nature. Likewise, the court's insistence that it does not attach a label in no way negates the opinions and reactions of the larger community. Despite homage paid to confidentiality and anonymity, the courtroom experience and the label "juvenile delinquent" have lasting and consequential influences on the individual's life.

The experience of being the object of a court hearing (which the juvenile may perceive as a trial) or being placed in detention or a correctional institution (which the child may interpret as prison) have profound influence on the development and life chances of a juvenile. In addition to the subtle impact of a potentially degrading experience of contact with the juvenile court, there is an extremely practical dimension: school personnel, law enforcers, and future employers may be significantly influenced by the juvenile's involvement with the court (Lemert, 1970:138–41; Wheeler and Cottrell, 1966:22–7; Flicker, 1977:1–14; Emerson, 1969:172–88).

> In effect, the juvenile justice labeling process works to single out adolescents from groups culturally alien to those in power. Those singled out, because of their powerlessness, are ill-equipped to stop the process or to intervene in it effectively to prevent themselves from having various and sundry tags imposed upon them by police, judges, probation officers, psychiatrists and others who are employed as agents of the juvenile justice system. (Martin, 1970:3–4.)

A major criticism of the juvenile system asserts that, rather than providing benevolent therapy, the court acts in an insidious manner to control and punish minorities and members of the lower class. Numerous researchers who have examined the relationships between delinquency and class, race, and sex contend that the juvenile system acts in a discriminatory manner toward minorities, females, and juveniles of low socio-economic status. Not only are law enforcers and court personnel viewed as predisposed against these groups, but the entire institutional structure is portrayed as systematically oppressing, dehumanizing, and controlling these individuals (Platt, 1977; Schur, 1971; Werthman, 1972; Martin, 1970; Cohen, 1955; Terry, 1967; Thornberry, 1973). Others contend that differential treatment is meted out on the basis of parents' marital status, or juveniles' age, physical attractiveness, powers of self-expression, or ability to display appropriate remorse (Schur, 1973; Davis and Chaires, 1973; Cicourel, 1968; Emerson, 1969).

Other theorists and researchers assert that the criticisms given above are unfounded and exaggerated and that there is no conclusive evidence to demonstrate bias in the court's dealings with juveniles. Accordingly, a youth's referral to court and subsequent treatment are determined by legal variables, that is, seriousness of the offense, the number of referrals, and the court's individualized evaluation of the juvenile's situation (Berg, 1967; Polk, 1974; Gordon, 1976; Cohen and Kluegel, 1978, 1980). Disparate treatment represents not capriciousness or unfairness, but, rather, the fruits of individualized justice and the tailoring of treatment to the particular juvenile.

But the accusation of discrimination persists, and, essentially, those who make this charge insist that, rather than dealing with juveniles as individuals, the juvenile court processes cases by categorizing juveniles according to social distinctions, chief among these class, sex, and race. This is the very opposite of individualization; one's qualities, personality, and needs are systematically overshadowed by the social category to which the juvenile is relegated. Individualized justice abdicates to assembly line justice.

Indicative of the lack of individualized justice is the extent to which juveniles and their families are denied an active, meaningful role in the everyday decision-making process of the court. As the narratives throughout this volume attest, court personnel are routinely the subjects, juveniles are most frequently relegated to the status of objects. Particularly within the courtroom setting, and to a lesser extent during informal sessions, individual juveniles and parents are encapsuled in their stereotyped roles, not treated as individuals. In addition to the undeniable fact that juveniles rarely are afforded an opportunity to engage in the decision-making process or even verbal interaction, a more subtle indicator of this is the manner in which court personnel relegate juveniles and their parents to superficial roles rather than treating them as "individuals." Rarely do decision-makers refer to juveniles and their parents as specific individuals, identified by proper names. Ms. Jones becomes "Mother"; Mr. Whitehouse becomes "Father"; and Samantha Taylor becomes "Juvenile"—titles not even preceded by an adjective.

This depersonalization, the converse of individualized justice, approximates the "non-person treatment" of mental patients described by Erving Goffman. The social presence of the juvenile is minimized and yielded ineffective. And in those rare instances when the void is bridged, juvenile "outpourings" are not treated as directly usable statements of information, but as symptoms of their "illness," delinquency, and primarily discounted (Goffman, 1961:341–44, 367).

A lack of understanding regarding the process in which they are involved, and the lack of avenues for meaningful participation in the determination of their fate combine to create a situation where the court's own procedures provide evidence of the extent to which the ideal of individualized justice has been tarnished (Bortner, 1980).

> . . . the tragedy of the juvenile court lies not in its stigmatizing so many, but in its "saving" so few. (Emerson, 1969:275.)

Closely related to the above criticisms of the juvenile system is the controversy regarding juveniles' human and legal right to treatment. Established upon the principles of humanitarian concern and scientific treatment, many critics charge that the court has failed to demonstrate sufficient knowledge to adequately explain, treat, or deter delinquency. It is this apparent inability to realize its aspirations which has prompted many to challenge the legitimacy and authority of the juvenile court.

These opponents contend that children have been deprived of their freedom of choice and movement in the name of therapy, but little evidence exists to demonstrate the existence or effectiveness of such therapy. Critics charge that not only is the juvenile system characterized by a shortage of personnel and facilities, but even more telling, the juvenile system lacks the knowledge or techniques to rehabilitate juveniles effectively. As Schullenberger (1973:126) has aptly stated, the juvenile court may soon be relegated to "the status of a well intended failure which survived for close to a century on the faith that its concept was so good it had to work."

Few deny that the espoused orientation of the court—treatment rather than punishment—is humanitarian, but many suggest that the inadequacies of the system outweigh its noble intentions. If the state is authorized to "arrest" and "imprison" a juvenile under the guise of treatment, the juvenile must demand a right to effective treatment (Schullenberger, 1973:120; Lemert, 1970:135–44; Haskell and Yablonsky, 1974:402; Ellis, 1976:697–732). In return for curtailment of freedom of movement and liberty in decision-making, juveniles have been promised individualized consideration and treatment. Many indict the juvenile justice system as failing to honor its promise.

It can be regarded as a bargain or agreement whereby the state, through the juvenile court, is permitted to intervene under broadly defined conditions of delinquency or violations of law, in the lives of families who have given up certain of their constitutional safeguards.

Unless the state is required to make good its promises, American juveniles have exchanged the precious heritage of individual freedom under law for the tyranny of state intervention. . . . (quoted in Rosenheim, 1962:22.)

Many have indicted the juvenile justice system for failing to realize its noble goals, and equally damning, many critics have accused the court of using its considerable power to systematically deny justice to juveniles. No longer in its infancy, the juvenile court has come of age and finds itself in a society extremely skeptical of its activities and achievements. The court now struggles to silence its accusers and reassert its role within modern American society.

The present journey inside a large metorpolitan juvenile court addresses many of these crucial issues. It discloses the process through which decisions are made and probes the social and legal factors that influence the wielders of power within the juvenile justice system. It seeks to provide an inside view of a juvenile court as it actually works and to assess the quality of individualized justice as operationalized in twentieth century America.

Notes

1. See Edward E. Waite "How Far Can Court Procedure be Socialized Without Impairing Individual Rights?" *Journal of the American Institute of Criminal Law and Criminology,* 12:339–47; Julian M. Mack "The Juvenile Court," *Harvard Law Review,* 23:104–22 (1909); Monrad G. Paulsen "Fairness to the Juvenile Offender," *Minnesota Law Review,* 41:547–76 (1957); Paul W. Tappan "Treatment Without Trial," *Social Forces,* 24:306–20 (1946).

2. Many have viewed this characteristic of criminal law—the excusing of certain individuals from punishment—as evidence of humanitarian influences within the society and legal system. As Judge David Bazelon has said, "Our collective conscience does not allow punishment where it cannot impose blame" (Blumberg, 1974:273–4). In such a view, concern for the individual compels the society to make exceptions, thus individualizing judgments and dispositions (Fletcher,

1974:1300). Likewise, the most appropriate method of dealing with the irresponsible individual is through treatment, not punishment.

From another perspective, the excusing of individuals from punishment is the result of logical and practical considerations regarding the purpose of conviction and punishment. If one primary objective of criminal law is the deterrence of future crime through the negative example of punished offenders, the irresponsible individual does not provide an effective example. Accordingly, no principle can be demonstrated, no public good accomplished.

3. For a thorough discussion of the historical development of the image and status of children see Aries (1962), Stern, Smith and Doolittle (1975), Marks (1975), Mennel (1973) and deMause (1974).

4. Thus, the juvenile court is instructed to combine the procedural safeguards of the adult criminal court with the informality and treatment ideals of the traditional juvenile system. Many question whether both objectives can be accomplished simultaneously. Others such as Judge John Steketle (1973:22–3) suggest that only through strict separation of adjudication and disposition can both objectives be realized: due process should be carefully observed during adjudication and treatment considerations should dominate the dispositional phase.

A further dilemma concerns the degree to which juvenile rights, granted by federal courts, are upheld in the state and local jurisdictions. Supreme Court decisions may challenge the existing structure, but they do not automatically insure full extension of those rights to juveniles. The true test of these decisions will be the extent to which they are implemented by the lower courts (Lefstein, Stapleton and Teitelbaum, 1969; Duffee and Siegel, 1971; Platt, 1977).

5. Despite the prevalent assumption that the basic concept of individualized justice is a benevolent and enlightened one, even if it has not been realized, dissenters suggest that, despite this facade, the very idea implies individualized punishment. "Punishment which is designed to fit the offender rather than the offense may be more coercive and intrusive than traditional penalties" (Platt 1977:15).

CHAPTER 2

Going Inside: The Examination of an Ideal

Getting inside a juvenile court can be a labyrinthian journey. By definition the court is confidential and closed to the public. Traditionally this statutorily dictated policy has been justified as a prerequisite to protecting juveniles from stigmatizing public exposure as "offenders." But within the past decade critics have denounced this confidentiality as providing a shroud for court personnel rather than privacy for troubled juveniles. Accordingly, juvenile courts have been depicted as demonic creatures wrapped in a cloak of secrecy: Thus, I began the research with considerable concern regarding its feasibility. I did not have an "in": I knew no one within the judicial bastion.

My introduction to the court was a conversation with a flamboyant social worker with strong opinions regarding the unrealistic, irrelevant pursuits of academics—especially as they pertain to the juvenile court. His pointed remarks that academics criticize the court without actually observing what goes on there elicited my reply that I wished to correct that fault in myself. At the end of our discussion I inquired whether or not it would be possible to observe a hearing; he referred me to one of the four presiding officers in the juvenile court, who, according to my new acquaintance, was "the friendliest person at the court." The presiding officer politely informed me the first hearing would begin shortly and invited me to step inside the courtroom. There I sat, alone, in a conference size room with flags, a long table, and the judicial bench. I could hear "them" in the outer office discussing the upcoming case. There they were—the intended objects of my study—and here I was, steadily observing inanimate flags, chairs and a gavel. Mercifully, the hearing began within a few moments and, despite the fact I only partially comprehended the proceeding, I was at last observing court personnel and their activities.

My integration into the courthouse setting was underway and I soon discovered a court open to my inquiries. I was permitted constant and uncensored access to court activities throughout the next nine months. During that time I observed over 250 juvenile delinquency hearings, including the activities of the presiding officers in their chambers both before and after hearings. Access to the latter made possible the present analysis, for without the benefit of informal discussions among personnel it is impossible to assemble the puzzle called the decision-making process. For as the following pages indicate so clearly, formal proceedings within the courtroom represent only one, relatively minor, aspect of decision-making. While participating in the daily life of the court I discovered the manner in which a juvenile court actually functions and found it to be far different than official rhetoric portends and far more complex than critics acknowledge.

Even when one is familiar with the general organizational structure, basic philosophy, and statutes regarding juveniles, each court represents a unique approach to the implementation of legislative edicts. Thus, it was necessary for me to become familiar with the organizational structure of this particular court, as well as the idiosyncracies of each courtroom. An understanding of legal jargon, procedures, and the function of various court personnel was prerequisite to examining decision-making within the juvenile justice system. An initial task was to identify the roles of various participants: Familiarity with seating arrangements within the courtroom and introductions to court personnel aided in eliminating my initial confusion.

Other difficulties which had to be overcome included gaining regular access to dockets (McCall, 1978), and, at a later stage in the study, arranging a schedule to observe cases in all four courtrooms. The kindness and interest of the court clerks and the receptionist were invaluable in affording access to such information without creating a nuisance. My acculturation to the courtroom setting was greatly facilitated by the extreme openness and generosity of courtroom participants, particularly one hearing officer and her clerk. Fortunately, court personnel volunteered much important information, as well as providing introductions to other court personnel essential to my understanding and indoctrination.

My presence within the courtroom was accommodated easily. Unlike many other fieldwork settings in which an "inactive" participant might be considered unusual and note-taking viewed suspiciously, a silent observer was appropriate within the formal atmosphere of the courtroom. Likewise, the role of the researcher resembles that of legal personnel such as court clerks or bailiffs. Silent participation is not unusual and the sedentary investigator does not interfere with the decorum.

The present analysis is derived from three major sources of information: daily observation of courthouse activities, including 250 hearings (trials); in-depth interviews with a random sample of decision-makers; and statistical analysis of all cases of juveniles referred to the court within the year (approximately 10,500 referrals for delinquent behavior).

The initial phase of the project was the observation of formal delinquency hearings. Formal hearings are distinquished from other proceedings in that a formal petition has been filed against ("on behalf of") the juvenile and if allegations are ruled true, the court is empowered to take jurisdiction and effect legally binding orders which supersede juvenile or parental desires. It is this action which truly initiates a juvenile's involvement in the legal system and makes her or him a candidate for more extensive state intervention. Delinquency hearings pertain to alleged juvenile behavior which is either analogous to adult misdemeanors or felonies, or status offenses, legally proscribed behavior unique to juveniles, such as incorrigibility, running away from home, truancy, violation of curfew, and consumption of alcohol.

The observations provided a very encompassing introduction to the manner in which this specific court implements the concept of individualized justice. They were conducted in four courtrooms, one in which a circuit judge presided (the official juvenile judge) and three in which hearing officers (referees) presided. A major objective of the observations was to focus on the interaction between official participants and to explore the manner in which they negotiated dispositions, including the resolution of any conflicts. A further concern was the manner in which the court implemented the legal rights of juveniles, including the role and influence of defense attorneys when present. Attention was also given to the actions of juveniles and their parents: A foremost concern was the extent to which they were either encouraged to participate actively or subtly relegated to a passive role in the decision-making process.

Narratives from the earliest observations, approximately one-fourth of the cases, were written immediately after leaving the courtroom; but the dialogues of the rest were recorded during the actual proceedings. In addition to the hearings, I had continual access to pre-hearing and post-hearing conversations, both official and unofficial. Likewise, court personnel were questioned informally regarding their recommendations and decisions, and frequently decision-makers volunteered explanations, justifications, or reservations regarding the cases.

First-hand observation of courthouse activities is essential, for it reveals the multitude of considerations that precede the court's final disposition of a juvenile's case. To understand decision-making one must delineate the process through which cases are handled, identify key decision-makers, explore the alternatives they have, and examine the organizational, legal, and social factors which shape their decisions. Interaction between official participants, resolution of conflicts between court personnel, and the roles played by juveniles and their families are all crucial elements of the process.

Understanding of the final disposition is possible only after observing the interaction between court personnel and the negotiation of decisions. Not only are official explanations for recommendations and decisions important, but the unspoken background expectancies which guide decision-making are even more revealing. In addition to noting the explanations and justifications offered by decision-makers, I sought to discover the frame of reference employed to provide such interpretations of the juvenile's case history, attitude, and behavior (Garfinkel, 1964:226; Cicourel, 1968:7–8). The dispensing of individualized justice is an exercise in reality creating, one in which negotiations and compromises dominate.

After observing hundreds of trials, I conducted interviews with the four presiding officers and a random sample of the prosecuting attorneys and court workers (probation officers, intake personnel, community service personnel), as well as the public defender assigned to the court. All of the decision-makers interviewed had been observed in both formal and informal settings during the previous months. The interview questions were designed to probe the many controversies which became apparent during the observations. The richness of the exchanges during interviews was enhanced by the decision-makers' familiarity and comfortableness with the interviewer. Court personnel frequently referred to past cases, framing their responses in terms of shared experiences.

The twenty-eight interviews ranged from one to three hours in duration and provided further explanation and insight into the roles of decision-makers. They focused on the alternatives available (as decision-makers perceived them), consultations with other decision-makers, and interactions with juveniles and their families. Decision-makers were asked to explain the factors which influence the decisions they make, with emphasis on the meaning of categories they use and the criteria they employ to decide the future of juveniles. They were asked to explain commonly used and infrequently analyzed phrases such as "a good attitude," "a stable family," or "hard-core delinquent." Their explanations, rationalizations, and opinions regarding their activities provide the backdrop for the following critique of the juvenile justice system.

In addition to the observations and interviews which form the bulwark of the following work, statistical analysis was used to examine several crucial decisions regarding a year's cohort of juveniles referred to the court for delinquency, approximately 10,500 referrals. The three major decisions examined are the detention decision (whether or not to detain a juvenile prior to adjudication), the screening decision (whether or not to process a case informally or formally), and the final disposition (the treatment or sentencing decision). The multivariate analysis provides a portrait of a large sample of cases, encompassing a much greater number of cases than would be possible to observe directly. It focuses on the influence juvenile characteristics exert on the decision-making process, exploring the impact a juvenile's social background and legal history have on the decisions of juvenile court personnel.

Once access has been gained to court records, statistical analysis would be possible without further interaction with court personnel or further inquiry into the court's organizational structure. Nevertheless, thorough analysis of statistical findings is virtually impossible without the insights gained from observational analysis. Official court files are sufficient to discover that certain variables are highly correlated with decisions, but extensive involvement in the everyday life of a court is necessary to explain *why* such variables are important.

The following pages consist primarily of the words and thoughts of decision-makers. Narratives of courtroom activities and opinions stated during interviews dominate the analysis. What emerges is the very subjective, human process of decision-making: It is a multi-dimensional portrait, one which involves not only the decision-makers and the juveniles whose lives they dominate, but it is a portrait which reflects the struggles of the larger society.

The words and actions of judges, attorneys and social workers reveal them to be not masters of socialized justice but limited human beings making decisions. They often appear as bureaucrats motivated primarily by organizational expediency and necessity; at times they appear as petty wielders of power over juveniles. But they emerge most clearly as finite human beings "doing justice" within a structure which espouses protection and guidance for juveniles but lacks the knowledge and ability to provide it. The court personnel appear not as individuals making noble or confident decisions, but as uncertain rulers choosing between equally bad alternatives. They are not champions of the ethic of individualized justice, nor saviors of children; rather, they are representatives of a judicial system in which individualized justice is deeply tainted with the uncertainty and inequity of the larger society.

CHAPTER 3

The Beginning of the Process: Court Personnel and the Detention and Screening Decisions

The juvenile court is in the business of making decisions regarding juveniles. Court personnel continually evaluate juveniles' situations and lives and take actions which greatly influence the futures of countless young people. There are numerous junctures in this complex process, and the decisions reached at each step influence subsequent decisions, as well as juveniles' experience within the system. The nature of those decisions made by court personnel and the criteria they use, objective and subjective, are among the major concerns of this book.

It is important to recognize that the juvenile court process is not a mechanistic one. Rather, it is a process which has numerous alternative paths, one which is determined to a great extent by the professional ideology and personal idiosyncracies of the decision-makers involved in a particular case, as well as by organizational dimensions of the particular court. Which social worker is assigned to the case, which judge conducts the hearing, and which correctional institution has available bed space are often more consequential in the outcome of a case than are the "facts" surrounding the alleged delinquency or the personality and life situation of the individual juvenile.

Although decisions, miniscule and great, are made throughout each case, there are three major decision points upon which we will focus. They include the decision whether or not to detain a juvenile in secure custody prior to trial; the screening decision of whether or not a juvenile's case should be handled informally or formally; and the final disposition regarding what action should be taken and whether the court should become involved in the juvenile's life on a continuing basis, that is, whether or not a juvenile should be put on probation, placed outside the home in an open setting or incarcerated in a correctional institution. To understand this complex system it is necessary to describe the roles of individuals involved in each phase of decision-making, delineate the organizational guidelines for processing referrals, and examine the factors which influence the exercise of discretionary power.

The Research Setting

The research was conducted at a large midwestern county juvenile court, one which serves the largest and most affluent county in the state. Approximately 4.8 percent of the population is black and an additional .4 percent is nonwhite. Of the county's population, 34.2 percent is below the age of majority and thus within the jurisdiction of the court. Juveniles account for an estimated 29.7 percent of the total police apprehensions and arrests in the county, excluding those for traffic violations.

The court serves over 90 municipalities, involving 30 police departments and 25 school districts. The court employs a staff of over 200 persons. Approximately two-thirds of the staff work with juveniles charged with delinquent behavior; there are nine delinquency-intake workers, 21 delinquency supervision workers (probation officers), 15 clinical services workers (psychological testing and family treatment), 38 short-term counseling workers for informal processing, and 35 detention staff members.

The court processes approximately 18,000 referrals a year, more than any other juvenile court in the state. Of those, approximately 58 percent are delinquency referrals. An estimated one-fourth of the delinquency referrals are processed through formal hearings, and the remaining are handled informally (dismissed by the legal department due to insufficient evidence or improper handling, informal adjustments, deterrence programs, short-term counseling, informal hearings). Approximately 21 percent of the delinquency referrals involve behavior analogous to adult felonies; 39 percent involve behavior analogous to adult misdemeanors; and 39 percent involve status offenses (offenses unique to juveniles).

The court is notable for both its affluence and diversity of programs. Residential treatment facilities used by the court include delinquency foster homes, county operated group homes, and private treatment facilities, including group homes and institutions licensed by the state and contracted with by the court. The court also uses the services of the Department of Mental Health and the State Department of Corrections. The latter is the state's juvenile correctional system which includes two secure institutions (a female and male prison) as well as group homes and a camp setting for males.

In addition to residential programs, the court operates numerous nonresidential treatment programs. Foremost among these are its General Equivalency Diploma (G.E.D.) Program designed to assist high school drop-outs to complete their education; and a "Youth Opportunity Program" designed to "offer services in employment counseling, motivational training, and job placement," as well as G.E.D. classes. The court also operates a federally funded family treatment unit as part of a program for the diagnosis and treatment of learning disabilities. The court maintains an extensive short-term counseling program designed to deter the majority of referrals from the formal courtroom process, as well as community-based shelter care facilities to minimize the number of status offenders who otherwise would have to be held in secure detention facilities.

The Decision-makers

The court maintains four courtrooms, one in which the juvenile judge presides and three in which hearing officers (referees) preside.[1] The juvenile judge is an elected member of the circuit court who is selected by that body to preside at the juvenile court. The term of office is two years with a possibility of a one year extension.[2] The judge presides over all adoptions, terminations of parental rights, and certification proceedings (transfer of juvenile offenders to the adult court).

The three hearing officers are attorneys appointed by the juvenile judge and serve at his pleasure.[3] Due to the rotation system among judges, hearing officers are frequently appointees of former judges. They serve in a capacity analogous to referees and preside over the bulk of cases involving status offenses, misdemeanors, as well as felonies. Together the hearing officers process approximately 80 percent of all cases referred to a hearing. In addition to delinquency cases, they hear all traffic violations in which certification to the adult court is not being considered. One hearing officer handles all neglect cases not set before the judge. All juveniles whose cases are heard before hearing officers have the right to appeal the decision to the judge, but this right is rarely invoked.[4]

In addition to the judge and hearing officers, three major groups of court personnel are routinely involved in the processing of delinquency referrals. They include those in the court's legal department, others in the psychological services department, and delinquency workers who are intake workers, members of the short-term counseling unit, and probation officers ("supervision workers"). The court was first in the state to establish a legal department as a permanent court unit, and has maintained such a unit for over ten years. Although the term "prosecuting attorney" is rarely used, members of the legal department (court attorneys) perform the same functions as the adult criminal prosecutors. Their primary responsibility is to provide legal counsel to the court's social work and psychological staff members.

As well as representing court personnel, the legal department often constitutes an independent voice in the decision-making process. In pretrial conferences and other informal discussions, the judge routinely requests the opinion of the court attorneys, and it is not unusual for them to offer suggestions which differ from the opinions of the court workers.

Most court workers insist that the legal department's sole responsibility is to represent court worker decisions. Although some members of the legal department concur with this view, others view themselves as serving as a legal representative for social workers *and* as a protector of community interests. Court attorneys espousing this viewpoint often suggest more severe dispositions than those recommended by court workers. Naturally, these differences in opinion are occasionally the source of conflict between decision-makers.

Members of the court's delinquency intake, short-term counseling, and probation units form the bulwark of court activity and decision-making. They participate in the screening of delinquency referrals, conduct social investigations into juvenile activities, prepare recommendations for the disposition of cases, provide short-term counseling for juveniles not going to a hearing, and serve as probation officers for juveniles over whom the court has taken jurisdiction.

Despite the fact that they prefer to be called court workers or juvenile officers rather than social workers, the activities and orientations of these individuals reflect the social work tradition. And although observance of due process and juvenile legal rights is among their responsibilities, they adhere to the casework orientation which emphasizes the rehabilitative, therapeutic potential of the juvenile justice system (Tappan 1949:3–30). Indicative of this viewpoint is the chief social worker's title, "Chief Juvenile Officer and Treatment Coordinator."[5] Although several have Masters of Social Work degrees, the majority of personnel loosely termed "social workers" have degrees in such areas as psychology, sociology, or criminal justice. The B.A. is required; approximately 20 percent of the workers hold masters degrees and many are working toward an advanced degree.

The clinical services department has a staff holding professional degrees in clinical and child psychology, as well as "social workers" who specialize in counseling or family therapy. The court also regularly uses private psychiatrists as consultants. The clinical services department conducts psychological testing, prepares dispositional recommendations, directs family counseling sessions, and is involved in the diagnosis and treatment of learning disabilities. Psychological evaluation of juveniles is often requested by social workers and occasionally by the presiding officer prior to disposition. The court is also statutorily empowered to order psychological evaluation of parents, although they rarely do so in delinquency cases. (It is more common in cases alleging parental neglect and abuse.) When psychological testing of parents is thought to be necessary, court policy is to seek voluntary compliance if possible.

In only one of 250 cases observed did the court request a parent undergo psychological evaluation. The case involved a 13-year old black male accused of forcing younger children to participate in sodomy. The presiding officer and court worker perceived the mother's reaction as one of dispassionate indifference and considered it both inappropriate and suspicious. The mother voluntarily underwent psychological testing upon the court's request.

Statutory Guidelines

State statutes reflect the traditional philosophy concerning the administration of juvenile justice in the United States:

> . . . to facilitate the care, protection, and discipline of children who come within the jurisdiction of the juvenile court . . . to the end that each child shall receive such care, guidance and control . . . as will conduce to the child's welfare and the best interests of the state. . . .
>
> JUVENILE CODE

The juvenile court has jurisdiction over all youths under the age of majority who reside within the county, as well as any juvenile alleged to have violated the juvenile code in that county. In order to take jurisdiction over a juvenile, the court must file a petition and rule the allegations contained in that petition to be true. Only when the court has taken jurisdiction may it enter legally binding orders which supersede parental or juvenile desires: such juveniles are under the court's jurisdiction.[6]

The Juvenile Code delineates four general conditions under which the court may become actively involved in the lives of children "alleged to be in need to care and treatment," and if allegations are found true, to take jurisdiction:

a) The parents or other persons legally responsible for the care and support of the child neglect or refuse to provide proper support, education which is required by law, medical, surgical or other care necessary for his well being. . . .
b) The child is otherwise without proper care, custody or support. . . .
c) The behavior, environment or associations of the child are injurious to his welfare or to the welfare of others. . . .
d) The child is alleged to have violated a state law or municipal ordinance. . . .

Of these four general allegations, the last two are germane in delinquency cases. According to administrative policy established by the legal department, the court relies mostly on the "behavior injurious" clause (c) as the statutorial headline in the majority of delinquency petitions. It employs the fourth alternative, "alleged to have violated a state law or municipal ordinance," only when entering a motion to certify the juvenile for transfer to the adult court. The court views its use of the general allegation "injurious behavior" as more consistent with its emphasis on treatment, rather than criminal prosecution.

In addition to a general allegation, the court is legally required to specify juveniles' behavior that brought them to the attention of the court. Although the statutes only require a descriptive statement, the court's legal department usually relies upon language contained in adult criminal statutes to specify the alleged activity. For example, rather than describing a juvenile's behavior as "attacking another," the petition will read "The juvenile's behavior, environment or associations are injurious to his welfare or to the welfare of others." It will then specify the date on which the alleged activity occurred and specify "assault with intent to do great bodily harm." Thus, although the juvenile code does not delineate specific offenses, the juvenile's alleged behavior will be described in terms similar to those used to describe adult crimes.

Although the court's use of the "injurious behavior" allegation is an attempt to minimize stigmatization of a juvenile, the specifications which are often stated in terms of adult criminal charges may negate that intention. Technically the juvenile has not been charged with a criminal act, but the language of the petition may be easily interpreted in that way by juveniles and parents.

The Referral Process

Referral to the juvenile court is the most severe legal option available to law enforcement officials, community agencies, school personnel, and parents (Piliavin and Briar 1964; Black and Reiss 1970; Ferdinand and Luchterhand 1970; Wilson 1968; Goldman 1963). This decision which initiates a juvenile's encounter with the court is beyond the purview of court personnel.

Accordingly, court personnel view their involvement with a juvenile as the response to community or family pressures.

The vast majority of referrals to the court, 96.7 percent are made by law enforcement officials. (This figure is somewhat misleading because in an incalculable number of referrals involving status offenders, especially runaways and incorrigibles, the police report merely reflects parental decisions to bring their child to court. Thus, what is officially recorded as a police referral originated as a parental referral.) Officially, parental referrals constitute only .1 percent of all referrals, school referrals 2.2 percent social agencies .1 percent, and "others" .9 percent. The final category includes referrals from other courts, police departments outside the court's jurisdiction, and private citizens.

Once the juvenile has been referred to court, there are several major decisions which effect the juvenile's subsequent involvement or non-involvement in the court system. Crucial junctures include the detention decision, screening decision, adjudication and disposition.

The Detention Decision

The decision to detain juveniles when they are first apprehended is the first major decision in the process. Despite the fact it is a decision which has tremendous impact on subsequent decisions about the juvenile's fate, the detention decision is an ill-defined and loosely controlled issue. Theoretically and statutorily, this decision is within the province of court personnel, but in actuality the decision is usually made by law enforcement officials.

When they take juveniles into custody, police have numerous options, including the alternative of taking the juvenile to the Juvenile Court Center for questioning and possible detention. Statutorily, law enforcement officers are required to question juveniles within the presence of a court worker and the final decision of whether or not to detain belongs to the court. Official policy notwithstanding, officers routinely decide whether to detain unilaterally. It is not uncommon for even juveniles allegedly involved in felonies to be questioned and released by the police—thus aborting the juvenile court's control over the detention decision.

Officially, there are three criteria for determining whether or not a juvenile should be held in secure custody prior to court action. Juveniles may be detained if they are considered a danger to the community, a danger to themselves; or likely to abscond prior to the hearing date (likely to flee the area prior to future court action in the case).

Although the official criteria for deciding on the advisability of detaining a youth are statutorily determined and seemingly straightforward, such is not the case. Numerous other factors come into play, organizational aspects of the juvenile court as well as extraneous factors over which court personnel have minimal control. In addition to police decisions preempting court procedure, parental desires on whether or not to allow the juvenile to return home are often crucial. There are numerous occasions on which court personnel feel a juvenile should not be detained, but parents insist to the contrary. Likewise, juveniles occasionally refuse to go home.

In addition to parental desires whether or not to allow the juvenile to return home, it is possible for juveniles to be held in "protective detention" because the court feels other members of the community pose a threat to their physical safety. In one case a court worker stated that a juvenile had been detained because he had been beaten severely by the police and the court worker felt his release would result in further confrontations.

The vast majority of juveniles, 83 percent, are not detained. Approximately 50 percent of those who are held in detention are released to their parents within four hours. Thus, few juveniles taken into custody remain in detention for an extended period of time. But for those juveniles who are held, the decision has far-reaching consequences.

State statutes stipulate that the juvenile court must conduct a detention hearing for any juvenile who requests such a proceeding and that such a hearing must be granted within four working days of the request. At the court under inquiry, detention hearings are not conducted automatically but must be requested by the juvenile. For numerous reasons not all juveniles request hearings: their parents may refuse to take them home; they may not fully understand their rights to such a hearing; or court personnel may discourage them from seeking such a hearing.

> Some [court workers] literally will say, "Well, you have the right to a detention hearing, but don't bother, because you can't get out anyway." Arguing against it without fully informing them that what that means is that the child has a very good chance to get out no matter what the worker's recommendation is. . . .
>
> PUBLIC DEFENDER

Due to the paucity of available information, the detention decision is extremely subjective. Not only do defense attorneys complain about the lack of objective criteria, but at least one hearing officer expressed great dissatisfaction with the hurried and ambiguous nature of the decision. It is not uncommon for detention hearings to be conducted in which no police report is available and/or no official charges have been filed by the court's legal department. The proceeding often degenerates into the intake or probation officer insisting that the juvenile *must* be detained and the juvenile's attorney insisting to the contrary. Most commonly, the presumption is in favor of the court personnel. In addition to legitimate concerns regarding the child's well-being, other less laudable factors may be crucial. One such influence is logistical in nature: if the juvenile is detained, the intake or probation officer will have daily access to the juvenile "to work up the case", thus making their jobs easier.

As will be demonstrated shortly, the fact that a juvenile is detained exerts tremendous influence on subsequent court decisions regarding the future, but, equally important, it has very immediate consequences for children. Juvenile justice rhetoric notwithstanding, those who are detained are essentially in jail.

Despite attempts to provide educational and recreational activities, detention is not a rehabilitation facility and the harsher dimensions of the experience are undeniable. Juveniles are in jail. They are detained against their wishes, confined to a limited space, afforded limited privileges, clothed in institutionally dictated apparel, and bedded in 9' x 12' locked cells. They are subjected to the potentially negative effects of incarceration such as the psychological trauma of confinement, exposure to more sophisticated offenders, and abuse from detention officials, psychological as well as physical. Even if they are not institutionalized at a later date, when they return to their classrooms and neighborhoods these juveniles know the experience of being unfree and bear the stigma of having been in jail.

It is impossible to assess whether these potentially damaging experiences outweigh the official and more positive justifications of providing protection and guidance of juveniles. But one irrefutable dimension of being detained is that it exerts tremendous influence on subsequent decisions made within the juvenile justice system.

If a juvenile is detained, especially if she or he requests a hearing and is denied release, it is often regarded as indication that further court intervention may be necessary. Minimally, the fact that juveniles have been detained is considered evidence that they are not able to deal with their problems and require immediate supervision and court involvement. Those juveniles who remain in detention are considered the more serious cases, despite the many outside considerations that influence whether or not they remain in detention. If a juvenile is detained, it is commonly regarded as a sign that there is a lack of self-control, problems are immediate, and the illegal behavior is likely to reoccur.

Thus, it is not surprising that juveniles who are detained receive more severe dispositions than those who are not detained: 38.4 percent are placed on probation and 14.0 percent are either placed outside their homes, committed to the Department of Corrections with a stay of execution, committed to the Department of Corrections or transferred to the adult court for possible prosecution. Of those who are not detained only 14.9 percent are put on probation and an extremely small number, 2.2 percent, receive the most severe dispositions.

Statistical analysis demonstrates that the nature of the offense and number of prior referrals to court are correlated with whether or not juveniles are detained prior to trial. Juveniles with prior referrals to court are more likely to be detained than are those who have not been referred to the court previously. The influence of the alleged offense is not as clear-cut, for juvenile social characteristics are also influential. For males, the more serious the offense, the more likely they are to be detained. Accordingly, those allegedly involved in felonies are more likely to be detained than all others, and those allegedly involved in misdemeanors are more likely to be detained than those allegedly involved in status offenses.

Such is not the case for young females: in fact, the opposite occurs. Female status offenders are more likely to be incarcerated than those who have committed misdemeanors or felonies. Young women who run away from home, violate curfew laws, are truant from school, or possess alcoholic beverages are more likely to be detained in secure custody than those allegedly involved in such major offenses as aggravated assault or robbery. As discussed in Chapter 10, differential treatment on the basis of sex is extremely evident in the juvenile court's first major decision regarding a juvenile's future. Overall, females are detained more often than males, but when the alleged offense is a felony, males are more likely to be detained.

Another social characteristic which plays an even statistically greater role in the detention decision is racial identity. Regardless of the offense, the number of prior referrals, or sexual identity, black juveniles are more likely to be incarcerated than white juveniles. Essentially, black children in similar situations as white children have a greater chance of being jailed prior to their trials.

It is extremely pertinent to note the influence of race and sex on this initial decision, for the impact of these and other juvenile characteristics cannot be over-emphasized. The juvenile court is empowered to conduct a total review of juveniles' life situations and to affect legal orders which will control juvenile futures. Recognition of the predispositions of decision-makers toward particular groups of juveniles influences whether or not justice is individualized.

Equally important, even though the impact of race and sex on decisions is demonstrated through interviews and observations of court activities, their influence becomes less obvious in statistical analysis of later stages in the process. (For further analysis see Appendix A). Statistically, race and sex do not figure as prominently in the screening and dispositional decisions as they do in the detention decision. For as juveniles become increasingly enmeshed in the court system, the impact of social characteristics is incorporated into newly defined legal variables. The detention decision and screening decision become much better predictors of final disposition than are race or sex alone. But what must be acknowledged is that these new "legal factors" are the products of previous decisions made by court personnel, decisions which are influenced by juveniles' racial and sexual identities. The impact of bias becomes statistically hidden to outside reviewers.

The Screening Decision

As a juvenile's case progresses through the system the next major juncture is the screening decision. It is here that the manner in which a case will be handled is determined, a decision which greatly influences all subsequent interaction between the juvenile and decision-makers. The alleged offense and number of prior referrals are crucial elements in this decision *as is the detention decision.* Juveniles who have been detained are likely candidates for further integration into the court system through formal processing and a formal hearing.

Most delinquency referrals to the court are screened by two major units, the legal department (prosecutor's office) and the delinquency intake department. The legal department is responsible for reviewing all serious felonies, i.e. murder, manslaughter, rape, arson, sale of drugs, and serious assault (assault with intent to do great bodily harm, assault with intent to kill). They may reject the referral on the grounds of insufficient evidence,[7] forward the referral to another jurisdiction,[8] file a petition and request that intake prepare a preliminary investigation or forward the referral to a delinquency unit for informal processing. It is regular procedure to file a petition on major felonies in which the prosecutors believe the case was handled properly by the police and there is sufficient evidence to make a case against the juvenile in court.

All other referrals involving juveniles not on probation are screened by the delinquency intake unit. These include status offenses, misdemeanors, minor felonies, and some major felonies. Cases involving juveniles held in the detention center but not on probation are assigned to an intake worker or a member of the short-term counseling unit the morning following the juvenile's detention. The short-term counseling unit is financed through a federal grant whose guidelines permit it to deal exclusively with specific juveniles with few referrals of a minor nature, especially status offenders and misdemeanants. They normally do not take cases involving a third referral for runaway, incorrigibles with a history of psychological problems, or juveniles with a history of truancy.

Referrals pertaining to juveniles already under the court's jurisdiction *or their siblings* are forwarded to the probation officer assigned to the family. This policy is both a matter of economics and convenience for court personnel, as well as an attempt to minimize the number of workers involved with the family. The family history and social situation have already been reviewed by the one child's worker; therefore, assigning the sibling to a different worker would create a duplication of the court's operation as well as an additional nuisance for the family. This policy is both rationally and economically sound. The fact remains, however, that such siblings are automatically involved with a probation officer, even if it is their first referral to the court. Thus, juveniles whose siblings are on probation are integrated into the court system more quickly than are juveniles from families not known to the court. This remains true even if they are referred for similar behavior. Although this policy is viewed by court personnel primarily as a matter of efficiency, it is also indicative of the court's assumption that if one juvenile from a family is involved with the court, others are more likely to be referred, and, when referred, require a more severe course of action. Thus, a policy which is economical for the court and perhaps initially less troublesome for families may function to the distinct disadvantage of a particular juvenile. However, court personnel suggest that such a policy works to the advantage of juveniles, for they are referred to "treatment" resources sooner than others.

The screening decision is extremely crucial, for it is at this point that it is decided whether or not a juvenile must go to court. Court-ordered probation or placement outside the home are *not* possible unless the child is given a formal hearing. The court's established policy is to deflect the majority of delinquency referrals from a formal court proceeding; approximately 74 percent of all delinquency referrals are processed informally. Only those juveniles whose cases are processed formally, after a petition has been filed, become subject to the full power of the court.

Informal and Formal Processing

Although there are numerous alternatives available to court personnel when they screen referrals, the options may be grouped into two broad categories based on the decision to handle the case *informally* or *formally*. Informal processing of a case does not entail the filing of a legal petition and therefore precludes the possibility of the court taking jurisdiction over the juvenile or involuntary placement outside the home. Major options within this category are dismissal with a warning letter, referral to the court's short-term counseling unit, or scheduling for an informal hearing. If a warning letter is issued, the juvenile has no face-to-face contact with court personnel. Referral to short-term counseling necessitates conferences between the juvenile and the family and a court worker on a voluntary basis for a period not to exceed six months.

The informal hearing is the only option in this category (informal processing) in which the juvenile faces the court and the judiciary. As opposed to a summons, parents and juveniles are requested to meet with the hearing officers for an informal discussion, which most often culminates in a verbal warning. A petition is not filed, and therefore no legal order can be entered.

The juvenile and parents may be requested to participate in "consent supervision" which is a voluntary agreement to work with a social worker for a period not to exceed a year. Although failure to cooperate with consent supervision would be viewed negatively by court personnel and thus influence their response to future referrals, there is no immediate legal sanction if a juvenile fails to attend counseling sessions. (*Voluntary* placement of a juvenile in a group home or hospital setting may also result from an informal hearing, but such action is infrequent.)

Hearings may be considered to be appropriate in cases involving younger children (nine to 12 years) allegedly involved in major offenses against property such as vandalism or shoplifting of goods worth more than $50. They are also used for juveniles who have been before a hearing officer previously, received a conditional dismissal, or their cases were taken under advisement, and subsequently returned to the court for a minor referral such as riding a motorcycle without a helmet or violating a curfew for the first time. Hearings are not conducted as extensively as they have been in the past since additional funding has been procured for the short-term counseling unit. Screening personnel prefer to send juveniles for counseling rather than introduce them to the courtroom atmosphere.

> I do very few informal hearings. And the reason for that is that normally those that would go for an informal hearing can go to short-term counseling and I'd rather have the kid talk to someone.
> INTAKE WORKER

Formal processing encompasses those cases in which a petition and allegations are filed against ("on behalf of") a juvenile. If the allegations are ruled to be true, the court may make legally binding orders which supersede parental or juvenile decisions; options include taking jurisdiction over juveniles, placing them on probation, or ordering placement outside the home. Thus, as is readily apparent, those juveniles whose cases are screened for formal processing are immediate candidates for further integration into the juvenile justice system. These cases then proceed to the adjudicatory and dispositional phases of the court system.

Notes

1. The court also has the option of maintaining a courtroom in which a commissioner presides. The commissioner is appointed by the circuit court, must have the same qualifications as a circuit judge, and may rule in all cases before the court.

2. The rotation system was initiated to discourage the establishment of "a personal kingdom" in the juvenile court. Prior to this system the term of office was unspecified and six to eight years was common. Now terms exceeding three years are highly unlikely.

3. The court has never had a female judge, nor has the juvenile court had a female commissioner, director of court services, or chief probation officer.

4. A written request for a rehearing must be filed within ten days of the original hearing. An appeal results in an entirely new hearing before the judge, not merely a review of the original proceeding.

5. This orientation is similar to that of delinquency workers observed by Matza (1964) and Cicourel (1968) who conceived of their activities in social work terms, but contrary to Emerson's subjects (1969) who rejected the social work image.

6. Jurisdictional powers of the juvenile court vary with the state. Most are defined according to residence and juvenile's age at the time of the alleged offense.

Others determine jurisdiction by the juvenile's age at the time of referral to court. Thirty-eight states grant jurisdiction to juvenile courts over juveniles under eighteen years of age. Eight stipulate 17 years, and four stipulate 16. For further discussion see Johnson, 1975:20–2 and Sussman, 1977:15–21.

7. The legal department also receives referrals from the delinquency intake department to be stamped insufficient and returned to the police department of origin. The legal department may not always agree with intake's interpretation of whether or not the police report provides sufficient evidence and may select to route cases into the court system. Likewise, the intake screening personnel may send cases into the court system which the legal department would have rejected due to insufficient evidence. The nonlawyer status of intake personnel creates this possibility, but their experience and familiarity with court procedures and standards minimizes the number of such incidents.

8. If the juvenile resides in another jurisdiction, the court has the option of sending her or him to that jurisdiction for adjudication and/or disposition. In referrals involving major felonies, especially if the juvenile is being held at the court's detention facility, adjudication and disposition will probably be dealt with at this court. Minor referrals are usually transferred to the other jurisdiction.

CHAPTER 4

Guilt and Punishment: Adjudication and Disposition

There are two major phases in formal juvenile proceedings, adjudication and disposition. In the former, the court seeks to establish a finding regarding the truth of the allegations against the juvenile; if the allegations are found to be true, the court decides what action should be taken in "the best interest of the child and community." Almost without exception, juveniles who are processed formally at this court are found guilty of something. The final disposition of the case is the primary issue, for it is there that the juvenile court has so much discretion.

In order for juveniles to be found "in violation of the Juvenile Code" (guilty), it is only necessary that they be adjudicated for one illegal act. Once this has been done, the floodgates are opened for the exercise of discretionary power within the juvenile court. But nothing is automatic or inevitable: the alternatives are many, ranging from doing nothing to sending the child to the state's juvenile prison. That is, there is no set penalty for a particular offense, and the treatment or punishment meted out by the court is totally discretionary. As demonstrated by cases throughout this volume, juveniles who have been found guilty of felonies may receive no punishment, have their cases dismissed and go home without even receiving probation or being ordered to pay restitution to victims. In contrast, juveniles convicted of status offenses may be put on probation or taken from their homes.

Undeniably, the major concern of juvenile court personnel is disposition, not adjudication. But before dispositional alternatives may be officially discussed, adjudication is necessary. Accordingly, the allegations brought against the juvenile must be reviewed and a finding rendered. There are three options regarding the adjudicatory phase. First, the judicial officer may elect to make no finding regarding the allegations and dismiss the petition, take the case under advisement, or make a conditional dismissal. If there is no finding regarding the allegations, there can be no disposition. Second, the judicial officer may rule that the allegations are not true and dismiss the petition. There will be no disposition. Third, the allegations may be found to be true, in total or part, and the court will proceed with disposition.

It is the adjudicatory, "fact finding," portion of the juvenile hearing which has been the object of Supreme Court rulings, and which theoretically must comply with strict legal procedure. No hearsay evidence is to be admitted, and even a police report (unsubstantiated by the officer's testimony under oath) is considered insufficient for a finding of guilty. Likewise, prior to taking any dispositional action, the court must prove beyond a reasonable doubt that the alleged violation of the Juvenile Code occurred (Faust & Brantingham 1974:507, 512–14; Neigher 1967:352–7).

The fact that most juveniles admit *some degree* of involvement in the alleged incident often abbreviates the adjudicatory phase of the proceedings. In order for the court to adjudicate the juvenile "delinquent," that is, in violation of the Juvenile Code, it is not necessary that all portions of the allegation(s) be found true. To the contrary, the juvenile's involvement in any act or portion of an act is sufficient to adjudicate and continue with the disposition.

There are three major proceedings during which a juvenile can be adjudicated delinquent: the initial hearing, the pretrial conference, and the contested hearing. Most adjudicatory decisions are made during pretrial conferences and initial hearings. In both instances a petition has been filed, and, if the allegations are found true, the court may take jurisdiction and enter legally binding orders regarding the juvenile's activities and place of residence.

The Initial Hearing

The initial hearing is analogous to the arraignment of adults, and 98 percent of such proceedings are conducted by the hearing officers. Parents are summoned to bring the juvenile to court, and both parents and the juvenile receive a copy of the petition filed by the court. The petition specifies the allegations against the juvenile and announces the date of the hearing. The summons lists the rights to have the allegations proved by competent evidence presented to the court; have an attorney present and if the family cannot afford an attorney, to have the court appoint one; receive written notice of the date of the hearing by summons at least 24 hours prior to the hearing date; question any witness who appears at the hearing; bring any witnesses or request the court to order persons to be present as witnesses; and appeal the court's decision to an appellate court. They are also informed that:

> If the juvenile is fourteen years or older and the petition alleges an offense which would be a traffic offense or which would be a felony if the juvenile were an adult, the court may conduct a hearing to determine whether the juvenile should be dealt with by the juvenile court, or whether he should be proceeded against as an adult, under the general law. If the juvenile is seventeen years or older and already under the jurisdiction of the juvenile court, and the petition alleges an offense which would be a violation of any criminal law or ordinance if the juvenile were an adult, the court may conduct such a hearing.
>
> If the court finds the facts in the petition to be true, it may make orders affecting the juvenile and his parents, guardian or other custodian concerning the care, custody and control of the juvenile, and the court may commit the juvenile to an institution.
>
> JUVENILE COURT SUMMONS

It is difficult to calculate the extent to which juveniles or their parents comprehend the rights and information contained in the petition and summons. One hearing officer routinely inquired whether juveniles and parents had read the petition and summons. Several indicated they had not read them at all; many stated they had not read them thoroughly, and others who had read them expressed confusion regarding their contents. Several probation officers also stated that most of their clients failed to grasp the process in which they were involved.

No witnesses are subpoenaed for the initial hearings, and, unless the hearing officer makes a specific request, no prosecuting attorney will be present. The major participants at the hearing are the hearing officer, the juvenile, and parents or guardians. A court worker from the short-term counseling unit, a delinquency intake worker, or a probation officer may be present, depending upon the juvenile's past involvement with the court.[1] Many initial hearings involve juveniles who have not had prior contact with the court, and therefore no court worker will attend.

Although they have been informed of the right to legal representation by the summons, less than 20 percent are accompanied by an attorney in the initial hearing. Thus, it is not uncommon for the participants at the first hearing to be the hearing officer, juvenile, parents, and court clerk. (The proceedings are tape recorded for purposes of appeal.)

When court workers are involved in a case, an informal discussion often is held between the worker and the hearing officer prior to the hearing. According to court policy, such conversations are permitted only if the juvenile's attorney attends them; if the juvenile is not represented, such conferences are prohibited. Official policy notwithstanding, informal, off-the-record discussions routinely are conducted whether or not the juvenile is represented by counsel. The discussions may entail merely a review of the allegations or the juvenile's past involvement with the court, but it often extends to a detailed analysis of the juvenile or family's history, associations, or attitudes. Many comments are speculative and prejudicial, calculated to demonstrate to the hearing officer the appropriateness of the social worker's recommendation. One hearing officer has not allowed such discussion unless the juvenile is represented by counsel at the hearing and the attorney is present for the discussion; extensive pretrial discussions are routine in the other two courtrooms.

At the beginning of the initial hearing juveniles are informed of the right to remain silent and to be represented by an attorney. They are also informed that if they are unable to afford counsel, the court will appoint one. The hearing officer then reads the allegations contained in the petition and outlines three alternative courses of action, one of which must be exercised. The juvenile may: admit to the truth of the allegations, deny the truth of the allegations, or make a statement regarding the allegations. If the juvenile denies the allegations, the hearing is adjourned and reset for a contested hearing.[2] In most instances counsel will be appointed for the juvenile, although this is not required.[3] The majority of juveniles elect to make a statement about the allegations.

The manner in which the initial hearing proceeds, the clarity with which juveniles are informed of their rights, and the extent to which the proceedings are explained vary with the personality and effectiveness of the hearing officer. For example, the manner in which juveniles are informed of the legal right to counsel varies greatly. One hearing officer routinely asks juveniles the direct question, "Do you want a lawyer?" Not surprisingly, more juveniles before that particular court request an attorney than do those in other courtrooms where the right to representation is only included in a list of statements.

There is often parental pressure for juveniles to continue the hearing without counsel. If the juvenile requests counsel, the proceeding will be stopped and reset for a future date. This, of course, necessitates another trip to court for the family, perhaps creating transportation problems or additional time away from jobs. The embarrassment caused by their child's appearance in court also makes parents desirous of settling the matter as expediently as possible. There is also financial pressure to proceed without counsel. For, when they are informed that the court will appoint counsel, parents are also notified that they will be required to submit a financial statement and contribute to the costs of the public defender as their resources permit.[4] Thus, for various reasons, parents urge juveniles to "just tell the judge what happened."

Court personnel also seek to avoid the inconvenience of rescheduling a hearing, but once in the courtroom, they seldom pressure juveniles overtly to continue without an attorney. Frequently there is indication that the court worker has not discussed the issue with the juvenile or parents fully, and occasionally they exert subtle pressure by suggesting that if juveniles or parents are dissatisfied with the outcome of the initial hearing, they have the right to a rehearing before the judge and may wish to retain counsel *at that time.* When juveniles are asked *directly* if they wish to have an attorney, they frequently discuss this issue with their parents; but in the vast majority of cases, they waive the right to an attorney without further discussion.

The initial hearing system was established in an attempt to maximize court efficiency while minimizing inconvenience for police and community witnesses. Before this policy was established, witnesses were summoned for each case; many of these individuals would endure long waiting periods in court hallways only to be dismissed because the juvenile admitted involvement in the incident. Under the current system, witnesses are required to make court appearances only in a minority of cases in which the juvenile denies involvement.

The system also minimizes the time spent by court personnel in the courtroom, particularly members of the legal department. Under the initial hearing system it is no longer necessary for a prosecuting attorney to attend each hearing. Thus, time formerly spent in hearings may be used to process referrals or prepare cases for pretrial conferences or contested hearings before the judge.

In over 95 percent of the initial hearings, the juvenile admits some degree of involvement in the alleged behavior. Often the hearing officer amends the original allegations to reflect the juvenile's version of the incident more closely. Only a portion of the allegation or one allegation among several need be ruled true in order to find the individual in violation of the Juvenile Code. Thus, most juveniles who admit any involvement are adjudicated delinquent, and most court orders indicate that the allegations (perhaps as amended) are true and by consent. Once the allegations are found true, disposition follows.

Although juveniles theoretically have the right to force the state to prove their involvement and guilt "beyond a reasonable doubt," few insist that the state make its case. As Hufnagel and Davidson have observed (1974:380), it is difficult for juveniles to understand this legal principle. Juveniles and their parents often consider it dishonest to force the state to make its case if they were involved in any way in the alleged incident. Also, defense attorneys may be reluctant to exercise this right for fear it will result in a backlash against the juvenile by court decision-makers.

Once a violation of the Juvenile Code has been established, the dispositional (sentencing or treatment) portion of the proceeding follows. Although this phase is occasionally postponed for further investigation, most commonly the dispositional follows immediately. The alternatives and process through which court personnel determine what is appropriate will be discussed shortly.

Contested Hearings and Pretrial Conferences

A contested hearing is analogous to the adult trial, including sworn testimony from the prosecution and defense. After testimony relevant to the adjudication, the presiding officer dismisses the allegations or rules the juvenile in violation of the Juvenile Code. If the allegations have been ruled true, the judge entertains testimony regarding the appropriate disposition. Less than 5 percent of the cases at the court under study involve contested hearings. Equally important, the court does not have bifurcated hearings, thus, adjudication and disposition are commonly finalized in the same proceeding.

The majority of cases scheduled before the judge are handled through a pretrial conference, usually followed by a brief session in the courtroom. Pretrial conferences are held in the judge's chambers and most adjudicatory decisions are reached within that setting. Court personnel who participate include the judge, the prosecuting attorney, and the court worker assigned to the case (an intake worker if the juvenile is not under the court's jurisdiction and the probation officer if she or he is). The chief social worker is often present, especially on more complicated cases or those in which his recommendation differs from the court worker's. Likewise, any psychological personnel involved in the case will attend. The juvenile and parents do not attend the pretrial conference, but all juveniles are represented by attorneys who do participate. Typically, the juvenile and parents wait in the hallway outside the judge's chambers.

Although pretrial conferences are not unusual within juvenile courts, the judge presiding over the court being studied here included not only the prosecuting and defense counsel, but also the court worker, who is the client of the prosecuting attorney (as the juvenile is the client of the defense attorney). In most pretrial conferences the attorney for each party is present, but clients are excluded. In fact, judges in the past have conducted pretrial conferences at which only attorneys were present; the court workers waited in the hallway with the juvenile and the parents.

Court workers favor the current arrangement for they often feel the prosecuting attorneys (their attorneys) do not or cannot fully explicate their cases to the judge. The judge also favors this system, for, in his view, court workers have the greatest knowledge of the experience with the juvenile and family, and therefore can render a more inclusive evaluation of the situation. This contention, however, does not explain the legal irregularity of allowing one client access to pretrials while excluding another. Court personnel are cognizant of this anomaly, as expressed by the following comment from a prosecuting attorney:

> Our system works a bit different than others. At pretrials clients are not present. We have the unusual system where we have one client present [the court worker]. . . .

In the established routine at a pretrial conference, the judge requests a report from the court worker and the juvenile's attorney; frequently he requests the opinions of the chief social worker and the prosecuting attorney. None of the particpants are under oath at this time, nor are the comments recorded.

The basic assumption underlying the practice of holding pretrial conferences is that a consensus can be reached between the court and defense counsel regarding adjudication, disposition, or both. Adjudicatory decisions are usually finalized at this stage, with the possibility of allegations being rewritten or modified to reflect agreement between the prosecuting and defense attorneys. If the juvenile's attorney admits the juvenile's involvement in any portion of the alleged offense(s), it is sufficient for the court to adjudicate the juvenile in violation of the Juvenile Code and proceed with disposition.

The public defender expressed her opinion regarding the defense counsel's role in adjudication:

> Adjudication has become a farce here, especially in the judge's chambers. . . . He doesn't need to find a child guilty of a major offense. He only wants some legal basis upon which to act. My role is almost nothing. Now I'm more into dispositional matters. . . .

In few cases does the defense counsel fight all the allegations against the juvenile; the majority consent to some portion of the allegation(s), permitting the court to adjudicate without going into the courtroom for sworn testimony. Following adjudication, private attorneys are more likely than the public defender to resist the court taking jurisdiction and becoming more involved in the juvenile's life either through probation or placement. But all defense attorneys concentrate their efforts on the negotiation of dispositions.

Bargaining plays a significant role in court procedures, but the term "plea bargaining" does not aptly describe the negotiations. The plea is almost invariably one of guilty (to something) and the bargaining revolves around disposition, not adjudication.[5]

Disposition

Most of the negotiations at the juvenile court pertain to the disposition of a case. If a juvenile has been found in violation of the Juvenile Code, the court must decide whether or not it should become more involved with the juvenile and the family. They must decide if the juvenile needs to be placed under the supervision of the court in probation or placed outside the home.

In many initial hearings the hearing officer makes this determination unaided by social workers or psychological personnel. This is usually the case when the juvenile has few or no prior referrals to the court. When the juvenile is on probation or an intake worker has prepared a preliminary investigation, the hearing officer requests a recommendation from the court worker. In all cases the judge receives the various opinions of the court workers, the prosecuting attorney, and the defense counsel.

Hearing officers accept the recommendations of court workers over 95 percent of the time. Some court workers report they have never had a recommendation refused. The hearing officers' dependency upon court workers is based on the fact that the court worker is most acquainted with the juvenile's background and behavior. Equally important, rarely are there defense attorneys present to offer contradictory evaluations. One indication of the extent to which the recommendations of court workers are followed is the fact that probation officers often attend hearings at which a member of the short-term counseling unit will recommend that the court take jurisdiction and assign a probation officer. It is assumed that the recommendation will be followed, and rightly so, for, in most instances, the hearing officer implements the court worker's decision, and, conveniently, the new probation officer is present to pick up the case.

During the pretrial conference in the judge's chambers the court workers' opinion does not go unquestioned, but the recommendations of court personnel are followed over 90 percent of the time. A major distinction is that, unlike hearing officers, the judge is frequently confronted with disparate recommendations from court personnel, the court worker, the prosecuting attorney, and psychological personnel.

In cases before the judge, dispositional decisions are usually finalized during the pretrial, with the defense counsel often leaving the discussions to negotiate with the juvenile and family to determine what they will accept or "go along with." A member of the legal department accurately depicts the pretrial conference:

> You've seen them. You walk in, there's a charge. Then there's the idea of what's he "good for" and if he's "good for" anything, should he be under our protection? And if he's under our protection, what can we do for him? . . . In most cases these kids need help. We usually can get them "good" on something in those charges. The public defender knows that because we do screen them.
>
> In most of these cases when they reach the level of the judge, he's got some case history behind him that brought him to court before, got a couple of strikes against him. So there's a lot going against the public defender when he or she tries to defend a child at a pretrial conference because *all that's kind of palpably in the air* concerning each case as it comes up.
>
> PROSECUTING ATTORNEY
(emphasis mine)

The disposition of juvenile cases is unique within the American judicial system. Supreme Court rulings have concentrated on adjudication, to the neglect of preadjudicatory or dispositional phases of the proceedings. The hearsay evidence theoretically excluded from adjudication is permitted during the disposition (Faust and Brantingham 1974:368; Emerson 1969:9).

Within the context of the informal, unrecorded pretrial conference, disposition becomes a negotiation between court personnel and defense counsel regarding the juvenile's future. Hearsay
and prejudicial statements are common, with court workers relating whatever information or opinions they consider necessary
to convince the judge that their recommendation is appropriate.

The atmosphere of the pretrial conferences is one which not
only permits but encourages speculation and statements that are
difficult to substantiate. Court personnel make comments they
would not make under oath and comments they would prefer
not to make directly to the juvenile or family. These speculations
most often concern the juvenile's past behavior and character, as
well as the family's ability or inability to deal adequately with the
juvenile's behavior. These comments may be laudatory or damning: "She thinks she's going to get off scott free!" "He thinks the
court can't touch him." or, "They're a very stable, cooperative
family." "He's not a *real* delinquent, just needs a little direction."
The comments are frequently offered as justification for a recommendation that other participants may view as too harsh or
lenient for the case at hand, that is, divergent from the disposition
often accorded a juvenile with a similar type and number of referrals. They are often geared to combat the defense attorney's
request for a less severe disposition or the prosecuting attorney's
insistence on a more severe disposition.

The defense attorneys also participate in hearsay discussions,
speculating on the family's and the juvenile's behavior and character. But they are usually at a disadvantage and on the defen-
sive, trying to counteract statements made by court personnel.
Likewise, defense attorneys are subtly pressured to allow such
conversations or to agree with negative comments about their
clients in order to demonstrate cooperativeness and good faith
to court personnel. A few derogatory comments can be endured
in the hope of eventually gaining a more favorable disposition.

Comments expressing the court personnel's interpretations of
the juvenile's life circumstances play a significant role in all proceedings at the court, for this is, indeed, the task of the juvenile
court: to interpret juvenile behavior and attitudes in order to arrive at a course of action "in the best interests of the child and
state." But the atmosphere of the pretrial conference is one in
which rules of evidence are relaxed greatly, accountability is

minimal, and juveniles are not present to hear either praise or condemnation, and, thus, are deprived of the right to object. Theoretically, juvenile interests are protected by defense counsel, but often attorneys' limited familiarity with the juvenile and family does not permit them to refute accusations or insinuations. And as has been suggested above, the pretrial conference is a court affair, one in which the judge rules and the opinions of court personnel are given preeminence.

The following pretrial conference and hearing pertain to a 13-year old black male ("Steven") charged with two common assaults on school grounds and trespassing on school grounds after being suspended. The juvenile had two prior referrals, but he had not been placed on probation.

Pretrial Conference

INTAKE WORKER: He's 13-years 11-months going on 25.* [Six months ago] he was referred for assault with a deadly weapon and armed robbery. He continues to drive the school crazy. Now he's here on two assaults, both on school grounds, and for trespassing on school grounds. He was expelled from regular school. We have a complete workup for special school.

JUDGE: What did we do with the other ones [the other referrals]?

PUBLIC DEFENDER: Witnesses weren't here so they weren't adjudicated [no finding of guilt].

INTAKE WORKER: Clinical testing shows his behavior is disordered. . . . There are eight other siblings. Steven has moved in with a brother and sister-in-law.

They tell all sorts of untruths, give a wrong address, change one number in the telephone number.

The mother can't handle him. I think she's afraid of him. He denies everything even before you say it. He's slick, he's slippery.

JUDGE: We don't have jurisdiction? [We have not taken jurisdiction?]

PUBLIC DEFENDER: No, you don't. I can't go along with a commitment to the Department of Corrections with a stay on two simple things from school.

[A joking exchange then occurs between the Public Defender and the Intake Worker.]

---

* "Going on 25 (years)" is a common court expression used to suggest that the juvenile is more streetwise and sophisticated than most juveniles of the same age.

INTAKE WORKER: Crockertown might be the place for the little booger.[Laughing.]

PUBLIC DEFENDER: Your whole unit's getting vindictive. [Laughing.]

INTAKE WORKER: He does what *you* say.

PUBLIC DEFENDER: He *does*. Maybe *I* should be his supervisor.

INTAKE WORKER: The police came over.

PROSECUTING ATTORNEY: I didn't ask them . . . Should we go with a commitment with a stay?

INTAKE WORKER: I think we need it.

PROSECUTING ATTORNEY: He needs to be told. It's the "D.O.C. Express."
[Brief phone call interrupts the discussion.]

JUDGE (TO PUBLIC DEFENDER): Well, you'll agree with jurisdiction but not commitment with a stay?

PUBLIC DEFENDER: Right.

JUDGE (TO INTAKE WORKER): Would this make it impossible for you to work with him?

INTAKE WORKER: No.

PROSECUTING ATTORNEY: He really needs to be laid into.
[Public Defender goes into hallway to talk with the juvenile.]

INTAKE WORKER: John Smaley [the probation officer who will get the case if jurisdiction is taken] says he wants a commitment with a stay. He says he can't supervise without it.

JUDGE: We can put one on the record vocally. If he doesn't go to school, shape up, he'll go to D.O.C. It's as good as putting it on paper.
[Public Defender returns after a four-minute conversation with the juvenile.]

PUBLIC DEFENDER: He'll admit to one assault and the trespassing.

JUDGE: All right. Let's go in [to the courtroom].

Courtroom [20-minute session]

[Prosecuting Attorney takes appearances (states the names of individuals present for the record).]

PROSECUTING ATTORNEY: Can we agree that Steven's birth date is October 1, 1964?

JUVENILE: October 1, 1965.

PROSECUTING ATTORNEY: When you come to see your worker please bring your birth certificate.

JUDGE: Let's review. It states in this petition that on December 13 you struck a girl and on January 8 you trespassed on school property.

JUVENILE: Yes, Your Honor.

JUDGE: In the original petition it says that on November 30 you struck an individual.

JUVENILE: Yes, Your Honor.

JUDGE: In the original petition it says that on November 30 you struck an individual.

JUVENILE: Yes, sir.

JUDGE: Did that happen?

JUVENILE: Yes, sir.

JUDGE: The intake department has recommended that the court take jurisdiction and place you under its supervision.

I understand you're not in school.

Young man, you have a lot of problems here. I want you to shape yourself up. They recommend special school here and I want you back in school. I want you to get with them. It's tough enough to make a living. You need an education.

I don't want any more trouble. Work with us.

If you get in any trouble you leave me no choice but to put you in the Department of Corrections. Understand?

JUVENILE: Yes, sir.

JUDGE: I want you to work with us. I don't want to have to send you to D.O.C.

You work with us.

I'll leave it there.

The tendency of the participants in a pretrial conference to speculate, and to make prejudicial comments is recognized by many members of the court staff. It presents a situation with which many individuals attuned to due process are extremely uncomfortable. The following quote comes *not* from the public defender, but one of the prosecuting attorneys:

> . . . [Such statements] are, can be prejudicial. Judges are human and, like anybody else, if they hear something that later is not admissible in court, maybe triple hearsay, it does have some effect . . . I think there are a lot of statements that are made to the judge and to hearing officers concerning cases, simply because they're there. It's a close building, everybody's working here together and you don't have separation.

When asked if hearsay or prejudicial comments in a pretrial conference are appropriate, another prosecuting attorney responded:

> That's a trick word. From my client's [court worker's] viewpoint, it's very appropriate. We win more cases that way . . . And usually

you have an attorney representing the child, that eases my conscience about the kid getting an unfair shot at it. [Pause.] Except
. . . I don't want to castigate any on the public defender but one
tends to see their cases are lost in the pretrials, what little they had
to go on, by allowing pretrials instead of going straight into trials.

The next question was whether or not defense attorneys have
a choice *not* to have a pretrial conference. The prosecuting attorney responded, "Not to my knowledge. No, they don't have
a choice. You'll have to ask the judge that one. . . ." Thus, from
the court's perspective, the juvenile's attorney should object to
any prejudicial comments, and if it is considered necessary, should
insist the pretrial conference should not be held. But, as the system presently operates, neither option is a viable alternative for
defense counsel. The majority of private attorneys coming into
the juvenile court have little understanding or experience with
juvenile procedures. They are trying to function within the juvenile system without blundering, trying to learn with whom they
should bargain, and simultaneously attempting to convince their
clients that they are providing effective representation. Their efforts are usually expanded negotiating with the court worker or
legal staff and then with the judge. Many have never participated
in a juvenile pretrial conference and have no experience on
which they can rely to object to the procedure. They run the risk
of antagonizing the judge if they object to hearsay or prejudicial
statements once they are in the conference.

Since the public defender handles the overwhelming majority
of cases which go to pretrial conferences, any effective challenge to the procedure might be expected to originate with this
individual. The following quote graphically describes the situation as perceived by the public defender.

Pretrials are prejudicial, period. That's your problem. Once you're
allowing it to happen you've already set the stage for all kinds of
hearsay. It's all hearsay, too, everything that the court worker says,
"The schools tell me this and the parents tell me this." 'Just quoting
a whole lot of people . . . All hearsay, a lot of it prejudicial, most
of it prejudicial. So what you're talking about is that I'd have to
insist on no pretrial, go straight into a hearing. . . . I tried everything including that, and the judge just said, "I want a pretrial. Who
cares what you want?" . . . [The former judge] wouldn't read any-

thing or hear anyone speak unless I said it was okay. He felt it was my legal right, that I had a legal right to go into a contested hearing if that's what I want. . . . There's nothing to object to. I can't appeal a pretrial conference. There's nothing on the record to appeal.

Well, pretrial conferences—I just can't believe that the real truth comes out there. I really can't because people are too loose about what they say since they don't have to worry about whether they're exaggerating. . . . A lot [of court workers] are getting sloppier in their work because they don't have to be careful about what they say: they don't have to go on the record, they don't have to take an oath, they don't have to substantiate it with something. Therefore, they just come in and they'll make those just grandiose statements and what can you say? First of all, there's no such thing as an objection, really. First of all, it's been said. It's been said and it's been heard, and if you object you're making it more exaggerated. So really once you're in the pretrial conference it's all downhill after that for the attorney. And then all I can go on is my own ability to persuade above the others . . .

I can demand a contested hearing but every time I'd demand a contested hearing with the judge he'd say, "Well, you're going to make me go to a contested hearing." And there's always a veiled threat: "He may end up in D.O.C. And if you did it today [at the pretrial conference] we just want to send him home or we just want to. . . ." I just got the feeling I couldn't really present my case the way I wanted to without a lot of pressure on me not to, so I just stopped doing it.

[You definitely felt pressure not to go to trial?]

Absolutely, absolutely. . . . I can't prevent him from having a pretrial, but I can insist on a contested hearing. So since I can't prevent the pretrial conference what he was doing was insisting on having them first. He'd make up his mind [regarding the case] and then say, "Okay, if you want to go to a contested hearing it's okay with me, but I've already made up my mind." And then what was the point? It's not an adversary system. . . .

PUBLIC DEFENDER

From the opposite perspective, the judge points out that every case he hears includes a defense attorney to protect the interests of the child, and it is that attorney's responsibility to put court personnel "on guard" about any unsubstantiated statements. He agrees that the rules of evidence are "somewhat relaxed," but maintains that court personnel don't have a tendency to make unsubstantiated comments. Rather, "they're just stating their views." When asked if defense counsel has the option not to have a pretrial conference, he responded:

> More or less. We will probably have it, because there are really two purposes of a pretrial or initial hearing. Number one is to try to see if there is a consent as to the referral and a consent as to disposition. If there is not a consent as to the adjudication or as to the facts of the referral, we can often at the pretrial arrive at a consent as to certain facts that are agreed upon. So that's helpful. We can often arrive at an agreement that we will adjudicate on these facts, but we can't agree on disposition. So that helps move the case.
>
> If the defense lawyer says we can't agree on anything, that ends the pretrial. But having a pretrial will sometimes bring at least some agreement, even the admission that maybe an officer who took certain types of scientific data need not be present because the data is here by a report. So that having a pretrial doesn't just mean you're going to dispose of a case. You may dispose of certain fact issues. That's why I insist on a pretrial. But again, the defense counsel may say, "We won't agree on anything, set your hearing." And that's it. That ends the pretrial. . . .
>
> JUDGE

Thus, the pretrial system represents one major advantage to the court, increased efficiency in processing juvenile cases. If agreement can be reached regarding adjudication, disposition, or a portion of either, it will greatly reduce the time and cost necessary to resolve a case. Court efficiency is maximized and inconvenience to police and citizen witnesses is minimized.

Court personnel also suggest that the pretrial system also has at least two distinct advantages for juveniles. First, the nature and seriousness of their alleged behavior are de-emphasized. Particularly in cases where the juvenile admits to major felonies, especially violent offenses, the pretrial conference eliminates a vivid depiction of those crimes. Under the present agreement, little time is spent contemplating the actual offense. The judge's knowledge of victims usually comes from a brief summary offered by court personnel. If witnesses were called to describe their victimization by juveniles, the judge would be confronted with a graphic portrayal of the juvenile's alleged behavior. Thus, dispositions for serious felonies might be more severe than those that are made at present.

This is an interesting hypothesis which deserves further study, but one which is beyond the purview of the present research. To explore this contention it would be necessary to compare felony cases settled in pretrial conferences with those settled through trials. Thus, it would be possible to discover whether or not trials with witnesses resulted in more severe dispositions. But if juveniles going to trial did receive more severe dispositions than those handled through pretrial conferences, it would also be necessary to determine whether or not the severe dispositions were due to the vivid depiction of their offenses or to extraneous factors such as the juvenile antagonizing court personnel by forcing them to go to trial.

From a different perspective, a few decision-makers suggest that the court's objective of detering future delinquency would be better served in the contested hearing. Accordingly, juveniles would be confronted openly with their behavior, forced to deal with the embarrassment or sorrow of their parents, and experience a more graphic encounter with the juvenile justice system. It is suggested that if they were to bear the full weight and consequences of their behavior, juveniles might be less likely to commit crimes in the future.

Nevertheless, most court personnel consider the pretrial system as advantageous for juveniles in that they are not forced to participate in a full-scale adversary proceeding, and thus avoid the traumatic experience of "being on trial." Juveniles have been granted the right to face and challenge their accusers, but little attention has been given to the potentially harmful nature of such an experience. Although there is little evidence probing this issue, few would suggest that exposure to pejorative comments or damning evaluations would be in any way therapeutic for juveniles. The force of this argument is illustrated by one contested hearing in which a juvenile listened to court personnel describe her as "cold," "shallow," "disordered," having "sociopathic tendencies," "a lack of remorse," and a "not fully developed" conscience. After several hours of testimony and cross-examination, the trial was aborted when the defense, convinced it could not win the case, consented to the original disposition recommended by the court, commitment to the Department of Corrections. The effect that such a negative evaluation has upon an adolescent (or anyone) is incalculable.

Defense attorneys are also confronted with the dilemma of deciding what would be "best" or "easiest" for juveniles and their parents. If they consent to the least severe disposition they can negotiate in the pretrial conference, they will avoid any such traumas. Thus, court personnel and defense attorneys often assert that handling a case in a pretrial conference spares the juvenile the experience of being labeled "criminal," and makes it possible to begin the prescribed treatment on a positive note.

However, the fact remains that, despite well-intentioned adult decisions regarding the "best interests of the child," juveniles have been granted the right to resist both adjudication and disposition. They have the awesome right to hear what is being said about them and to know the basis upon which decisions regarding their futures have been made.

It is also crucial to ask if the negative effects of being labeled in the open courtroom would be perhaps less harmful than the experience of being adjudicated and disposed of while waiting in a hallway outside the courtroom. As the public defender suggests, parents often articulate frustration regarding the proceedings.

> What they're desperately upset about is that they have absolutely no idea of what's being said about them and what the decision was based on. And they don't know if they were sold out by me.

As suggested above, reliance on pretrial conferences to process juvenile cases is extremely controversial. Paradoxically, its potential for both protection and abuse of juveniles is great.

> I think the pretrial represents the greatest potential abuse of a kid in a system. Because you're operating on the premise that you'll arrive at consent, it opens up the greatest potentiality for plea-bargaining. . . . As a result of that kind of potential abuse, I think that it needs to be scrutinized pretty carefully.
>
> There are some benefits not only to the court but to the kid—cost benefits, clearly. And there are also benefits in not forcing an adversary proceeding against youngsters which, I think, have, in some cases, some pretty negative effects on kids, either through a labeling process or through creation of a fair amount of guilt.
>
> You've kind of got to balance it off. . . . Negatives are that it opens up potentiality for abuse and coercion. I would be amiss, I

guess, if I said that some of those abuses have not taken place in this system. I think they have. Although in the main I suspect that the benefits have been greater than the potential loss.

I'm not quite sure that we're able to communicate to kids and their parents as clearly and noncoercively as we ought of their right to a full-blown hearing. . . . The check on it, again, I guess, goes right back to the quality of people doing it. . . .

CHIEF SOCIAL WORKER

Courtroom Sessions

If both adjudication and disposition have been resolved at the pretrial conference, a short session of five to 50 minutes in the courtroom usually follows. These sessions are held most often to formalize decisions reached in the conference. This is also the only time the juvenile will face the primary symbol of the court's authority, the judge. In addition to summarizing what has been determined during the pre-trial conference, the judge often takes this opportunity to advise, lecture, or congratulate juveniles and their parents on their behavior. The tone of these comments ranges from friendly encouragement for families to continue their excellent cooperation with the court to a stern warning, "If you want to spend the rest of your life behind bars, just keep going on the way you are."

The nature of the discussion is determined by the judge's appraisal of the cooperativeness, attitude, and needs of the juvenile and family. Remarks are often geared to impress juveniles with the gravity of their actions and to inform them of the possible consequences of similar behavior in the future. The judge often takes this opportunity to instruct juveniles regarding the benefits of "the cloistered, informal setting of the juvenile court," reminding them that the atmosphere in which they now find themselves is in sharp contrast to that of the adult criminal court.

The judge may also question juveniles in an attempt to determine the extent to which they understand the court's decision. Juveniles most frequently reply in the affirmative to the inquiry, "Do you understand what this means?" But when the judge requests they explain the disposition, their comments indicate that their understanding is less than complete. At this juncture the judge usually attempts to clarify the situation or suggest that the defense counsel will do so after the session. The encounter usually ends with an encouragement from the judge for the juvenile and family to "work with the court" and to make the best of the opportunity to do better in the future.

If adjudication has been resolved but disposition is still contested, sworn testimony will be taken in the courtroom. Witnesses most often include the court worker assigned to the case, the chief social worker, and any psychological personnel involved. The defense counsel may cross-examine or present contradictory testimony. The defense's case usually consists solely of cross-examination of court personnel. The defense frequently challenges the appropriateness of the court worker's recommendation, questioning whether or not all possible alternatives have been explored. Although they may do so, defense attorneys rarely use independent expert testimony (social workers, psychologists, or psychiatrists) to refute court personnel. Likewise, juveniles are infrequently called to testify in their own behalf.

At the conclusion of testimony and cross-examination the judge may announce a decision or adjourn until a future date. Usually the decision is announced immediately, and in almost all cases, the disposition is the one that was recommended by court personnel during the pretrial discussions.

Alternative Dispositions

Once the juvenile has been adjudicated, there are numerous dispositions available to the court. A brief description of the major alternatives follow. They are listed from the least to most severe, as determined in a poll of court personnel.

Dismissal

The court dismisses the petition and will not become further involved in the juvenile's activities at this time.

Conditional Dismissal

The petition is scheduled to be dismissed in an established period of time, usually six months or a year. The court does not become involved in the juvenile's activities at this time, and if there are no further referrals in the intermittant period, the petition will be dismissed on the designated date. The juvenile is not required to return to court at the time of dismissal.

Taken Under Advisement (Synonymous with Held in Abeyance)

The court elects not to impose a disposition. The matter is usually taken under advisement for a period of six months or a year and will be reviewed at that time. Although the juvenile is not officially assigned to the supervision of a worker, the court worker keeps the case and is expected to make periodic checks with the juvenile and to loosely monitor future developments. The petition will be dismissed at the review session if the juvenile has not been referred to the court again and the family report is favorable.

Jurisdiction and Supervision

This represents the court's official involvement in a juvenile's activities. The court takes jurisdiction over the juvenile and places her or him under the supervision of a court worker, an arrangement commonly known as probation. The juvenile or family meet regularly with the worker and construct a "treatment plan" for dealing with the juvenile's problems. The court worker decides whether the sessions will take place at the court, the juvenile's school, or home. If the juvenile fails to comply with conditions stipulated by the court worker, such as regular attendance at school and conferences, the court is empowered to have the juvenile brought to detention and held pending further dispositional action. Although the court has officially entered the juvenile's life on a regular basis, the child continues to reside at home.

Placement Other than Department of Corrections

The court orders the juvenile to be removed from the parent's or guardian's residence and placed in a delinquency foster home, a court operated group home, a privately operated group home, or a privately operated institution. The settings are environments in which juveniles are monitored and supervised. Although the placement may terminate the juvenile's stay, the court retains ultimate power to enter orders stating whether or not the juvenile is released. The majority of the facilities are within 30 miles of the juveniles' homes to encourage family visits.

Commitment to the Department of Corrections with a Stay

The court may commit an offender to the jurisdiction of the Department of Correction, *but* the order will not be executed immediately. The juvenile may remain at home, or if the stay is combined with placement in another setting, the juvenile may be placed in a group home or privately operated institution. The stay cannot be lifted, and the juvenile cannot be sent to the Department of Corrections without a court hearing. Although further referrals may result in placement under the department, such action is not automatic.

Commitment to the Department of Corrections

The Department of Corrections includes several state-operated facilities for the rehabilitation and control of juveniles. Some are group homes, but the major facilities are two institutions formerly called "state training schools." The girls' facility is approximately 200 miles from the metropolitan area; the boys' is approximately 150 miles from the metropolitan area. Both are secure facilities. Once the juvenile court has committed an individual to the Department of Correction, it relinquishes jurisdiction and the release decision becomes the responsibility of the department. Sentences are indeterminate and confinement is possible until the juvenile's twenty-first birthday, but few are detained beyond the age of majority (legal adulthood).

Certification (Transfer) to Adult Court

The Juvenile Code empowers the court to transfer any juvenile 14 years of age or older to the adult court if the allegations would be considered as a traffic offense or a felony if the juvenile were an adult.[6] Although it is commonly referred to as a "disposition" within the present court, the decision to waive jurisdiction and transfer the juvenile to adult court for possible prosecution must be made prior to any adjudication for the alleged offense. Before such a transfer is ordered, the court must conduct a proceeding to address the issue of whether or not the juvenile is amenable to treatment within the juvenile system. If the judge determines that the juvenile system has no treatment facilities to offer, the juvenile court will dismiss the petition against the juvenile and notify the adult prosecutor of its decision. The adult prosecutor has the option to file criminal charges against the juvenile. In major felonies such as murder or rape this is virtually automatic, but in less serious felonies the prosecutor may decide against pressing charges.

Probable cause and amenability to treatment are the two most common criteria used in making the decision whether or not to transfer a juvenile to the adult court. The former addresses the issue if whether or not there is sufficient evidence to suggest the juvenile was involved in the alleged offense, and the latter addresses the issue of whether or not the facilities and resources of the juvenile system are appropriate for this particular juvenile.[7] In the state under examination, amenability to treatment is the only official consideration in the decision.

Accordingly, the juvenile court's decision to certify is not based on a finding regarding the allegation; the court need not be convinced of the juvenile's involvement in the alleged offense to transfer to the adult court. The court's action is based on a decision of whether or not the juvenile system has treatment facilities appropriate for this particular juvenile. Although in practice certification is not considered unless the legal department believes there is sufficient evidence to prove the juvenile's involvement, the facts of the allegation are not considered at the certification hearing.

If the court decides against certification, the juvenile's case will then be processed for adjudication and disposition. In the present jurisdiction, certification to the adult court applies only to the allegation being reviewed at the time of the hearing. Even if a juvenile has been certified in the past, any subsequent referrals prior to the age of majority will be forwarded to the juvenile court. At that point the court must determine whether to deal with the juvenile in the juvenile system or to transfer to the adult court. The foregoing has been a description of the process through which juveniles are reviewed and a delineation of the alternatives available to court personnel. The following chapters will examine the organizational exigencies and defendant characteristics which influence the alternatives chosen by decision-makers.

Notes

1. If the child has been dealt with by the short-term counseling unit at an earlier date, the worker will attend the initial hearing. If the juvenile is already under the court's jurisdiction, the probation officer assigned to the case will attend.

2. If the hearing officer presiding in the initial hearing reads the police report or discusses the case with the juvenile, parents, or court workers, and the case is reset for a contested hearing, it will be docketed for another hearing officer.

3. Juveniles must be informed of their right to counsel, but the court is not obligated to appoint counsel if the defendant does not request it. I observed several contested hearings at which juveniles were not represented. Hearing officers generally appoint counsel if they believe either the juvenile or parent to be mentally retarded.

4. The court theoretically considers a juvenile's request for counsel without regard to parental financial resources, but the newly established policy requires parents to pay for the lawyer even if they do not agree with their child's desire for counsel.

5. Although Cicourel (1968) emphasizes the negotiation of dispositions, Emerson (1969:20) states that bargaining played a minor role at the court he observed. In a more recent study, Hufnagel and Davidson state that 90 percent of the sentences they observed were bargained (1974:377).

6. Although the Juvenile Code establishes 14 as the age for transfer, the court rarely certifies juveniles under 15.

7. Thirty-six states specify conditions for transfer to the adult court. For further discussion see Sussman, 1977, and Johnson, 1975.

CHAPTER 5

External Considerations and Pressures

Although the exercise of discretionary power by court personnel is the major concern of the present inquiry, it is important to recognize that numerous crucial decisions lie beyond the control of court personnel. The initial decision to refer juveniles to court and parental desires regarding court involvement greatly influence the final decision of the court. As has been suggested previously, referral to court is the most severe legal option available to societal institutions in their dealings with juveniles. The court is *not* the source of a juvenile's encounter with the juvenile justice system. This paramount decision lies within the province of law enforcement officials, school personnel, and parents.

Once a juvenile has been referred to court and (if) allegations are ruled true, court personnel must decide upon an appropriate disposition. But even in this aspect of court involvement, outside considerations become important. Not only are there statutory and budgetary limitations on alternatives, but court personnel must also deal with outside treatment facilities which often thwart court desires and limit options. The decision-makers within the juvenile court do not act unilaterally: Their alternatives, and consequently their encounters with juveniles, are greatly influenced by other decision-makers.

Police Involvement in Court Action

As numerous authors suggest, law enforcement officials exercise vast discretionary power in their encounters with juveniles.[1]

Their actions, although beyond the control of the juvenile court, greatly influence future interaction between juveniles and court decision-makers.

The court under examination deals with over 30 separate police departments, each of which establishes and implements procedures for handling juvenile cases. The resulting lack of uniformity is not only inevitable but extremely problematic for court interaction with juveniles and their parents. A major problem is the manner in which cases are handled by various police departments; for the manner in which juveniles are questioned and taken into custody often impedes further court action. Approximately 2 to 4 percent of police referrals are rejected by the court's legal department because they do not provide sufficient basis for court action.[2] Both the potential needs of the community and juveniles are obstructed by such mishandling.

In addition to the necessity of rejecting referrals, court personnel may also find themselves processing cases which have been poorly prepared by police. The following case involved a felony referral, one representing potential danger for the community and juvenile, but the court was forced "to settle" for voluntary cooperation from the juvenile due to questionable police practices.

#170: Pretrial Conference [Judge's Chambers 12 minutes]

Judge
Prosecuting Attorney
Public Defender
Court Worker
White Male, 14 years old ("Tim")
Referral#1:   Peace Disturbance
       #2:   Arson
JUDGE: He set fire to a trash can, that beats burning a bush.
PUBLIC DEFENDER: No, no. . . .
JUDGE: Oh, he did that later.
COURT WORKER: The bush, unfortunately, was close to a house. Luckily the police were there close on the trash incident, and followed to the bush.
JUDGE: What do we have?
COURT WORKER: A father and boys. Tim is the second youngest. I'm recommending jurisdiction and supervision [probation], Your Honor. The

boy will be living with his grandmother on a 230 acre farm in Smith County.

JUDGE: I keep shipping people to other places.

COURT WORKER: He's very typical, sort of grinning and all that. The poor kid hasn't had a mother. It's a sad story. His sisters raised him. The police say the father's been taken to the station several times intoxicated.

PROSECUTING ATTORNEY: This one there was a witness.

PUBLIC DEFENDER: No, he [witness] doesn't say he saw the juvenile set the fire. Tim pointed it out to me [in the police report], I didn't see it. This was badly done by the police. My problem with the case is that the history shows this kind of behavior, but on the other hand, these two incidents. . . . In investigating the trash can incident they were looking for this boy by name. They took him to the station without a parent or a court worker. At first he denied it—that's not in the report. It's circumstantial testimony—they saw the matches. All evidence was gathered from questioning him—when they shouldn't have without a parent present. I don't like admitting to it. They even questioned him on the street.

JUDGE: Which department was it?

PUBLIC DEFENDER: They never called his parents, they never read his rights. Basically, they don't know how to prepare a proper case. They said they were looking for Tim by name. In their own minds they knew he did it. It's really difficult for me to admit to it.

JUDGE: Is there anything we can do without jurisdiction [without taking jurisdiction over the juvenile]?

COURT WORKER: We can do consent supervision with short-term counseling. It would probably be difficult to get the father in for the appointments.

PUBLIC DEFENDER: If he consents they would have a volunteer working with them.

COURT WORKER: The father isn't available. The wife was in a mental insititution even before the boy was born. It's very unstable. But nothing psychological was indicated with the boy. I thought we'd get jurisdiction.

We always look for something psychological with arson, but they saw this as situational delinquency. There may be other psychological problems because of all the instability in the family. If they sign the consent, we could work with them.

PUBLIC DEFENDER: I know they would do that. I talked with them about the court helping the family; they agreed.

COURT WORKER: Once they got here, they were very cooperative.

PUBLIC DEFENDER: I would feel much better about it that way.

JUDGE: If we've got a bad statement, and it looks like we do, it would

be best to informally adjust by consent supervision. Is this a first referral?
COURT WORKER: Yes.
JUDGE: Well, they've gotten along well for 14 years. If he comes back,
we'll get it (jurisdiction). See if they'll agree.

The public defender goes to the hallway to discuss the situation with the juvenile and his father. They agree to consent supervision (that is, they voluntarily agree to the court's supervision). There is no courtroom session. The juvenile and his father
have been sitting in the hallway for two hours, including the time
spent talking with the public defender. They never go into the
courtroom or see the judge.

Court personnel may also encounter hostility from juveniles
and parents who were informed by police that they would not
have to go to court if they "cooperated." Accordingly, parents
and juveniles are disturbed when they receive summons to appear in court, and, subsequently, the court must deal with their
expressions of frustration and anger. Thus, the interaction between the court and the juvenile begins in an antagonistic manner. The court must then explain that once a report is filed, law
enforcement officials do not make the decision of whether or
not the juvenile will be required to appear in court. As explained
in Chapter 3, this determination is made by the court's legal department and intake personnel.

Further police involvement in a crucial court decision also creates confusion and impedes court action. The decision to detain
juveniles at the time of apprehension is technically within the
purview of court power. The state statutes instruct court decision-makers to detain those juveniles whom they consider to be
a potential danger to the community or themselves. Rather than
allowing court personnel to make this decision, police often act
on a unilateral basis to release or detain juveniles. Thus it is extremely difficult for the court to establish uniformity in decision-
making, for they are frequently denied the opportunity to make
such decisions. This lack of control may result in such inconsis-
tencies as juveniles charged with felonies being released while
others are detained. And as court personnel have commented,
police decisions may be based on factors other than potential
danger to community or self.

One specific police policy often results in difficulties for court personnel: in order to protect the identity of undercover agents responsible for reporting potential juvenile involvement in drug traffic, it is common for police to delay filing referrals with the juvenile court. Although this policy is understandable from the perspective of the demands of law enforcement activities, it presents an awkward and often impossible situation for court involvement. It it not uncommon for the juvenile court to receive a referral on a sale of drugs (a felony, regardless of the amount or kind of drug sold) six months or a year after the incident allegedly occurred.

A further complication arises when such referrals involve juveniles close to or over the age of majority. For, although the youths have been sent to the juvenile court because the alleged act happened when they were legally minors, they are beyond the age of the court's jurisdiction when court involvement actually begins. The age of the juvenile eliminates many treatment resources, for, as will be discussed, many placements prefer not to deal with juveniles over 16-years old. The court can be confronted with a major referral and then must decide if it should take the case under advisement, dismiss the petition, conditionally dismiss the petition, and not become actively involved. Otherwise, it can take a much more serious course of action, namely certification to the adult court for possible prosecution. Thus, the alternatives available to the court (if the allegations are ruled true) are restricted severely.

Allegations of police harassment or brutality may also influence court interaction with juveniles. Of the 250 cases observed, there were 26 cases in which this was claimed. Again, the court's involvement with juveniles begins on a negative note, with juveniles seeking redress for perceived or actual mistreatment from law enforcement officials.

It is difficult for court personnel to ascertain if allegations of harassment or brutality are legitimate, and some suggest that such allegations are "in vogue" and greatly exaggerated. Others suggest that because of disgruntlement with the court's handling of juvenile offenders, police administer "treatment" before bringing juveniles to court facilities. When confronted with parental or juvenile allegations charging police misbehavior, some court personnel choose to ignore them, asserting that "We're here to talk about your involvement." Others suggest that juveniles and parents file a complaint with the FBI, which conducts these investigations. Regardless of their response to such allegations, accusations of police brutality or harassment remain a volatile issue which influences the court's attempts to deal with juveniles.

The court is also subject to police and community pressure to take strict disciplinary action against juveniles.[3] Court personnel receive inquiries and pressures from law enforcement officials regarding pending court action. Police often lobby for placement of a juvenile and they sometimes express pleasure that a juvenile's family has had to retain an attorney to handle the case, that is, that the family has had to "pay" for the juvenile's actions.

In addition to withstanding police pressure to dispose of cases in a particular manner, the court must also combat community pressures. Persistent or numerous calls to the police may result in referrals to court which are "not good," as illustrated by the following case.

#173: Pretrial Conference [*Judge's Chambers 16 minutes*]

Black Male, 14 years old ("Alan")
Judge
Prosecuting Attorney
Public Defender
Court Worker (probation)
Court Worker (Intensive Treatment Unit)
Referral#12: Truancy
        #13:   Insufficient Evidence
        #14:   Insufficient Evidence
        #15:   Insufficient Evidence
        #16:   Insufficient Evidence

JUDGE: What do we have?

COURT WORKER: He's 14-years old and was on probation for 11 months about a year ago. A month ago the police got all kinds of calls, a slew of delinquent activity. The police aren't able to get the kid on anything.

We got a call from Lou Warton [TV news reporter] and it's been taken up by the city council. Three weeks ago the police got a call on stealing bicycle parts. I called the school; he's been truant, too. The truancy is our only good case.

PROSECUTING ATTORNEY: Number of kids in the family?

COURT WORKER: Seven or eight.

PROSECUTING ATTORNEY: On the rest of them, they're just junk. They're set for informals—all together. [The rest of the children are scheduled for informal processing.]

PUBLIC DEFENDER: This is a black family in a white neighborhood—I think that's an important part of this.

COURT WORKER(PROBATION):   I have his brother. A lot of time the parents aren't around, the kids are outside. They're not doing anything.

JUDGE: Maybe it's a neglect situation.

PUBLIC DEFENDER: I sure wouldn't call it delinquency. The police said to me "We've got to get this kid out of the community." There's a lot of community pressure.

I talked to the boy. I told him not to make a statement. They wanted to question him about everything. I believe this is a little bit of a farce. We're not here about a truancy.

PROSECUTING ATTORNEY: Not really. What happened is the community got upset, called the police. I looked at the files—there's nothing here [no good referrals].

JUDGE: I don't think we ought to be pressured. Maybe we ought to refer them to Family Services.

COURT WORKER (PROBATION):   Apparently there was a worker out once, no parents around.

PROSECUTING ATTORNEY: It was referred to the hotline [neglect hotline]—didn't work out.

JUDGE: If the best we've got is truancy and he's been downstairs (held in detention) for 25 days. . . . All due respects to the Moonvale people. . . .

COURT WORKER (ITU):   He was put in public school out of special school district. He had done well in special.

PROSECUTING ATTORNEY: Will the family sign informal supervision?

PUBLIC DEFENDER: I don't know why this child should be treated differently from the others [other brothers and sisters].

JUDGE: Let's put them all together. I don't think he should be downstairs.

COURT WORKER (ITU):   I just think the kid needs supervision.

JUDGE: I'm sure he does—but that's not reason to keep him.

COURT WORKER (ITU):   [inaudible].

JUDGE: That's the old deal—we do treatment because we can't make the other. I want him released today. Get the whole group in on an informal. Maybe the child care unit. Hell with the community.

PROSECUTING ATTORNEY: We'll dismiss this and enter an order to put him with the others.

JUDGE: Keep Family Services on this. I'm sure they're [the kids] aggravating the hell out of the neighborhood, but that's not enough.

COURT WORKER (ITU): At the detention hearing none of the referrals had gone through legal [referrals were later found "insufficient" by legal department]. The hearing officer denied release from detention, on danger to community.

JUDGE: [*To Court Worker*] Anything you want to add?

COURT WORKER (Probation): The one kid is doing very well.

JUDGE: What do the parents do?

COURT WORKER (ITU.): The father is a union worker—good job. The mother works in the school offices in some capacity. A girl, 14, takes care of them when no one's there.

COURT WORKER (PROBATION.): I'm sure Family Services could go out there.

JUDGE: We won't be very popular at Moonvale.

Courtroom Discussion [two minutes]

JUDGE: We've been discussing why we're all here. First of all, I want Alan released today. The court worker working with him says he's been doing fine. The juvenile needs some help. I understand you're going on vacation in July.

MOTHER: Yes.

JUDGE: When you come back we'll set it down [for an informal hearing]. Here's the problem. Idleness breeds problems. What we've had is a series of piddly things—add them up, everybody gets upset. [To the juvenile] Did we treat you all right?

JUVENILE: Yes.

JUDGE: Food all right?

JUVENILE: Yes.

JUDGE: I'm going to sign off right now.
     We want to work with you.

Post Hearing

A third year law student doing an internship with the public defender represented the juvenile at the detention hearing. He says the juvenile was detained on the basis of the truancy referral. He says the same information the judge received from the court workers today was available at the time of the detention hearing. Even though the referrals hadn't been reviewed by the legal department at the time of the detention hearing, the hearing officer knew the charges were "not good" and wouldn't be filed. The hearing officer detained the juvenile anyway.

School Decisions

Another institution integral to court activities is the educational system. The court must deal with over 25 school districts and hundreds of schools. Schools are, of course, the source of truancy referrals to the court, but they may also make referrals for the use of drugs, ungovernable behavior, and trespassing if a student returns to school grounds after being suspended. Although court personnel have no control over school decisions, they often must deal with the aftermath of such actions. And whether or not the referral is school-related, court personnel routinely discuss a child's participation at school. As a result, they often find themselves confronted with confused or angry parents and juveniles who look to the court for an explanation and perhaps redress of penalties school administrators have imposed.

School suspension practices are a major issue: these policies vary greatly and may result in increased idleness for juveniles and supervision difficulties for parents. Court personnel are often unable to explain school action. For example, a school administration suspended a juvenile in February for the remainder of the school term after he was found in possession of one marijuana cigarette. The hearing officer was unable to reply satisfactorily to the mother's accusation that the school's action constituted "cruel and unjust punishment" and that this would "encourage juvenile delinquency" (because the suspension would result in idleness).

Approximately 5 percent of the court's delinquency referrals involve truancy. When attempting to deal with such referrals, court personnel often encounter parental frustration and juvenile boredom with the educational system. Court personnel have several options: they may become reluctant apologists for the school's failure to interest and challenge their students. They might locate the problem within the individual child and reprimand for failure to perform well. Or they also might lecture the juvenile on the virtues and necessity of education.

The court must also deal with untimely truancy referrals, for it is common for school administrators to wait until the end of the school term to submit cases of truancy for the past nine months. Obviously, it is difficult to deal effectively with truancy during summer vacation. If the court decides to take jurisdiction over the juvenile, a review hearing may be scheduled for late fall to re-discuss the issue. If the court does not take jurisdiction, they merely lecture and wait for any future truancy referral from the school—which may arrive at next summer vacation time!

The court must also deal with the varying policies of school districts regarding court referrals. Some districts regularly rely on the court to arbitrate truancy and disciplinary problems; others make few referrals to court. These decisions lie beyond the control of the juvenile court. Consequently court personnel may become involved in matters which would be better resolved by school personnel and parents in many cases, but in school districts which are reticent to make court referrals, court personnel may become involved in juvenile problems long after they have begun, and their opportunity for effective action is greatly curtailed.

Parental Referrals

The juvenile court is often depicted as a monster snatching children from grief-stricken parents. There are numerous cases in which parents do not desire court involvement. (Chapters 10 and 11 explore the circumstances under which families can prevent unwanted court involvement). Nevertheless, some parents do bring and, in some cases, abandon their children to the court, be it out of desperation or abdication of parental responsibility.

The high number of referrals for incorrigibility, approximately 4 percent of all delinquency referrals, indicates that some parents seek outside help in dealing with their children. Although such referrals are officially coded law enforcement referrals, the "offense" originates as a parental request to police or court personnel for aid in controlling their child. In such instances, the court becomes involved only in direct response to parental pleas for help.

Although some parents view the stigma of placing their children under court supervision as greater than any benefits the court can afford, some families view them as the appropriate means to resolve their conflicts with their children. Others seek court involvement as a last resort in their attempts to maintain control over their children. The lack of alternative community services is an important factor, especially for poorer families. Such families frequently do not desire court involvement any more than do their more affluent counterparts, but they often have less latitude in their attempts to raise teenagers in a troubled society.

Parents often request that police take their children to detention for a few hours "to cool off" or for an extended period of time. The court *must* become involved in such instances. Likewise, placement outside the home is almost inevitable when parents continue to refuse custody of their child, a juvenile refuses to return home, or continually runs away when returned home. The vast number of runaways, 1423 or 13.8 percent of all delinquency referrals further indicates the magnitude of the problem.

The following cases are illustrative of constant court efforts to encourage a reconciliation between parents and their children. In the first two cases a temporary, albeit tenuous, resolution is achieved, in the third case it is impossible.

#107: Initial Hearing [28 minutes]

Black Male, 15-years old
Hearing Officer
Juvenile ("Leroy")
Mother
Father
Fraternal Uncle
County Clerk
Referral #5:   Assault with intent to do great bodily harm (felony), amended to common assault (misdemeanor)

Prehearing

Father comes in to speak to Hearing Officer
FATHER: I'd like to sign for Leroy to be kept on week days and come home on weekends because he won't go to school.
HEARING OFFICER: Do you mean Leroy should be kept in this building?
FATHER: Not necessarily, but in some court place.
HEARING OFFICER: We'll see how the hearing goes.

Hearing

HEARING OFFICER: Have you read the petition? Do you have any questions regarding the wording?

JUVENILE: I didn't do anything like "bodily harm."

HEARING OFFICER: We're just talking about the wording right now. Parents, do you have any questions?

FATHER: No. Sir.

HEARING OFFICER: You have the same rights as an adult. You don't have to say anything, and if you do, you can stop in the middle of a sentence. All we have here today is a police report which is hearsay evidence and not admissible evidence. Now you have three choices today: you can deny, admit, or make a statement. Which one?

JUVENILE: Make a statement.

I went to a friend's, then his girlfriend and a friend came. . . . Girls came walking by, we dumped a cigarette out the window and it almost hit them. They said "Watch it, nigger." And then I said, "I'll slap you," and she said she'd kick me in my privacy. I went like I was going to slap her, she hit me. Her friends grabbed me. She went into the house. I told them to tell her I was sorry, but she didn't come out again.

HEARING OFFICER: When did the police talk to you?

JUVENILE: They came down and talked to me at my sister's one time.

HEARING OFFICER: Is this a girl in the neighborhood?

JUVENILE: No, she live in Lake City.

HEARING OFFICER: Do you go to school with this young lady?

JUVENILE: I didn't see her but once.

HEARING OFFICER: You sure you didn't have anything in your hand?

JUVENILE: No, nothing.

HEARING OFFICER: How many of your friends were there?

JUVENILE: Couple. One was going to come with me, but it's too early. He don't get up this early.

HEARING OFFICER: The allegation is true as amended. Strike out. . . . the way it'll read is "did willfully and knowingly assault upon and did strike with hands with force likely to do bodily harm." Great bodily harm and death are stricken.

All you have to do is strike with an open hand to constitute assault. There's no provocation. Just because someone calls you names is no reason to strike them. It's assault and battery. Self-defense is different.

You just don't strike someone, a girl, as long as you live. We men don't strike women unless she has a gun or something like that.

JUVENILE: Next day, at school, group of kids was fighting. We. . . .

HEARING OFFICER: You're not charged with that—it's not in the allegations. Sticks and stones may break my bones, but words will never hurt me, you know. How's school?

JUVENILE: Got put out.

HEARING OFFICER: What reason? You ended a sentence with a preposition, but go ahead.

JUVENILE: Late—I tried to tell the man how it was, he sent me to the principal. I tried to tell him how it was. He suspended me.

HEARING OFFICER: When was that? What month?

JUVENILE: I don't know what month.

FATHER: October [seven months previously].

HEARING OFFICER: What have you been doing in all this time?

JUVENILE: I went to the Job Corps.

FATHER: He only stayed a week.

HEARING OFFICER: You [to Mother] said he went "two weeks ago."

MOTHER: I thought he did. I called his father.

HEARING OFFICER: Expelled from school seven months ago, when did he go [to Job Corps]?

FATHER: Two and half weeks ago.

HEARING OFFICER: You did go then. Where?

JUVENILE: Utah.

HEARING OFFICER: How'd you get there?

JUVENILE: Greyhound [bus].

HEARING OFFICER: How long did that last?

JUVENILE: Around a week. I called my sister and said I was supposed to go to court. I didn't like it up there no way. I just came home.

HEARING OFFICER: Who'd you contact?

JUVENILE: Mr. Johnson with the employment office.

HEARING OFFICER: He hasn't had a court worker assigned?

MOTHER, FATHER: No.

HEARING OFFICER: He's not 16 until next Januray, has to go to school.

JUVENILE: I'm going next year. It wouldn't make any sense at the end of the year. They said I could come back.

HEARING OFFICER: He got out of school seven months ago but didn't go to Job Corps 'til this month.

JUVENILE: I've been trying to go to Job Corps. It takes a good month just to get your tickets.

HEARING OFFICER: What didn't you like?

JUVENILE: The weather, the food, lot of people out there . . . too many mountains up there.

HEARING OFFICER: The court will take jurisdiction, custody will be continued with the father with supervision by the juvenile officer. Any questions?

MOTHER: His father and I have been discussing and would like to talk in private.

FATHER: I already talked with him.

HEARING OFFICER: We'll do that after we adjourn. [To juvenile] Are you looking for employment this summer?

JUVENILE: I'm looking for a job.

HEARING OFFICER: I know it's tough. Keep trying. If a guy keeps trying he can always find work, whether it's picking up trash or what. [To Uncle and Juvenile] Will you step outside while I talk with the parents? [Uncle and Juvenile leave.]

MOTHER: Leroy has high temper. He's not doing what his mother and father want. Could we put him where he could be in during the week and come home on weekends?

HEARING OFFICER: I can't think of a facility—but maybe if his school accepts him back, he could go to school this summer.

MOTHER: What I'm asking is there any way he could be kept?

FATHER: What she's trying to say is he gets kicked out everywhere he goes.

HEARING OFFICER: The thing to do when his worker is in touch with you, he'll set up an appointment, he'll explain the whole process. You should express your opinion then.

MOTHER: If he won't go to winter school, will he go to summer school?

HEARING OFFICER: I'm behind now [in the docket]. The guy to talk to is the worker.

FATHER: If a day can be set up. . . .

HEARING OFFICER: It will be set up whenever's best for everyone. I'm sure it'll be in the evening if that's best. Keep trying.

FATHER: Sometimes I think all of my trying is in vain.

#103: Detention Hearing [22 minutes]

Hearing Officer
Prosecuting Attorney
Public Defender
Probation Officer
Juvenile ("Mark)
Father
White Male, 16 years old
Referral #14:   Arson

The judge requested a detention hearing be held for the juvenile. At first the parents said they would not take the juvenile home; they later said they would take him home but wanted to have a hearing to discuss it.

All but one of the juvenile's first 13 referrals to court were for status offenses. On the last referral the court worker assigned to the case recommended the juvenile be committed to the Department of Corrections. The juvenile and parents were opposed to such action. Subsequently, the judge closed the case and instructed detention workers not to accept the juvenile in detention on another status offense. This time the referral was arson [a felony]; parents called police because the juvenile was throwing matches on the rug at home.

Hearing

PROSECUTING ATTORNEY: I would like to ask Mr. Paulis for a report.

PROBATION OFFICER: Mark was brought to detention last Monday on a charge of arson. . . . Parents stated that the juvenile was involved in injurious behavior, also set fire to and burned carpeting.

He was under the supervision of the court for one and a half to two years. There have been numerous placements: with an aunt and uncle, Methodist Home, Sunnyvale, Teen Refuge, [group homes, private placements]. The parents also put the juvenile in several placements. Many lasted from two to four months.

Six months ago we had a hearing and the case was closed. The family and boy were not willing to accept Crockertown [Department of Corrections main facility]. In the court order the judge stated that Mark was not to be taken into detention on another status referral.

HEARING OFFICER: How is the home situation?

PROBATION OFFICER: Chaotic, they've had a difficult time. The parents brought Mark to detention on status offenses a couple times, he wasn't taken. This charge is arson. The parents refused custody when he was brought to detention.

HEARING OFFICER: In your opinion, will he return for the hearing?

PROBATION OFFICER: Yes.

HEARING OFFICER: Is he a danger to himself or the community?

PROBATION OFFICER: I hope not. No.

HEARING OFFICER: Mr. Jones [Father], would you like to make a statement?

FATHER: There's more involvement than just arson. It's Mark's tempo of setting up a power play—threat of bodily harm, set the fire. He threatens to hit his mother if she calls me about his behavior. I will not condone any bodily harm. He was using the dog as a target for knife throwing. Maybe that's a part of growing up, but I will not condone it. So there's more to it than a fire.

HEARING OFFICER: Have you had an opportunity to talk with Mark?

FATHER: His mother did on the phone.

HEARING OFFICER: Are you willing to take him home?

FATHER: If he's on probation with restrictions. If there's more trouble I will come with the proper attorneys to have him taken from the home. He has a brother 14. . . .

HEARING OFFICER: How about school?

FATHER: He doesn't particularly like to go, almost uneducable. He's had two jobs—fired from both. He refuses to take orders. He was making about $100 a week.

HEARING OFFICER (to *Public Defender*):   What would you like to add?

PUBLIC DEFENDER: I'd like to let Mark speak for himself. My involvement has been when Mark went before the judge and the only thing the court hadn't tried was the Department of Corrections. No one felt comfortable with that and the family didn't want it. I was encouraging the family to use their own resources. There's not much left that the court can do.

HEARING OFFICER: Mark, what would you like to say?

JUVENILE: When I threatened my parents it was only because they threatened to send me to Crockertown. I've been placed in several institutions. I'd crumble in there. No matter what my faults, I'm not that kind of kid.

HEARING OFFICER: Do you understand that only a hearing officer with the judge's consent could send you to Crockertown?

JUVENILE: I thought parents could.

HEARING OFFICER: Do you wish to be released?

JUVENILE: Yes.

HEARING OFFICER: If I release you, there shouldn't be any further threats to your family.

JUVENILE: Yes.

HEARING OFFICER: There's not a lot the court can do. You must try to get along with your family. Under no circumstances, unless you've threatened yourself, there's no reason to threaten anyone.

JUVENILE: OK.

HEARING OFFICER: It's my understanding and expectation that you'll get along at home and try to get another job. Did you quit or get fired?

JUVENILE: Got fired. You see, in the back you're allowed to use your fingers to mix the salad bowl. I used my fingers out in front. And I stepped on a lady's toe. She was a stockholder. . . . I got fired.

HEARING OFFICER: Let's give it some effort.

FATHER: He has a new job [explains new job]. Of course, the destruction of property at home must stop too.

HEARING OFFICER: I hope Mark will do his part. And I hope you and your wife will refrain from saying you'll send him to Crockertown.

FATHER: If Mark will try to do his part—If there's any more, I'll sell the house, dissolve the business and be gone.

HEARING OFFICER: I don't think statements like that help.

FATHER: The harrassment of 17 years gets a little much.
HEARING OFFICER: It's a two-way street.

#27: Initial Hearing [approximately 40 minutes]

Hearing Officer
Court Worker (short-term counseling)
Juvenile ("Wanda")
Mother
Court Clerk
Black Female, 15 years old
Referral #1:   Runaway

Prehearing

[Hearing Officer, and the court workers are present in the hearing officer's office.]

Worker from short-term counseling states that when Wanda ran away from home she told the police she was afraid to go home, was afraid of being beaten because she had broken a light chain. Mother instructed the police to put her in detention; Wanda was transferred to Shelter Care (open facility for detaining status offenders). Wanda was interviewed by present worker when she first came to detention.

Wanda doesn't want to return home, "never." She says her mother beats her for the smallest things. Prior to the hearing Mother has shown no interest in Wanda's returning home. She has made statements such as, "Tell her she has no family any more." Mother denies she has a daughter by the name "Wanda." "Has said she doesn't want the juvenile back because, "She left when I really needed her." Mother has several other children, about 11, 8, 1 years and a baby 1 month old. Mother's boyfriend lives with the family and they plan to marry. He is outside with Mother waiting for hearing, but Wanda has pleaded with Court Worker for him not to be admitted to the hearing.

Hearing Officer states that since he isn't her father he doesn't need to come to the hearing.

Worker states that Wanda's older brother was formerly to court. The probation officer present was the brother's worker. They feel there is little hope Wanda will ever return home. The psychiatric testing indicated a severe depression; and if Wanda didn't exhibit so much fear of going, hospitalization would be indicated according to the clinical services department. Since she has been away from the disturbances at home, Juvenile is "holding her own." Feel depression is caused from Mother's rejection of her, but Wanda seems to be accepting this rejection and dealing with it. Wanda hasn't been allowed to see her brothers and sisters, but the counselor from school took her to see the other kids at their school park. The other kids said they were painting the house and had moved into Wanda's room.

Court Worker states that when she visited with Mother she asked if perhaps Mother's minister might mediate between Mother and Wanda. Mother is extremely religious. Mother said okay, Court Worker contacted the minister, tried to arrange a meeting, but when the minister contacted the family he was told to stay out of it.

Foster home situation is going quite well. Only potential problem is that the foster mother is a Pentecostal minister which is quite different from Wanda's background as Baptist. Wanda has stated that she feels the foster mother's religion is strange and very different. Court Worker will arrange for the juvenile to go to her own church if she wants to and will make certain there's no pressure for her to participate in the foster mother's religion.

Hearing

[The mother, and the juvenile join court personnel in the hearing room]

Hearing Officer discusses arrangements for foster-home placement.

Mother asks if she can return with a lawyer, and states that she is not going to take any more of this "being led blind."

Hearing Officer asks why she feels she needs a lawyer.

Mother says she doesn't know what's going on but, she knows her rights.

Hearing Officer says that court normally seeks to return juveniles to the home and reunite families, but there seems to be little chance of that. Therefore, the court is seeking a foster home placement for Wanda.

Mother says she hasn't signed anything yet and that she wants a lawyer.

Hearing Officer asks Mother what her position is and if she wants Wanda to come home.

Mother discusses how Juvenile urinated in a trash can in her bedroom, and didn't keep her room clean. She states that when the court worker came to her house she proposed the mother make a contract with the juvenile about keeping her room clean. Mother says she doesn't make deals with any kids and no kid of hers is going to be dirty.

Hearing Officer asks if Mother wants Wanda to return home with her.

Mother states that she hasn't signed anything and the court can't put Wanda in a foster home without her permission.

Hearing Officer asks again if Mother wants Juvenile to return home with her.

Mother says, "Give me something to sign to put her in a foster home. I have babies at home—one in a crib—that I need to take care of."

Hearing Officer states that there's no need to sign anything to put Wanda in a foster home. The court will take jurisdiction.

Mother leaves the courtroom angrily saying, "I haven't signed anything yet."

As Mother leaves Wanda drops her head and says, "Fuck."

Hearing Officer states that the court will take jurisdiction and will place the physical custody with a foster parent.

Wanda says she thinks her mother will come and drag her away from the foster home if she changes her mind. She tells the hearing officer she'd better give her mother something to sign.

Hearing Officer states that Mother can't come and get juvenile; custody has been given to her foster mother. Any decisions Mother makes are not relevant now, the court has jurisdiction.

Wanda says her mother will come and get her and tell the foster mother she didn't sign anything and that she wants the juvenile back. Her boyfriend will find out the address.

Hearing Officer states that the court won't tell her mother where she is, they'll take the foster address off the court order. Foster mother knows the arrangement with the court and knows she has custody. If Mother comes in and insists on taking juvenile, the foster mother will call the police and they will not permit it to happen once they see the court order. They'll take Mother to jail if necessary.

Wanda says she understands.

Hearing Officer states court normally likes to get the family together but that will be impossible unless Mother is willing to be in counseling. In her present state of mind she isn't.

Wanda says her mother never will be willing.

Juvenile Officer asks Wanda if she understands she might not be going home.

Wanda says yes, she doesn't ever want to go home.

Hearing Officer asks Juvenile about her discussion with the foster mother, particularly the religious part and asks if she thinks the arrangement will work.

Wanda says it'll work.

Hearing Officer says she hopes everything works out for Wanda. Encourages her to get in school and give it all she has. She says Wanda is a good looking young girl who has a lot going for her and wishes her good luck.

Juvenile thanks Hearing Officer. On way out of the courtroom she tells

Court Worker she thinks her mother was trying to embarrass her when she said that about her bedroom.

Thus, at the very outset of a court's involvement in the lives of juveniles, crucial decisions are made by law enforcement officials, community members, school personnel, and parents. Other decision-makers exercise the option to initiate court involvement: the court receives the problems and often the mistakes of other societal institutions and is expected to rectify situations where others have failed.

Treatment Facilities and Outside Agencies

In addition to decisions by individuals and agencies referring juveniles to court, court personnel must also deal with outside agencies when choosing among dispositional alternatives.[4] Not only do budgetary limitations and legislative edict restrict the alternatives available, but the policies of outside treatment agencies greatly influence court action.

Juvenile treatment facilities with which the court contracts for services have the prerogative of narrowly defining the "type" of juvenile they consider appropriate for their programs. Especially when such criteria are unofficial or unspecified, an agency may reject the court's application for any juvenile they find unsuitable either after examining the juvenile's file and psychological scores, or after a pre-placement visit and interview. This tendency is particularly characteristic of private agencies, many of which have superior facilities to offer juveniles. For even though many court personnel assert that public facilities are upgrading their services, many use state facilities as a final alternative.

The following cases illustrate the extent to which the decisions of outside agencies shape court action and juvenile futures. In the first case the juvenile "falls through the gaps" and no services are available. In the second example, the court worker attempts to secure placement at numerous facilities, but the juvenile is rejected because his I.Q. is too low, then too high, and his attitude is "inappropriate." Placement in a state facility becomes the only alternative.

#104: Contested Hearing Scheduled

Hearing Officer
Public Defender
Court Worker
Representative from:
Special School District Division of Mental Health
Juvenile ("Bobby")
Father
Referral #3:   Destruction of Property (misdemeanor) and Flourishing a
              Deadly Weapon (felony)
Prior Referrals:#1:   Injurious Behavior
              #2:   Truancy

Prehearing Discussion [20 minutes]

[Hearing Officer, Public Defender, Court Worker, representatives from Special School District and Division of Mental Health are present.

PUBLIC DEFENDER: The entire police report is confusing. The allegation against the juvenile [flourishing a knife] is in the midst of a report regarding a shooting of two people. Juvenile not involved. I can't see how you have a case.

HEARING OFFICER: We don't have a case. We'll dismiss this, but we can see if we can get him some help. Worker says the victim's father went to school to pick him up [to bring to court to testify], but he had run away from school. Last time the case was set, the victim was sick. We do have a witness on the destruction of property, but the legal department says we can't make a case.

We won't take testimony on either allegation. We'll have an informal discussion regarding possible help, but the court can't be involved [doesn't have jurisdiction].

SPECIAL SCHOOL REPRESENTATIVE: He has a history of atypical behavior, violence, threatening behavior. We have tried to get medical and psychological aid, but have been unsuccessful. We're not able to contain him in the classroom. He's so restless, so violatile in temperament that we're unable to contain him. He cussed out and threatened other children; cussed out the teacher and said he was never coming back. Not only can they not contain him, but the situation requires a high degree of specialization that Special School is not able to provide.

COURT WORKER: He needs therapeutic treatment. DMH [Division of Mental Health] is one of our sources. He's quite hyperactive, was on medication but would always be falling asleep. He will not take medication now because it makes him sleepy. He has been an out-patient with the county hospital. And has been a resident at Maple Hospital.

SPECIAL SCHOOL REPRESENTATIVE: The juvenile's behavior is too difficult for Child Center to handle on a day basis. He requires institutionalization.

REPRESENTATIVE FROM DIVISION OF MENTAL HEALTH: The psychiatrist says day-basis is not enough. He's so high-functioning that he would be inappropriate for many of the programs, I hate to sound like he's falling through the gaps, but. . . .

HEARING OFFICER: Should he make contact with the psychiatrist on an out-patient basis?

REPRESENTATIVE FROM DIVISION OF MENTAL HEALTH: She [psychiatrist] has the records.

HEARING OFFICER: Something should be provided!

PUBLIC DEFENDER: Somebody has to do something. They can't all say they can't do anything!

SPECIAL SCHOOL REPRESENTATIVE: We would pay educational funds to another program if the Division of Mental Health was able to find a program.

Courtroom

[Juvenile and Father join others in hearing room for five minutes]

HEARING OFFICER: I just wanted to say to you, Bobby, and Father, the public defender is available, and the court's worker is available to help if you run into a snag. You have to do this on your own because the court doesn't have jurisdiction. Bobby, do you understand what we've done here today?

JUVENILE: No [shakes head].

HEARING OFFICER: We're going to dismiss the petition, but we still want to help. Will you go see Dr. Stanley at the state hospital?

JUVENILE: [No response for several seconds.] Yeah.

HEARING OFFICER: All right, we'll dismiss this and waive the court costs. [Public Defender and Court Worker talk with Juvenile and Father.]

#171: Review Hearing

Judge
Prosecuting Attorney
Public Defender
Probation Officer
Representative from Special School District

Juvenile ("Carl")
Mother
Clinical Services Worker
Black Male, 15-years old
Referral #10:   Incorrigible; Possession of Marijuana (minor)

Pretrial Conference [17 minutes]

[Judge, Prosecuting Attorney, Public Defender, representative from Special School District are present; in judge's chambers]

COURT WORKER: This is the fourth or fifth review on this case. I've made at least five referrals to various institutions, not in a punitive sense. He needs to be out of the community and have a chance to get an education.

PUBLIC DEFENDER: What have you looked into?

COURT WORKER: Marydale, but because of his record and their past experience with this type of boy they feel he wouldn't fit it. I don't agree wholeheartedly. Others there have been successful.

PUBLIC DEFENDER: Was his I.Q. a problem?

COURT WORKER: In all the referrals. Sunset [another group home] wasn't my original choice, but. . . . It's not so much that he tested out low, about 65, but they would have to deal with him attending school in the community. They didn't want the responsibility of having him leave [the group home] to attend school because of the problem with controlling his behavior. Catholic Children's Home originally accepted him. They were number 3 on my list. After they got the psychological they rejected him. The problem was they aren't able to control him if he has to go to school outside.

I toyed with the idea of Oakland [another placement center]. He could possibly get accepted, but I don't know if he would comprehend the rules. But during the pre-placement screening he was rejected. They didn't feel he had the right kind of attitude.

I contacted the Division of Mental Health. I suggested the possibility of some assistance, perhaps feedback between them and an institution. He tested out too high to be committed to the Division of Mental Health. They suggested they might possibly set up a special program if he's placed at Hilltop.

The Department of Corrections would take him, at Maynard [a particular setting within the city]. It's contrary to what I had in mind, but I don't have any alternative. There's no control. The mother is violently against commitment to the Division of Mental Health and Crockertown [a major facility of the Department of Corrections approximately 150 miles away]. All the placements I considered were relatively close, she had access to visit.

I explained the new program at Maynard. I told her I'd try to get that set up. He hasn't been to school since November [eight months]. He was kicked out of Special School for a number of reasons. There's a new referral, strongarm robbery and taking a watch. The mother is wishy-washy. The juvenile is kind of erratic, but not that many referrals. He doesn't have the ability to decide what he wants to do now that Orin Peters [another juvenile with prior court involvement] is out of the neighborhood. I've come to the conclusion that he has to be out of the community. He comes in at 3 o'clock in the morning and all other hours.

PUBLIC DEFENDER: When was the latest I.Q. test?

PROBATION OFFICER: August—came in on rape. He tested out mildly retarded, it's more a function of no general information. He should be educable.

PROSECUTING ATTORNEY: Who knows about I.Q. . . . .

PROBATION OFFICER: Special School thinks he can test out of there.

CLINICAL SERVICES WORKER: The difference between verbal and performance scores may be a function of not wanting to do it. The social comprehension is up, school-oriented things drop.

JUDGE: You're recommending Department of Corrections?

PUBLIC DEFENDER: This is a bizarre case. People say he's too high [referring to his I.Q.] or too low for their programs.

CLINICAL SERVICES WORKER: I had another girl who was perfect for a program. She tested a couple points too low—it was more the test than her.

PUBLIC DEFENDER: I still don't know. For sure Maynard?

PROBATION OFFICER: Yes. They won't send him to Crockertown.

CLINICAL SERVICES WORKER: Are they using peer pressure? I think that would be appropriate.

JUDGE: They've reduced from 40 to 20 [the number of juveniles in the facility].

PROBATION OFFICER: The education's important for him. He's been out too long.

JUDGE: Do we have jurisdiction? [Has the court taken jurisdiction over the juvenile previously?]

PROBATION OFFICER: Yes.

PROSECUTING ATTORNEY: We never did anything with the rape charge.

JUDGE: It was held in abeyance last December.

PROSECUTING ATTORNEY: Whatever that means.

JUDGE: Well, held in abeyance. . . .

PROBATION OFFICER: We didn't put this other referral on the petition. It's fairly weak.

PROSECUTING ATTORNEY: It's not bad.

JUDGE: As juvenile cases go—they're just borderline bad. Poor Carl, we can't even get a good rape case. I imagine he's lonely since Orin Peter's gone.

COURT WORKER: Yes. [A discussion of the other juvenile's progress takes place.] Another problem is that Mother is going on nights at the hospital. [She is a hospital maintenance worker.]

[The Public Defender leaves the conference to talk with the juvenile and his mother. After an eight-minute discussion she returns and is joined by the Court Worker to discuss the problem with the juvenile and his mother.]

Courtroom [Six minutes.] [Juvenile and Mother join others.]

PROSECUTING ATTORNEY: [Takes appearances of individuals present.] The two supplemental petitions will be dismissed. There's nothing to come back to, the record is clean. It is the recommendation of the juvenile officer that the juvenile be committed to the Department of Corrections. I further recommend that he be detained [held in the juvenile detention center pending transfer to the institution.]

JUDGE: As I understand this is a commitment that is consented to?

PUBLIC DEFENDER: Yes, Your Honor.

JUDGE: [To the juvenile] You have agreed to go to Maynard?

JUVENILE: Yes, sir.

JUDGE: Mom, you understand that DOC is not run by the court, it's run by the state. When we commit it's their province what to do. They've told us you'll go to Maynard. You'll stay with us until then.

[Juvenile begins to cry.]

JUVENILE: Want to stay with my mother.

MOTHER: I didn't understand he had to stay here today.

JUDGE: What about it, Tom [Probation Officer]?

PROBATION OFFICER: It's the practice of DOC to detain. Ninety-nine percent of the time they come here expecting the boy to be here.

JUDGE: I'll do this. I think it's evident to me Carl and Mom weren't aware what might happen today. Why don't you and Carl go home and come back in the morning?

MOTHER: Okay, what time?

JUDGE: Any time in the morning, around noon.

PROSECUTING ATTORNEY: I suggest when they appear would be the appropriate time to make the order.

JUDGE: The reason I'm doing this is because your probation officer is right. They're [DOC] not going to sit around on this. They'll probably be out tomorrow since Carl is going to be in the city. I know you weren't expecting to stay today, so go home for tonight.

Posthearing

JUDGE: Think he'll be back?
PROSECUTING ATTORNEY: That's why I didn't want to sign the order dismissing all this. If he doesn't come back, we might want to certify.
PUBLIC DEFENDER: This problem is common. A child with his I.Q. He'll be here tomorrow. It was just staying overnight he didn't understand. [Juvenile came back to court the next morning as agreed at last hearing. He has been in detention since then (9 days).]

Dispositional Hearing [Judge's Chambers 12 minutes.]

The Public Defender is concerned regarding the juvenile's ability to understand commitment to the Department of Corrections. The Prosecuting Attorney is concerned that the Public Defender is not going to sign a consent order. The Public Defender says she will sign after the people from the city facility come and accept the juvenile. They have already said they will take him, but she feels more comfortable if assured it will be Maynard.

PUBLIC DEFENDER: Carl's terrified with detention, something happened there. . . . Carl and Mother keep changing their minds. He keeps making wild sobs, something about the staff. I couldn't understand what he's saying. He's been in detention five times.
PROSECUTING ATTORNEY: We'll get a hearing, have the Probation Officer make his recommendation on the record.
[Prosecuting Attorney takes appearances of persons present. Has the bailiff call Father's name three times.]
BAILIFF: Your Honor, he answers not.
PROSECUTING ATTORNEY: Juvenile Officer is dismissing [two] supplemental petitions. We will continue with the disposition, the court already has jurisdiction. I would like to call Mr. Allen.
[Probation Officer takes the stand.]
PROSECUTING ATTORNEY: Please give your name and occupation.
PROBATION OFFICER: Mr. Tom Allen, Probation Officer.
PROSECUTING ATTORNEY: Is part of your duties supervising Carl Reeves?
PROBATION OFFICER: Yes, since March.
PROSECUTING ATTORNEY: Did you prepare the (present) reports?
PROBATION OFFICER: Yes.

PROSECUTING ATTORNEY: Please accept these as the juvenile officer's exhibit number one.

JUDGE: Has the Public Defender had the opportunity to examine them?

PUBLIC DEFENDER: I have, Your Honor.

JUDGE: Accepted.

PROSECUTING ATTORNEY: In your report did you recommend that the court explore placement alternatives?

PROBATION OFFICER: Yes. Four placements [which he lists].

PROSECUTING ATTORNEY: Have they all been explored?

PROBATION OFFICER: Yes.

PROSECUTING ATTORNEY: Did any accept the juvenile?

PROBATION OFFICER: No. They all rejected the juvenile.

PROSECUTING ATTORNEY: Did you receive two more referrals since this report?

PROBATION OFFICER: Yes.

PROSECUTING ATTORNEY: What is your recommendation?

PROBATION OFFICER: Because of his record, a commitment to the Department of Corrections. There is the potential for resources on the campus at Maynard with access to facilities at the Division of Mental Health. He may possibly need psychological therapy and a neurological workup. It's yet to be verified.

PROSECUTING ATTORNEY: Is it your recommendation he be held in detention until transferred to Maynard?

PROBATION OFFICER: Yes.

PROSECUTING ATTORNEY: And that the court take your recommendation under advisement?

PROBATION OFFICER: Yes.

PUBLIC DEFENDER: Have you talked with the Division of Mental Health?

PROBATION OFFICER: Yes. They felt that a commitment (to Division of Mental Health) was improper due to testing, test scores and psychological makeup.

PUBLIC DEFENDER: Who suggested Maynard is the appropriate place?

PROBATION OFFICER: Mr. Sakes, treatment coordinator for DOC.

PUBLIC DEFENDER: No further questions.

PROSECUTING ATTORNEY: No further questions.

JUDGE: When should we expect to hear from Maynard?

PROBATION OFFICER: Within 24 hours.

JUDGE: Take it under advisement.

The reason I wanted to have a hearing is there is a doubt in my mind whether Carl really understood commitment to the Department of Corrections. We're not asking Carl or you [Mother] to consent. The court will make the order on its own.

DOC is an agency run by the state. Where a person is placed [which of their facilities] is within their discretion, not ours. They tell us they expect Maynard and I expect it. But we should all understand it may not be, but I've never known them to go back on their word. But say they place you there and things don't work out, they may move you someplace else.

DOC's average stay is five or six months, the aftercare is about the same. You need some help—work with these people. You're rapidly approaching the age when you won't be in the juvenile court. I don't want you to get in any problems and be before a court and jury. I want you to get some schooling.

[juvenile begins to cry softly.]

JUDGE: Will you try that for me?

JUVENILE: Yes sir.

Another difficulty confronted by the court personnel is the paucity of job opportunities for juveniles. Even when decision-makers feel a job and the resulting income would benefit a juvenile's life situation greatly, jobs are difficult to provide. The court is unique in that it maintains a program financed by local industry to provide youths with pre-vocational career planning assistance, but the program is limited to juveniles 16–21 years old who have quit high school and is only able to accommodate approximately twenty persons at one time. Thus, there are many juveniles for whom jobs would represent a positive change, but these opportunities are not available. The court does have the option of referring juveniles to work projects within the county, but has no input on the acceptance or rejection of applicants.

#241 Review Hearing [Judge's Chambers for nine minutes]

Judge
Prosecuting Attorney
Public Defender
Court Worker
Black Male, 17-years old ("Danny")
Referral #4:   Assault with intent to do bodily harm (felony)
          #5:   Shoplifting (record album—misdemeanor)
          #6:   Trespassing (misdemeanor)

COURT WORKER: I've been working with him since our last setting. He's been attending G.E.D. [General Equivalency Diploma], transportation has been a lot of trouble. He applied for a job with the county, but for reasons unknown he didn't get the job. He hopes to re-enroll in school.

JUDGE: We set the review for after his birthday [age of majority].

COURT WORKER: That was three months ago. He was suspended from school after the assault. He's setting himself up for failure, but wants to go back to school. He had a truant problem, attitude. But he's changed. G.E.D. speaks highly of him, but he's below average academically. I had in mind a continuance (for three months) so the court can be involved.

JUDGE: The problem is if he's picked up, we have an open petition. . . . He'd end up in some jail. . . . I think we almost have to close it. We can urge him to keep in touch with us.

COURT WORKER: OK.

JUDGE: I remember him.

COURT WORKER: Yes. He had a couple things, all handled. He's not a violent boy, Your Honor. He said he was retaliating, the victim called his younger brother a name. . . . Mother's a typical welfare woman, operating on a minimum.

JUDGE: How much longer does he have to go in school?

COURT WORKER: He'll have to start eleventh [grade]. He got kicked out in January.

JUDGE: That's a long way. He'll never make it. Why didn't the county hire him?

COURT WORKER: He didn't fit their requirements.

JUDGE: I'd sure like to know who they hire!

PROSECUTING ATTORNEY: Sons of the people who run the government.

COURT WORKER: He had a shoplifting, minor, something like peanut butter. The trespassing was when he went to school [after being suspended].

JUDGE: We ought to send this to [the job program], see what they'd do with this boy. What's their recommendation, they just criticize. If we sent him over, certify, nobody'd convict him.

PROSECUTING ATTORNEY: He'd just have a record and then the next time he'd be a double offender. . . .

JUDGE: Great county youth program. They won't even give him a job. They'll [the school administrators] find some reason to kick him out. Well, dismiss it. . . . . Isn't there anything we can get for him? I'd like to write a letter: "If you didn't take this kid, who do you take?"

Although it is beyond the scope of the present analysis to discuss all the outside pressures and considerations which influence court actions, the preceding may provide some appreciation of the extraneous factors with which court personnel must contend.

Contrary to stereotypical images, decision-makers within the juvenile court do not function in a vacuum. Numerous agencies, schools, communities, and parents exercise discretionary power which greatly influences the juvenile court's involvement with juveniles and their families.

Notes

1. See Williams and Gold, 1972; Erickson and Empey, 1965; Goldstein, 1960; LaFave, 1962; Kadish, 1962; Piliavin and Briar, 1964; Black and Reiss, 1970; Goldman, 1963.

2. A case may be rejected if no police lab report is received, there is insufficient evidence connecting the juvenile to the crime, the Miranda rights were not read to the juvenile, no adult was present during the interrogation, or no court worker was present at the reading of the rights.

3. Although the court (and police) receive considerable community pressure, in this state the wishes of the complainant or victim are not determining factors in court action. The court decides whether to file a petition, citizens cannot "press charges."

4. Emerson (1969) comments extensively on the juvenile court's relationship to outside agencies.

CHAPTER 6

The Basis for Decision-Making

In accordance with the purpose of the juvenile justice system, court personnel are called upon to make numerous decisions regarding a juvenile's life situation. The basis for these decisions varies with the role of the decision-maker. On the juvenile's first referral to court, many decisions are based on "paper profile": the police report; the nature of the referral; the age of the juvenile. In particular, members of the court's legal department have little person-to-person contact with juveniles and their families outside the courtroom. The suggestions and actions of these attorneys are based upon their evaluation of the police report, the nature of the offense, and their past experiences, especially their opinions regarding the appropriate action for a specific type of offense. If a juvenile has prior court referrals, prosecuting attorneys will take into consideration the nature and number of past referrals, as well as any previous interaction they may have had with the juvenile and family. These attorneys have access to information contained in the social file prepared by court workers as well, but they rely less on this material than do other decision-makers.[1]

Hearing officers rely on numerous sources of information in order to make decisions, including reports on the nature of the offense, number of past referrals, court workers' recommendations, and their own interaction with juveniles and families. In many initial hearings, the hearing officer must make dispositional decisions without the advice of social workers. In these instances, the hearing officers must incorporate the more legalistic information (nature of offense, number of referrals) and their impression of a juvenile's family situation and needs. This complex process takes place during the 15–30 minute interaction in the hearing.

When a juvenile is under the court's jurisdiction, the probation officer assigned to the case will offer a recommendation to the hearing officer. In felony referrals, a member of the court's delinquency intake department will have conducted a preliminary investigation and provided a recommendation to the hearing officer. The intake department becomes involved only in those cases where the juvenile is not under the court's jurisdiction. If psychological testing has been done, the hearing officer may also receive the psychologist's or psychiatrist's report and recommendations. Likewise, if the juvenile is represented by counsel, the hearing officer will receive the opinions and suggestions from his lawyer.

All cases docketed for the juvenile judge will have an assigned court worker and are represented by defense counsel, thus the judge always has input from these sources. The court's clinical services department or a private psychiatrist may also provide an evaluation or recommendation. The chief juvenile officer may also enter a case to review the court worker's evaluation and recommendations.[2] The judge also frequently requests the opinion of the prosecuting attorney assigned to the case. Thus, in addition to his own experiences and predilections, the judge has considerable information upon which to draw when making a decision.

> I read the court [legal] file to see the nature of the referral. If it's a referral that involves some type of person-to-person crime, robbery, a homicide, that causes me to have in my mind a red flag as to disposition. Then I try to rely on my own experience as a judge which now exceeds eight years. I try to rely on my own experience as a human being, having raised my own family, and common sense, hopefully. And, obviously, I put a lot of reliance on my court workers because I know that they are skilled and I rely on them very heavily. In the serious referrals I put a lot of reliance on the report of the psychologist or, if there is also a psychiatrist, the report of the psychiatrist. So that scientific data coming from the court worker, the psychologist and psychiatrist are of great help to me in making a decision and obviously I put a lot of reliance in the attorney for the child and the attorney for the court worker.
>
> JUDGE

Court workers have the most prolonged and intense interaction with juveniles and their families, and for this reason, their recommendations are followed regularly. The following comments from the hearing officers reflect their reliance upon the evaluations of court workers.

[When you have court workers involved, do you usually feel their recommendations are appropriate?]

Yes, I do. . . . On one or two occasions maybe I've differed with their recommendation, but the large majority, no. They're the guys in the trenches as far as I'm concerned. They're out there and they've been with them and they know the entire picture so doggone much more than a guy sitting in a courtroom listening to some conversation for about 15 minutes. No, I really give credence to whatever their recommendation is.

HEARING OFFICER

[Do you usually feel a court worker's recommendations are appropriate?]

On the whole, yes. But it is just that, it is a recommendation. And I think, yes, on the whole their recommendations are sound. I have disagreed at times and that is obviously why we have a hearing. . . .

[When you're confronted with differing opinions from two court workers, or someone from clinical services or a psychiatrist, how do you decide which recommendation to accept?]

I suppose it doesn't happen, you know, very frequently. It does happen. I would say basically what I do in a situation like that is just pretty much draw on general knowledge that I feel I've had or experiences I've had, or experiences with other children with maybe similar problems. . .

HEARING OFFICER

[When you have a recommendation from a court worker do you usually accept the recommendation?]

Oh, I think better than fifty percent of the time I do. But I look upon the recommendation as just that, a recommendation. . . . . I really base what the court should do as to what has developed in the courtroom in terms of information. Sometimes the recommendation might be two or three weeks old or something like that and there may have been something happen in the interim or we may hear some facts from the parents or the youngster that would warrant maybe partial acceptance of the recommendation. I just think it's my position to decide what happens and I would like to have a recommendation. If it's a good one and it's up-to-date, then chances are we'll go along with it. If it's not up-to-date, and sometimes they aren't, or if it's not based on what I think has been continuous contact with the youngster and parents, I might not follow it at all. That happens sometimes.

[What would you do in an instance when you felt you weren't getting sufficient information?]

Well, as I did on a couple of those cases, I told them I didn't like what I was hearing and I continued it for a couple of weeks for them to provide updated information about a placement or a recommendation. When they really couldn't answer some questions other than about the one they were recommending, and I wanted to know why were they recommending it and they really couldn't tell me. In one case they really didn't know what the program was all about and that's ridiculous.

. . . I want some alternatives. A reasonable alternative, not just one. There's no one thing usually for a youngster. There may be one best thing but, and that's when I find that the workers fall down the most. They usually just zero in on one thing. It's hard to defend one position if you haven't explored some other alternatives. They should explore more alternatives and then they can make a recommendation as to one of those that they like, that they feel is the best. But they shouldn't just come in here and say, "Okay, I'll send him to Crockertown." without having explored other alternatives that are available for a kid that age, with their problems.

HEARING OFFICER

If the juvenile or the juvenile's sibling has been under the court's jurisdiction for months or years, the probation officer has a long history of encounters and impressions upon which to base decisions, as well as information gathered in the social file. If the juvenile has been involved with the short-term counseling unit of the court, the social file will contain the impressions and evaluations of that court worker. In felony referrals, the delinquency intake unit will conduct a preliminary investigation with the juvenile and family.

Because the court routinely handles both adjudication and disposition in the same hearing, the social investigation is conducted prior to adjudication.[3] Thus, although the juvenile has not been adjudicated in violation of the Juvenile Code, the court worker must prepare a dispositional recommendation to be presented after the juvenile has been found guilty. Such recommendations are based upon the information and impressions gathered regarding the juvenile's life situation; especially crucial is the interview with the juvenile and family. Some recommendations are based on two or more sessions, but due to heavy caseloads, busy schedules, and crowded dockets, it is common for the recommendation to be based on one 45-minute to two-hour interview.

Court policy requires that if juveniles are held in detention, a court worker should visit them daily. Thus, the court worker has more opportunity to review and evaluate juveniles' situations and personalities during the two to five week period in which they are awaiting a hearing. The public defender also has increased access to juveniles held in detention.

The Social Investigation and File

The social investigation and its product, the social file, have been the source of much criticism and controversy within the juvenile justice system. Those who advocate curtailment of the discretionary power exercised by court personnel condemn the court's review of a juvenile's life situation as an invasion of juvenile and family privacy. Proponents of the juvenile court assert that the social investigation is the primary resource on which the court must rely to fulfill its major objective, the evaluation of juvenile problems and needs. Regardless of the critics, court personnel are statutorily empowered to conduct social investigations in order to appraise a juvenile's situation and recommend the disposition of cases. The social investigation is symbolic of the juvenile court's espoused purposes: Discussions are not limited to a probing of facts pertaining to the alleged violation of the Juvenile Code, but include the entire social situation of the juvenile. The purpose of the social investigation is not legalistic, rather it is designed to facilitate the court's functioning as a social agency.

The present court requests parents to sign a "release of information" form granting permission for the court worker to investigate outside sources. Juveniles do not sign this form, but they may be requested to give verbal consent. Compliance is voluntary, but the vast majority of parents agree to the review. In those instances when parents refuse permission, the court worker can request that the judge enter an order to allow the court worker to make an investigation. A variety of information may be deemed relevant to the evaluation of a juvenile's case: family living conditions, economic circumstances, neighborhood conditions, friends and associates, past family involvement with the court, school records, reports from social welfare agencies, and psychological evaluations. Some court workers approach only those who the parents agree they can, and rely primarily upon written reports submitted by outside agencies. Others consult with the police to inquire whether a juvenile is known on the street, and hold conversations with school officials and other juveniles under the court's jurisdiction.

A major basis for the evaluation and recommendation is, of course, the interviews between court workers and juveniles and their families. Participation in such interviews is voluntary, although court workers vary in the extent to which they inform parents and juveniles of their right not to participate, as well as their right to refrain from answering any inquiry.

The following comments from court workers indicate the various types of information gathered and the manner in which court personnel integrate and interpret such material.

> [When you get assigned to a case, what decisions do you have to make right away about how to handle that particular case?]
>
> Well, the most important thing, I think, is to try to get factual information about just what's going on in the person's life. You will be aware automatically of what the offense was. . . . If someone else from a different [court] unit hasn't done a real assessment of the case, which is possible, because in certain situations you have cases that go to initial hearings where no one has ever even talked with the child other than a policeman and they're scheduled for a hearing and placed under supervision. If another worker has done a complete assessment then you just need to verify the facts, important facts like how many people are in the family, where do you go to school, where do your folks work, are they home much, what are your activities, in other words the facts of day-to-day life so you know how to reach the person basically . . . and also get some idea of what the kid's relationship is with his parents. That's really what you'd call an initial assessment and we try to do that as much as possible.
>
> PROBATION OFFICER
>
> [When it's your responsibility to compile a social file, what sources do you usually contact?]

Well, okay, the school and the home. . . . I meet with the schools, parents, and counselors, and so on like that, on a regular basis and with the police department. . . . I meet with the "short-term counseling" workers. . . . So there's not much left out really.

I'm in touch with the juvenile police officers and so I have a lot of people who give me input without my asking. They say, "Hey, we have a kid for you." So as far as looking for information, usually it comes to me. You know, I'll get a kid and the school will say, "Hey, our psychological department wants to talk to you." and so on. These are the sources, the counselors, the principals, police, "short-term counseling" workers, and so on.

[On the information you get, how do you decide which of it is accurate or which will be useful to you?]

You never destroy anything. Even what you don't write down you put in the back of your mind. I feel that way, that you always look at the smoke. There might be something underneath it. The only thing I think we have to be aware of is there's a lot of smoke when kids talk, especially about their parents. . . . Unless it's in a serious counseling session, because they tend to, if you're just sitting around with kids, they tend to exaggerate and so on. But most of my work is too serious to even bother with that sort of thing. That's usually hearsay, for example parents will say, "Why, over here, do the kids say all this type of stuff?" I say, "Forget it." Kids exaggerate, but otherwise . . . I put it in the back of my mind, most of it.

PROBATION OFFICER

[If you add to a social file whom do you contact?]

Depending on the situation, cases are so different and I really do treat them all individually and I don't do anything standard in each one. If the kid is in Special School District I'll write to them and get a report, their evaluation. If they're in the city schools or one of the schools I deal with, I usually don't get a [written] report from them. I'll talk to them and get just some information on what kind of grades this kid had and how they're behaving in school, are they posing a truancy problem, anything like that. But I usually don't send away for a formal report from them unless I'm going to have a court hearing and I need some actual documentation or if I'm going to place the child. If I'm going to place the child when I get all that stuff, but usually I just do it verbally otherwise because I'm over at the school seeing the kids there and I just talk to people about it. And it's, really, you get more information when you talk to somebody than when you say send me information in writing. They don't come across with the same stuff as when you talk to them. You get the more helpful information when you talk to them.

[Do you ever talk to neighbors or other kids about the juvenile?]

I rarely, I never talk to neighbors. I do talk to other kids. I really don't talk to them, they more tell me things. You know, "So and so, you're my worker and I know you're his worker too and. . . ." They'll start blabbing stuff to me and I don't usually have to ask. Once in a while I'll go out looking for a kid and if I don't know where they're at I'll ask them a question, "Have you seen so and so?" And they'll give me information. Kids are real free with information.

[Of the information you gather for the social file, how do you decide which of it is accurate?]

I just have to know the kid long enough to make my own impression. I can't really go, I don't use it really. As I said, the papers, the information you get in writing, I really don't rely on very heavily at all. I mainly get it just because you're supposed to get it and you need it when you make a referral anywhere, any type of referral, for some type of service in the court or a placement somewhere. That's really the main reason I get it because I find that sometimes I've gotten reports on kids saying they are looney, they are off the wall. Then I find the kid doesn't ever give me any trouble at all, as good as gold. I never see any of that crazy behavior they talk about, so I don't rely on that that much. I make my own impression.

PROBATION OFFICER

The sources of information for court decisions are many and varied, as diverse as the personnel who gather it. Decision-makers must, of course, sift through all the material gathered and summarize a juvenile's social history and situation. Crucial variables in this process are multitudinous: there are the more easily identified variables such as age, the nature of the offense, the number and nature of past referrals, school grades, and psychological testing scores. But of even greater import are those difficult-to-define, less-calculable such as juvenile demeanor and attitude, the evaluation of the home situation, family stability, and the prognosis for future behavior.

Although it is a distortion of the decision-making process to consider these variables separately, the next chapters will attempt to explore the major legal and socioeconomic factors which influence decision-making in the juvenile court. In addition to examining these variables individually, it is crucial to examine the final product of this complex interaction, "the great synthesis," that process through which court personnel integrate and interpret the vast of miniscule amount of data they have obtained and the manner in which they incorporate their impressions into their recommendations and orders. The great synthesis is that all-important matrix of fact, experience, bias, professional ideology, personal preference, and intuitive knowledge which culminates in an evaluation of the juvenile's life situation and produces a decision which will greatly influence that juvenile's future.

Notes

1. The court maintains two separate files: the legal file which contains only court orders and petitions, and the social file which contains all the information gathered by court workers on the juvenile's social situation, including school reports, psychological/psychiatric information, and court worker evaluations/reports.

2. The chief juvenile officer may enter a case on his own initiative, or at the request of the prosecuting attorney or the court worker assigned to the case. He is frequently involved when the referral is a major felony or when there is disagreement between the court worker and court attorney regarding the appropriate disposition.

3. In those juvenile courts which use bifurcated proceedings (two separate hearings), it is possible for the court to refrain from making a social investigation until after the juvenile has been officially adjudicated delinquent. Although many support this approach because it minimizes the possibility of unnecessary court involvement in juvenile and family affairs, bifurcation may also increase the amount of time necessary for processing cases due to the delay between adjudication and disposition.

In the present court, court workers must prepare a recommendation in case a juvenile is found guilty. One intake worker stated, "You see our trouble is that we have to make a recommendation based on the fact that he probably is good for it (the offense charged) but otherwise how can you make a recommendation until it's been tried?"

CHAPTER 7

Legal Variables: The Offense

Judicial discretion is a hallmark of the present juvenile justice system; it enables the judge to individualize the treatment for each offender and *to treat the offender rather than the offense,* and I support its retention in the juvenile justice system.

HEARING OFFICER (emphasis mine)

Traditional juvenile justice philosophy emphasizes the needs of the juvenile rather than punishment for an offense. Thus, it is consistent with that philosophy that the nature of the allegations against a juvenile *not* be the major criterion by which court decision-makers choose among alternatives. Although the nature of the allegation against a juvenile is, indeed, considered crucial, the court's evaluation of a juvenile's social situation, including home and school circumstances, is also important. Two major considerations are what court personnel perceive to be the needs of a juvenile and what they feel the juvenile justice system has to offer a juvenile. For this reason, the offense may serve as a preliminary clue for the evaluation of a juvenile's social situation or provide insight into a juvenile's character, but the offense, in and of itself, is not the major factor in court decisions. It is merely a starting point.

As discussed in Chapter 3, the nature of the offense does influence a major decision made by court personnel, the decision whether to process the referral informally or formally. Major felonies must be processed formally according to court policy (with a petition filed and a formal court hearing scheduled); most felonies are handled in this manner.[1] But when the allegation is a misdemeanor or a status offense, the court may deal with the case informally or formally. Court personnel may file a petition and schedule a formal hearing, but they also may take informal action such as issuing a warning letter, scheduling an informal hearing, or suggesting short term counseling.[2] Thus, the nature of the offense provides an initial, but limited, guide for court personnel in their dealings with juveniles.

Unlike adult offenses, it is difficult to define "seriousness of offense" within the juvenile justice system. For although court personnel generally define seriousness in terms of "danger to the community," the child-oriented approach of the court places more emphasis on "potential danger to the juvenile." Many decision-makers consider the latter criterion as most appropriate for determining the seriousness of an act. Thus, although when requested to rank offenses from the least to most serious, most court personnel list status offenses, misdemeanors, felonies, and felonies against persons, the interpretation and operationalization of these rankings vary greatly during actual decision-making situations.

Although status offenses are seen as the least serious in terms of danger to the community, such cases are more often viewed as needing court involvement than are misdemeanor cases. Unless a juvenile has been referred a number of times, such crimes as shoplifting under $50, minor destruction of property, or peace disturbances are commonly viewed as situational delinquency, that is, behavior that, although undesirable, does not necessarily indicate a pattern of delinquent behavior.

The court's policy is to process most misdemeanor referrals informally, thus not involving the juvenile in a courtroom proceeding or formal probation. In those cases processed formally, if the juvenile is not having problems at school and there are no major family conflicts, the usual disposition is either conditional or outright dismissal of the petition. Of all misdemeanor allegations, 86.4 percent are afforded the least severe dispositions. In 11.6 percent of such cases the court takes jurisdiction over the juveniles and places them on probation; in only 2 percent of such cases does the court place the juvenile outside the home or make a commitment to the Department of Corrections with a stay of execution.[3]

Unlike misdemeanors, status offenses are often viewed as indicative of deeper, perhaps undisclosed, home or school problems. Truancy, running away, and incorrigibility are rarely interpreted as isolated or situational occurrences. Although they pose minimal threat to the larger community, all of these behaviors may be viewed by court decision-makers as indices of severe family-juvenile problems; they are often regarded as warning signals urging court involvement to break established behavior patterns. Likewise, intervention may be recommended to prevent future delinquency, for many court workers express the conviction that, if not dealt with immediately, status offenses will lead to more serious delinquency.[4]

Approximately 23.8 percent of juveniles involved in status offenses are placed on probation; 4.8 percent are placed outside their homes. Thus, the likelihood that status offenders will receive more severe dispositions is greater than those who commit misdemeanors. The danger to the community as well as the school and home situations are examined by court personnel. Those juveniles who are seen by court personnel as experiencing difficulties at home or school will be classified as requiring ongoing court services.

In accordance with general statutory guidelines, felonies are regarded as very serious acts and given much attention by court personnel, in particular, person-to-person offenses such as murder, rape, assault with intent to do great bodily harm, assault with intent to kill, and armed robbery. Not only do court decision-makers reflect the dominant societal and legal response to such behaviors, but they also view involvement in such crimes as indicative of a juvenile's character and problems. It is more than the offense which causes concern for court personnel; rather, it is what the act symbolizes that is crucial. Such behavior from an adolescent is commonly regarded as an indication of serious problems, problems which may necessitate further, perhaps extensive, court intervention in a juvenile's life situation.

> Well, I treat the personal-type crimes differently than non-personal. I did in the adult system. I think most judges do. As I say, I read where they say the juvenile judges should never, or some juvenile judges never consider the offense and I think that's just not so. Obviously I treat a forcible rape, which is a distasteful type of an offense, differently than I do a consensual statutory rape. If, now again, I'm generalizing, if I'm talking about a statutory rape, and

we've had a lot of them, where you're talking about a 16-year old boy and a 16-year old girl or a 16-year old boy and a 15-year old girl that have sex together. I can't get all charged up about that as I can about the 16-year old that beats up an 11-year old girl and rapes her. So, yes, you do react more to that, obviously, I think. Not just because of the nature, the heinous nature of the crime, but because you're dealing with a different type of person. It's demonstrative of the type of person you're dealing with. The person who takes a gun into the Quick Shop and holds it at the head of the 68-year old social security type of proprietor is going to be treated by me differently than the kid who grabs another kid on the school grounds and steals his lunch by threatening to hit him in the head with a ball bat. Now they're still person-to-person crimes, but they're two kids fighting as opposed to something that I consider to be a lot worse.

JUVENILE JUDGE

Although the seriousness of an offense does influence the decisions the court may make, it would be erroneous to suggest that it is the major determinant of such decisions. For once the nature of the offense has been noted, court personnel also consider mitigating or explanatory circumstances, which can alter the decision-maker's initial impression of a juvenile based solely on the offense. These factors include the number and nature of prior referrals to court, the degree of involvement in an offense, the court's evaluation of "known about" delinquency (which has not resulted in official referrals to court), and most importantly, the court's evaluation of the juvenile's home and school situation.

Accordingly, it is crucial to examine those situations in which mitigating circumstances or extraneous considerations either satisfactorily explain a juvenile's involvement in a serious offense, and perhaps explain that involvement to the extent that further court involvement is seen as unnecessary; or convince court personnel that further intervention is necessary, even though the seriousness of the offense alone does not dictate further court involvement.

The following two cases provide examples of both extremes. In case #196 a juvenile is charged with assault with intent to do great bodily harm, the allegations are found true, but the disposition is one of the least severe possible, a conditional dismissal. In the second case, #166, the juvenile's only prior referral is incorrigibility. Having been placed outside her home, she has returned to court on a "failure in placement" referral. The dispositional recommendation is commitment to the Department of Corrections, a severe disposition.

#196: Full Contested Hearing

Hearing Officer
Defense Counsel (Private Attorney)
Prosecuting Attorney
Court Worker #1 (Short-term counseling)
Court Worker #2 (Probation)
Mother
Father
Juvenile ("Tom")
Witnesses
Court Clerk
White Male 16 years old
Referral #2:   Assault with intent to do great bodily harm (felony)

Pretrial Conference [18 minutes]

[Hearing Officer, Prosecuting Attorney, Private Attorney, Court Workers.]

COURT WORKER #1:   There are so many circumstances that led up to the fight, if it all gets settled in the courtroom it might resolve it.

DEFENSE COUNSEL: It's my understanding that there's been a long-time feud in the neighborhood factions among the juveniles.

HEARING OFFICER: Salt and pepper?

COURT WORKER #1:   Yes.

DEFENSE COUNSEL: Tom saw others throwing garbage outside the house and called the police. Chased them into a field. He [juvenile] was advised that Craig (victim) was going to beat him up. Craig attempted to trip him, said he was going to get him. Tom met another boy who said Craig was going to get him. He [defendant] took off his shirt and got the first punch in.

PROSECUTING ATTORNEY: It looked very serious from what the witnesses said. Serious injuries to the boy [victim], and nothing in the home to correct the situation. Perhaps it was being fermented by the father.

COURT WORKER #1:   My concern is that Tom learn some alternative way to deal with his frustration.

DEFENSE COUNSEL: With all due respect, what was his alternative that day? "You're going to get yours." Would it have been better for *him* to have a broken jaw?

PROSECUTING ATTORNEY: You have a man leaning over a drinking fountain and Tom coming down with a blow and breaking his jaw. It's too dang serious.

COURT WORKER #1: Tom, by nature, isn't an assaultive person. I understand his frustration with the neighborhood. I'm mainly concerned that he learn that another incident like this will get him in serious trouble.

PROSECUTING ATTORNEY: He'll be 17 in seven months.

DEFENSE COUNSEL: It's a two-way street.

HEARING OFFICER: I seriously hope there hasn't been any further altercation.

DEFENSE COUNSEL: He got beat up the next day, hit several times. The father has taken the attitude they can't live in the neighborhood and just have to move. The family relates there's been damage to the house. The father's a policeman, has an unlisted number, but they still get all-night phone calls.

COURT WORKER #1: I truly feel for the family, they have been harrassed.

DEFENSE COUNSEL: It's an ugly situation. There's no way I can condone it. But placing myself in the situation, I don't know how long I could run.

HEARING OFFICER: It's a fine line—but there's a legal and right way to do things.

COURT WORKER #1: It's the manly thing to stay and fight, and he feels some pressures to be manly, but he needs to explore other avenues.

PROBATION OFFICER: It's the Mayland police. Father . . . .

HEARING OFFICER: Other children?

DEFENSE COUNSEL: Just the younger brother.

PROSECUTING ATTORNEY: We have witnesses. How shall we handle it?

HEARING OFFICER: Sequester them?

DEFENSE COUNSEL: I'd appreciate it.

Hearing [52 minutes]

[Prosecuting Attorney calls first witness who was the victim (16-year old white male).]

PROSECUTING ATTORNEY: Craig, how old are you?

VICTIM (CRAIG): Sixteen.

PROSECUTING ATTORNEY: Were you a student last semester?

VICTIM: Yes.

PROSECUTING ATTORNEY: Were you present at school on May 3?

VICTIM: Yes. I was going to my second hour class. It was on the third floor on the left side of the hall.

PROSECUTING ATTORNEY: Do you know the individual seated across from you?

VICTIM: Yes.

PROSECUTING ATTORNEY: Did you see him at 8:30 on May 3?

VICTIM: I saw him earlier in the morning.

PROSECUTING ATTORNEY: Did you speak to each other?

VICTIM: No.

PROSECUTING ATTORNEY: Did you pass in the hall?

VICTIM: Yes. Then I went to class.

PROSECUTING ATTORNEY: What happened after class got out?

VICTIM: I went to my locker, then I went to get a drink. That's all I remember. Next thing I knew there was someone on top of me.

PROSECUTING ATTORNEY: What is the last thing you remember?

VICTIM: Getting hit.

PROSECUTING ATTORNEY: Were you leaning over?

VICTIM: Yes.

PROSECUTING ATTORNEY: Where were your hands?

VICTIM: On the fountain.

PROSECUTING ATTORNEY: How long did you not know what was going on around you?

VICTIM: A few minutes.

PROSECUTING ATTORNEY: Did you recognize who was on top of you?

VICTIM: Not until they pulled him off. It was Tom.

PROSECUTING ATTORNEY: What injuries did you receive?

VICTIM: The bone here (pointing to jaw) was fractured. Another bone was wired back together.

PROSECUTING ATTORNEY: Were you hospitalized?

VICTIM: Yes. For one and a half weeks.

PROSECUTING ATTORNEY: Are you fully recovered?

VICTIM: Yeah.

PROSECUTING ATTORNEY: Was there any impairment to the muscle structure?

VICTIM: No.

PROSECUTING ATTORNEY: Was this the first time you were in an incident with Tom?

VICTIM: Yes.

PROSECUTING ATTORNEY: How would you describe your relationship?

VICTIM: Not good. We didn't care for each other.

PROSECUTING ATTORNEY: Did you ever let him know that?

VICTIM: In a way, I guess.

PROSECUTING ATTORNEY: You were never in a prior fight with him?

VICTIM: No.

PROSECUTING ATTORNEY: Do you know what motive he might have for the fight?
VICTIM: No.
PROSECUTING ATTORNEY: Has there been any type of incident since then?
VICTIM: No.
PROSECUTING ATTORNEY: Will you attend high school this fall?
VICTIM: Yes.
PROSECUTING ATTORNEY: Thank you. No further questions.
DEFENSE COUNSEL: Do you remember what happened May 3?
VICTIM: Yes.
DEFENSE COUNSEL: Were you bent over a fountain when you were struck?
VICTIM: Yes.
DEFENSE COUNSEL: You know of no reason why this occurred?
VICTIM: No.
DEFENSE COUNSEL: No reason at all?
VICTIM: We never got along.
DEFENSE COUNSEL: Do you have any idea why he may have thought you were out to get him?
VICTIM: No.
DEFENSE COUNSEL: Will you direct your attention to the day before? Were you in the neighborhood of Tom's house?
VICTIM: Yes.
DEFENSE COUNSEL: Were boys throwing trash at the house?
VICTIM: I heard about it afterwards.
DEFENSE COUNSEL: How long afterward?
VICTIM: Fifteen to twenty minutes.
DEFENSE COUNSEL: Were you in a field near the house?
VICTIM: I came later.
DEFENSE COUNSEL: Were you present when the boys were arrested?
VICTIM: No.
DEFENSE COUNSEL: What were the names of those arrested?
VICTIM: [Names the juveniles.]
DEFENSE COUNSEL: Are they friends of yours?
VICTIM: Yes.
DEFENSE COUNSEL: You were in no way involved?
VICTIM: No.
DEFENSE COUNSEL: Were you ever involved with damage to the house?
VICTIM: No.
DEFENSE COUNSEL: Did you ever have bad words with Tom?
VICTIM: Yes. Things going on in the subdivision, everyone blamed on him. I don't know if it was him.
DEFENSE COUNSEL: Did you ever talk with him?
VICTIM: Yes.
DEFENSE COUNSEL: Did you ever accuse him?

VICTIM: I never told him I thought he was responsible.

DEFENSE COUNSEL: Have you ever threatened to fight him?

VICTIM: A couple of years ago.

DEFENSE COUNSEL: What are the names of the boys being questioned by police?

VICTIM: [Names the boys.]

DEFENSE COUNSEL: Do you know a boy named Oliver McKay? Is he your friend?

VICTIM: Yes. He's in my second hour (class).

DEFENSE COUNSEL: Did you mention to him that you were going to fight with Tom because he called the police on your friends?

VICTIM: No.

DEFENSE COUNSEL: Besides yourself at the fountain was anyone there present?

VICTIM: Harold Armour.

DEFENSE COUNSEL: Was he one of the boys taken into custody by police?

VICTIM: Yes.

DEFENSE COUNSEL: No further questions.

HEARING OFFICER: I have one question. I believe you stated you contemplated a fight with Tom a couple of years before.

VICTIM: It wasn't really nothing. He missed the basket. I said something.

HEARING OFFICER: How long have you been acquainted?

VICTIM: About three years.

HEARING OFFICER: You're excused. (He explains to the juvenile that the hearing would be confidential).

PROSECUTING ATTORNEY: I'd like to call the next witness.

PROSECUTING ATTORNEY: How old are you?

WITNESS (WHITE MALE):   Fifteen.

PROSECUTING ATTORNEY: Do you attend Garvey High School?

WITNESS: Yes, I was in ninth and will be a sophomore.

PROSECUTING ATTORNEY: Do you know the individual across from you?

WITNESS: Yes.

PROSECUTING ATTORNEY: Were you present on May 3?

WITNESS: Yes.

PROSECUTING ATTORNEY: Were you interviewed by the police?

WITNESS: Yes.

PROSECUTING ATTORNEY: What happened?

WITNESS: Well, before first hour Tom (defendant) said he was going to fight with Craig. We saw Tom take off his shirt, he gave it to his younger brother. Craig was getting a drink. Tom hit him. Craig fell on the ground with Tom beating him.

PROSECUTING ATTORNEY: Do you know any motive Tom might have?

WITNESS: No.

PROSECUTING ATTORNEY: Did he have any weapon?

WITNESS: No.

PROSECUTING ATTORNEY: Did you see the victim attempt to strike the accused?

WITNESS: No.

PROSECUTING ATTORNEY: No further questions.

DEFENSE COUNSEL: What is your age?

WITNESS: Fifteen.

DEFENSE COUNSEL: Are you in the same class as the victim?

WITNESS: No.

DEFENSE COUNSEL: Is he ahead of you?

WITNESS: Yes.

DEFENSE COUNSEL: Do you live in the same neighborhood?

WITNESS: Yes.

DEFENSE COUNSEL: Is he a good friend?

WITNESS: Yes.

DEFENSE COUNSEL: The day before were you there when they were throwing trash at the house?

WITNESS: I was standing there.

DEFENSE COUNSEL: You and [names juveniles] are all good friends?

WITNESS: Mel is in [another city] now.

DEFENSE COUNSEL: Have you had trouble with the accused in the past?

WITNESS: Yes.

DEFENSE COUNSEL: Were you ever present when the two said they were going to fight?

WITNESS: No. Craig didn't know.

DEFENSE COUNSEL: Are you talking about several incidents?

WITNESS: All I know of is the one with the garbage.

DEFENSE COUNSEL: Who was down there?

WITNESS: Me and Carl Borger.

DEFENSE COUNSEL: Were you stopped by the police?

WITNESS: Yes.

DEFENSE COUNSEL: Did you run?

WITNESS: Yes.

DEFENSE COUNSEL: Police brought you here?

WITNESS: Just talked with us.

DEFENSE COUNSEL: No action was taken?

WITNESS: They wanted to tell us not to bug Tom.

DEFENSE COUNSEL: Did you talk with the accused after that evening?

WITNESS: No.

DEFENSE COUNSEL: Do you know Steven King?

WITNESS: No.

DEFENSE COUNSEL: When you went to the second floor. . . .
WITNESS: Third floor.
DEFENSE COUNSEL: Craig got hit after?
WITNESS: Getting up from the drink.
DEFENSE COUNSEL: Where were the victim's hands?
WITNESS: Down to his side.
DEFENSE COUNSEL: Where was he facing?
WITNESS: To the side.
DEFENSE COUNSEL: Did you see anything else?
WITNESS: I seen Tom on top of Craig.
DEFENSE COUNSEL: Did you hear anything after they pulled them apart?
WITNESS: No.
DEFENSE COUNSEL: Were you at school the day after?
WITNESS: Yes.
DEFENSE COUNSEL: Did you hear about Tom being beaten?
WITNESS: No.
DEFENSE COUNSEL: Have you heard about it since then?
WITNESS: Yes.
DEFENSE COUNSEL: Do you recall the name of the person who did it?
WITNESS: Darrell Osgar. He moved about a month ago.
DEFENSE COUNSEL: That's all the questions I have.
    [Hearing Officer instructs juvenile on confidentiality of hearing, and
    adds, "Keep it to yourself. You make a good witness. You're ex-
    cused."]
PROSECUTING ATTORNEY: I'd like to call my next witness.
PROSECUTING ATTORNEY: What is your name?
WITNESS (WHITE MALE):   Sam Thomas.
PROSECUTING ATTORNEY: Do you attend Garvey High School?
WITNESS: Yes sir.
PROSECUTING ATTORNEY: What grade are you in?
WITNESS: Junior.
PROSECUTING ATTORNEY: Were you present on May 3 at 8:30 A.M.?
WITNESS: I was.
PROSECUTING ATTORNEY: Did you witness a fight?
WITNESS: Yeah.
PROSECUTING ATTORNEY: Had you seen either person involved earlier?
WITNESS: No.
PROSECUTING ATTORNEY: Will you tell us what you saw?
WITNESS: Before first hour kids told me there was going to be a fight.
    Tom took off his shirt, walked over to the fountain. I didn't know the
    kid [the victim].
PROSECUTING ATTORNEY: What position was the victim in when he was
    struck?
WITNESS: Just getting up from the fountain.

PROSECUTING ATTORNEY: Where were his hands?
WITNESS: I think they were on the fountain.
PROSECUTING ATTORNEY: Did you see the victim strike Tom [defendant]?
WITNESS: Maybe when they were on the ground, not before then.
PROSECUTING ATTORNEY: Are you acquainted with either juvenile?
WITNESS: Yes, Tom [defendant].
PROSECUTING ATTORNEY: Are you a friend of his?
WITNESS: Yes.
PROSECUTING ATTORNEY: No further questions.
DEFENSE COUNSEL: You said you heard about a fight. Did you hear names?
WITNESS: Just Tom.
DEFENSE COUNSEL: Nothing further.
HEARING OFFICER: How long have you known the accused?
WITNESS: About ten years.
HEARING OFFICER: Live in the same neighborhood?
WITNESS: Three years ago I lived down the street.
   [Hearing Officer explains regarding confidentiality of hearing, excuses
   witness.]
PROSECUTING ATTORNEY: I'd like to call the next witness.
PROSECUTING ATTORNEY: Are you a student at Garvey High School?
WITNESS: Yes.
PROSECUTING ATTORNEY: What grade?
WITNESS: Sophomore.
PROSECUTING ATTORNEY: Do you know Tom [defendant]?
WITNESS: Yes, sir.
PROSECUTING ATTORNEY: How well do you know him?
WITNESS: I'm not sure.
PROSECUTING ATTORNEY: How long have you known him?
WITNESS: One year.
PROSECUTING ATTORNEY: Do you reside in the proximity?
WITNESS: No, sir.
PROSECUTING ATTORNEY: Were you present at the fight?
WITNESS: Yes, sir.
PROSECUTING ATTORNEY: What did you see?
WITNESS: A punch.
PROSECUTING ATTORNEY: Who struck whom?
WITNESS: Tom just drew back and hit him on the side of the face.
PROSECUTING ATTORNEY: What position was the victim in?
WITNESS: He just turned around.
PROSECUTING ATTORNEY: Do you know of any motive?
WITNESS: No, sir.
PROSECUTING ATTORNEY: Do you know of any subsequent altercation that
   Tom was in?
WITNESS: No, sir.

PROSECUTING ATTORNEY: No further questions.
DEFENSE COUNSEL: On that day did you have any conversation with Tom?
WITNESS: I seen him and talked with him.
DEFENSE COUNSEL: What was the conversation about?
WITNESS: About school.
DEFENSE COUNSEL: Anything else?
WITNESS: Girls.
DEFENSE COUNSEL: Did you discuss the victim?
WITNESS: No, sir.
DEFENSE COUNSEL: Did you discuss the incident the day before?
WITNESS: No, sir.
DEFENSE COUNSEL: No further questions.
[Hearing Officer explains the confidentiality of the hearing and excuses witness.]
HEARING OFFICER: [To private attorney] Counselor, is there anything further you wish to include?
DEFENSE COUNSEL: I'd like the court to hear the juvenile's and the family's statements. [Addresses defendant.]
DEFENSE COUNSEL: What is your age?
JUVENILE ("TOM"):   Sixteen.
DEFENSE COUNSEL: Do you live with your mother and dad?
JUVENILE: Yes.
DEFENSE COUNSEL: What grade were you in?
JUVENILE: Tenth.
DEFENSE COUNSEL: Are your grades average?
JUVENILE: Average.
DEFENSE COUNSEL: Your attendance record?
JUVENILE: Four days excused absences.
DEFENSE COUNSEL: Were you ever reprimanded or disciplined at school before this incident?
JUVENILE: No, sir. Well, when I was in junior high I was in two fights.
DEFENSE COUNSEL: How old were you then?
JUVENILE: Fourteen.
DEFENSE COUNSEL: Looking back to the day before May 3 did anything unusual happen?
JUVENILE: Yes.
DEFENSE COUNSEL: What time?
JUVENILE: About two-thirty. I changed clothes. Me and my brother took the dogs out directly across the street. Some boys were laughing at the dogs. They were calling me and my brother "puss," throwing rocks, and garbage. We called the police. By that time the boys were in the woods. Me and the policemen chased them in the woods.
DEFENSE COUNSEL: Was that the end of that incident?
JUVENILE: Yes.

DEFENSE COUNSEL: What happened at school the next day?

JUVENILE: I walked into school and went to my locker and got my books. I went in the cafeteria and talked to Sam. He told me he heard a lot of talk that Craig was after me because I called the police on his friends. He said he was going to kick my ass.

DEFENSE COUNSEL: Those were his words?

JUVENILE: Yes.

DEFENSE COUNSEL: Continue.

JUVENILE: I went by a table and two others told me the same thing. The bell rang and I went to my locker. I saw Craig and two other boys. They walked down the hall. I was walking past and Craig said, "You're dead, puss." I didn't say anything. I just kept walking. Everybody knew about it. I thought if he was going to start something I'm going to be ready for him. If it looks like he's going to hit me I'll stick up for myself. I was standing next to my room, and I figured if he's going to start anything he was going to start it then. He got a drink. I took my shirt off. He got up from the drinking fountain, was walking away. As I walked by he said, "You're dead, puss." with a clenched fist. I hit him. We went down and I hit him three or four more times.

DEFENSE COUNSEL: Mr. Legarski broke it up?

JUVENILE: Mr. Legarski picked up Craig. Mike walked over and kicked me. Mr. Legarski got him, was screaming at him. He took us to the office. We sat in the office. The police came and got our story. I went to the hospital and got my hand in a cast. That was it.

HEARING OFFICER: Well, your story is contrary to the testimony of four witnesses regarding the action of the victim. I will find the allegations true. Now we go to the second part of the hearing, the disposition. I'll ask Mr. Cavender (court worker) for a report.

COURT WORKER #1:   I've met one time with the juvenile and parents, and have had phone contact with the juvenile. My impression is that he is likeable, outgoing. He has a background of being very involved in sports, basketball and baseball. He has average grades in school and real good attendance. Given the longstanding nature of the problems in the neighborhood my feeling is I can understand Tom's frustration. There are real problems. However, to put himself in a situation like this and to end up with a charge like this by handling his problems this way can only lead to more problems.

HEARING OFFICER: This is a second referral?

COURT WORKER #1:   The first referral was ridiculous. A neighborhood girl spit on him and he kicked her for it.

PROSECUTING ATTORNEY: Why does the neighborhood have an antipathy with the family? There are thousands of families with police officers.

COURT WORKER #1:   There was another police officer in their home who didn't get along with the neighborhood. They bought the home from another police officer. Some of the feelings carried over. I don't know firsthand if Tom has been part of continuing or fostering the problems.

HEARING OFFICER: Are there problems on the adult level also?

FATHER: It's useless to even talk with the neighbors. We were there less than a week before the first incident, slapping Tom, calling him "pig lover." I went to talk with his [the other juvenile's] father, rather than calling the police. I made a mistake. I should've called the police. I can relate incident after incident.

HEARING OFFICER: [To juvenile.] What I'm going to tell you I'm certain your father and attorney have told you. The reason you're in the juvenile court is because you're [under the age of majority] and live with your parents in this county.

COURT WORKER #1:   I'd like to add one point. I'm not sure if Tom or his parents see any alternative to handling the problems. My feeling is through the court we can explore something.

HEARING OFFICER: The only thing I can think of is moving out of the neighborhood.

FATHER: Tom's involved in sports, he plays basketball, umpires other games.

HEARING OFFICER: That's a tremendous plus.

FATHER: He will not be going to Garvey High School this fall. He's had little contact with those juveniles since school [summer vacation]. He keeps so busy.

HEARING OFFICER: My main concern is that I want you to understand the seriousness of the situation. If your father did the same thing to me, if he went before a circuit court before a jury, convicted it would be two to four years in the penitentiary. He could not use the defense of self-defense until physically threatened. There's a legal and a right way to do it. Correct, counselor?

DEFENSE COUNSEL: No doubt about it.

HEARING OFFICER: If you were 17-years old. . . . You're way above average, you've got too much going for you. Don't get conned into it. If you make a serious mistake, learn from it. Don't do it again. [To the Court Worker.] What is your recommendation?

COURT WORKER #1:   Conditional dismissal or probation because of the seriousness of the offense.

HEARING OFFICER: Do you feel he has learned a lesson?

COURT WORKER #1:   Yeah. . . . I doubt he will put himself in a position to be the first to strike.

HEARING OFFICER: Another incident you could possibly be certified to stand trial as an adult.

COURT WORKER #1:   I think we need to discuss what the consequences would be if he strikes after being hit.

FATHER: I explained that after the first blow is struck he can legally defend himself.

HEARING OFFICER: That's right. Correct, counselors?

DEFENSE COUNSEL: Yes.

PROSECUTING ATTORNEY: [He says nothing.]

HEARING OFFICER: [To Court Worker #2] Are you recommending a disposition?

COURT WORKER #2:   No, Your Honor.

PROSECUTING ATTORNEY: I might explain about the records. This is a confidential record. When you [reach the age of majority] you may ask the court to destroy the social record and seal the legal and police department records.

HEARING OFFICER: If there's any intimidation, if there's any harrassment, your father can tell you how to handle it.

Conditional dismissal.

[Court costs were levied and the juvenile and parents waived their right to a rehearing before the juvenile judge. There was no discussion regarding retribution to victim.]

In the preceding case, the charge against the juvenile was extremely serious, a person-to-person offense. The hearing officer ruled that the allegations were true. The juvenile was "found guilty" of assault with intent to do great bodily harm, but he was not even put on probation. The decision was greatly influenced by the hearing officer's positive evaluation of the juvenile's family situation and his belief that the juvenile's actions were the result of past harrassment. Rather than emphasizing the juvenile's acts, the hearing ended with the hearing officer and father advising the juvenile to protect himself from future harrassment. The nature of the offense was overshadowed greatly by other considerations.

The following case is also illustrative of the fact that the nature of the offense can be minimized, except this example involves a juvenile who is before the court for "failure in placement." The original allegation was a status offense, incorrigibility. This case also affords an example of the impact of the court worker, who was convinced that a severe disposition should be given the girl because she "is known" to be involved in drug use and sale. Although this was not an official charge, much of the conversation revolves around the worker's opinion. The home situation was also evaluated negatively, the mother was accused of prolonged neglect of the juvenile and viewed as unable to deal effectively with the perceived problems. On the basis of these considerations alone the judge may have been willing to commit the juvenile to the Department of Corrections, but the fact the girl would reach the age of majority and become a legal adult before a disposition could be enacted greatly influenced the judge's actions and resulted in the juvenile's release and the case being closed.

#166: Pretrial Conference [Judge's Chambers for approximately 50 minutes]

Judge
Attorney from Public Defender's Office
Prosecuting Attorney
Court Workers
Referral #2:   Failure in Placement
Previous Referral: Incorrigibility
Attorney from Public

DEFENDER'S OFFICE: Nancy [a public defender regularly assigned to the court currently on vacation] asked me not to get involved in this case. But I understand the court's position.

JUDGE: Where does that put us?

PROSECUTING ATTORNEY: If we let it remain the Public Defender's case? The Chief Juvenile Officer, Probation Officer and I are in full agreement regarding this recommendation.

JUDGE: I understand the child isn't consenting. Tell me about it.

PROBATION OFFICER: The child was originally in Peirpoint Hospital for an attempted suicide. She went to Wayside [a group home] as a last-ditch chance. On the basis of the data available it looks like she's been doing drugs since 11 [years old]. She's been selling, but not caught. She has no inner controls and her mother can't control her. There are only two referrals, incorrigible and failure in placement. She was brought to the building [detention] on the failure in placement. That's her present status. Mother can't control her.

JUDGE: What are Mother's resources? Like taking her over to probate [court], getting her declared. We don't have to hang on. Why doesn't Mother go and do that if the girl's that incompetent?

PROBATION OFFICER: She [juvenile] says all the right things. "I'm not going to do drugs."

JUDGE: Everyone's saying. . . .

PROBATION OFFICER: She needs structure, time to a self-examination.

ATTORNEY FROM PUBLIC DEFENDER'S OFFICE: If she's that sick, it won't work.

JUDGE: If I appoint a lawyer, I can't fire her to have an emergency hearing to send her client to Salem Heights [Department of Corrections main facility for girls]. I won't do it. Nancy has a right to her days off, if she doesn't want to come in on a case [during her vacation]. Mother better get hopping. We had her [the juvenile] under jurisdiction [on probation].

PROBATION OFFICER: The things she's been doing have never been brought to court.

JUDGE: I'm doubtful if we ever could help her. If she's an adult [within a few days], we're hitting six years [of drug involvement]. I don't think I've ever had one like that that made it.

PROBATION OFFICER: We talked Mother into taking her home from detention. It was okay the first few weeks, then. . . .

JUDGE: Whether we like it or not she'll be 17 on Monday. I can't send her. I don't like it.

PROBATION OFFICER: It would give her a year's more supervision.

JUDGE: I like DOC [Department of Corrections], but I don't think I can send her on this. She's going to say, "I've been railroaded." Why should she change?

PROBATION OFFICER: I'd hope she'd gain some insight.

COURT WORKER #2: (assigned to juvenile's younger brother). I've had her brother's case since last week [about eight days]. I've seen him twice. It's my understanding, I do not know the girl, that what we have basically is an unreported six-year neglect. Father's up in Topper, miles away. From what Father and Brother tell me, Mother just can't control her.

JUDGE: How about getting her back with Father?

COURT WORKER: If the girl goes in, the whole household will go. . . .

JUDGE: Is he aware? Any relatives?

COURT WORKER: Grandmother, she's not able. . . .

JUDGE: I'll get her in, tell her where she's going. She's dodging the cops. It's her life and she chooses to lead it . . . I don't know what can change her.

COURT WORKER: If it's a six-year neglect, she deserves some help.

JUDGE: I'd be willing to do it if she were willing. But she's not. You can't drive this into her brain. If it's been since she was 11 . . . forget about her. That's hard to say. [To attorney from Public Defender's Office] How many do you save in the adult system?

ATTORNEY FROM PUBLIC DEFENDER'S OFFICE: Not very many.

JUDGE: I don't know what to tell kids on this junk.

PROBATION OFFICER: Mother won't do anything.

PROSECUTING ATTORNEY: [To attorney from Public Defender's Office.] Have you talked with her?

ATTORNEY FROM PUBLIC DEFENDER'S OFFICE: No, Nancy didn't want me to.

PROSECUTING ATTORNEY: I wish you would talk with her and explain.

ATTORNEY FROM PUBLIC DEFENDER'S OFFICE: At least I can let her know Nancy will be back Monday.

JUDGE: We can set it down [have a hearing] for Monday, if she's changed her mind.

ATTORNEY FROM PUBLIC DEFENDER'S OFFICE: I can see.

JUDGE: Tell her for me that if she changes her mind I'll send her. [To the Probation Officer] I'm sorry, I just couldn't.

PROBATION OFFICER: Well, I thought there might be a chance you wouldn't.

JUDGE: If this girl's hooked. . . .

PROBATION OFFICER: When she came in here she was spaced out on valium.

JUDGE: They're gone. The only time you see them is getting methodone. And then they're only changing one drug for another. We won't let her go until her birthday. I'd like to say something (to her).

PROBATION OFFICER: She'll be in jail three months.

JUDGE: I'll put it in the order—if *she* wants to go.

PROSECUTING ATTORNEY: Nancy said she didn't want Joan [other attorney] to get into it.

JUDGE: I think a lawyer's entitled to that. I can't say to the Public Defender, "Come in here and play games."

Second Pretrial Conference [six days later; Judge's Chambers: approximately 25 minutes.]

Judge
Prosecuting Attorney
Public Defender
Chief Juvenile Officer
Probation Officer
Court Worker (Brother's case)

[Public Defender regularly assigned to the case has returned from vacation. A different prosecuting attorney is present because the original Prosecuting Attorney is taking the day off.]

PROSECUTING ATTORNEY: We're looking at the definitions of child . . . 12 or over, can continue jurisdiction until 21.

JUDGE: I say we have the right to commit her [to Department of Corrections] because we have jurisdiction up to 18. There's nothing in DOC legislation that says 17. 041 uses the language "child" to refer to one committed.

Anabelle [original Prosecuting Attorney involved in case] felt that if we had the hearing before she was 17, there would be no problem.

PROSECUTING ATTORNEY: Why doesn't her faction get together and decide what to do?

JUDGE: There's no use having a hearing if we don't have the right [to commit her to DOC].

Once you've got her downstairs [held in detention] you have to set a date. [To Prosecuting Attorney.] You want to offer expert testimony [psychological testimony]?

PROSECUTING ATTORNEY: Yes.

PUBLIC DEFENDER: What do you mean "get our heads together?"

PROSECUTING ATTORNEY: Well. . . .

JUDGE: Department of Corrections would take her?

COURT WORKER: Yes.

JUDGE: I think we better set this down for a hearing. [To Public Defender.] You tell me when.

PUBLIC DEFENDER: That puts a burden on me.

JUDGE: What?

PUBLIC DEFENDER: It's my understanding that Bud [the hearing officer who held the juvenile's detention hearing] said, "You can stick it out [in detention] 'til your birthday." She thought she was leaving today.

JUDGE: Joan [another attorney from Public Defender's Office] told us you didn't want her to come into the case, so I said I wouldn't want her to. I said, "Talk with her." She said under no circumstances would she [the juvenile] consent. I said I wouldn't fire her lawyer. . . .

I don't know why they brought the psychiatrist. I didn't want to bring him in. If her birthday is the critical day, then it doesn't make any difference.

PUBLIC DEFENDER: You ought to figure out the legal aspect. If they don't want to commit there's no reason to hold her. Maybe by tomorrow we'll know if we'll have a hearing.

JUDGE: The best way to do it is to have a hearing and you raise it.

PUBLIC DEFENDER: It's a little awkward from my position. . . .

JUDGE: You could do it on behalf of your client. I don't know. I'd like to get in here and see if case law says anything. . . .

PUBLIC DEFENDER: Do you have reports? The psychiatrist's?

JUDGE: Why don't you [addressing the Public Defender] discuss this with the psychiatrist so you'll be ready for cross-examination? Why don't you and Chad [the Prosecuting Attorney] talk with him [the psychiatrist] together? We'll continue this until tomorrow. We'll continue it every day 'til we get it settled.

[The decision was reached to release the juvenile from detention without a hearing and dismiss the petition. Case closed.]

Notes

1. It is technically incorrect to refer to juvenile allegations as "offenses" or to label them "felonies" or "misdemeanors," for, officially, there are no such terms in the juvenile system. The correct designations would be "delinquent behavior analogous to an adult felony" or "delinquent behavior analogous to an adult misdemeanor." Nevertheless, the more familiar and convenient terms "felonies" and "misdemeanors" will be used throughout this discussion (as they are used commonly by court personnel).

2. For a review of these options see Chapter 3.

3. State statutes do not permit the certification of misdemeanors, so this option is not applicable to such referrals. Status offenses cannot be certified, for the behaviors they proscribe would not be illegal in the adult court.

4. It is interesting to note that one of the hearing officers ranked status offenses as the most serious type of offense—above all misdemeanors and felonies.

CHAPTER 8

Additional Legal Factors: Past Referrals; Degree of Involvement; Legal Representation; Presiding Officer

Number and Nature of Past Referrals

A juvenile's past encounters with the juvenile justice system influence court personnel's response to any new referrals. If the juvenile has not been referred to the court before, the court might deemphasize the seriousness of the present allegation, especially when the case involves an older juvenile whose school and home situations are evaluated positively. Conversely, when a juvenile has been brought before the court a number of times before, new referrals may be viewed as indicative of a pattern of delinquency requiring further court intervention in the juvenile's life.

The following armed robbery case involves a juvenile with no prior referrals to court: this fact, combined with the boy's minor involvement in the incident and the court worker's sympathetic view of the home situation, results in a less severe disposition of the case.

#130: Pretrial Conference and Hearing

Judge
Prosecuting Attorney
Public Defender
Court Workers

Supervisor for Court Worker
Chief Juvenile Officer
Black Male, 15 years old
Referral #1:   Armed robbery

Pretrial Conference [Judge's Chambers for 8 minutes.]

COURT WORKER: (INTAKE)   There were three boys together. One has moved out of town.
JUDGE: Who was the victim?
COURT WORKER: A 64-year old man walking through. . . . One juvenile fired a shot, threw something in the bushes. The gun was originally at one of the juveniles' homes.
JUDGE: What do we have?
COURT WORKER: This is a first referral. Happened in April [four months earlier], nothing since. Father is deceased, Mother has a history of health problems. Father was shot and killed. The killer intended to shoot the 20-year old son of Father. Mother is depressed from all of it. The school situation has deteriorated. Juvenile complains of being bored. He's a third grade repeater and wasn't promoted to ninth. He's primarily a loner. Says one of the other juveniles [involved in the robbery] is his best friend, but he doesn't seem to have many friends.
  Mother's not seen as particularly the most capable parent; she almost seemed lethargic, as if under medication. She's immobilized. Juvenile needs help regarding school and friends.
  I'm against certification. He neither had the gun nor fired it. Also his age and no prior referrals. I'm recommending jurisdiction/supervision [probation]. I think we need a review in six months.
INTENSIVE TREATMENT UNIT WORKER: Mother struck me as severely depressed. She lost Juvenile's father, her own father. There's no supervision for the juvenile. Mother works, then goes to sleep.
SUPERVISOR OF WORKER: I don't think the request for a review should be part of the order. Let the worker decide.
CHIEF JUVENILE OFFICER: I agree with that. The key is who we assign, but Ron (court worker) can handle it. If it wasn't going to be Ron, I'd recommend more severe action.
JUDGE: [To the Public Defender.] How do you feel about it?
PUBLIC DEFENDER: I don't disagree.
JUDGE: These scare me; they really bother me. He was involved peripherally. . . . I have extreme reservations, anyone who's a part of this. . . . I'll feel better if Ron will be on it.
CHIEF JUVENILE OFFICER: He seems to have done well until these events entered into his life.

Courtroom [six minutes.]

[Court personnel joined by the mother, the juvenile ("Jim"), and an adult cousin.]

[Prosecuting Attorney takes appearances, verifies juvenile's birth date.]

JUDGE: As I understand it, the juvenile is admitting to the allegation.

PUBLIC DEFENDER: Yes.

JUDGE: It is my understanding from our pre-trial discussion that on April 23 you and other people were involved in a robbery. Who were the others?

JUVENILE: [Names others.]

JUDGE: What happened?

JUVENILE: In the evening. . . .

JUDGE: Did one of the fellows have a gun?

JUVENILE: Uh, huh.

JUDGE: I think Jim knows what he's saying. What is the recommendation?

PROSECUTING ATTORNEY: Jurisdiction and supervision [probation].

JUDGE: [To the juvenile.] Do you understand what that means?

JUVENILE: Yes, sir.

JUDGE: I'm very reluctant in any type of armed robbery to do anything like this. Most times I don't just put someone under the court's supervision. It takes an exceptional case. You've never been in court before, and you were not directly involved. That's the only reason I'm allowing just supervision.

I want to caution you. I consider this to be a very serious matter. If you were a year older you would be up before the court and jury. The minimum sentence would be five years; sentence would be five years; sentence can be five years to life imprisonment.

Aside from the serious nature of this, anyone who takes from someone else is just wrong. Young man, you have a lot of life ahead of you. I don't want you to mess it up. You're lucky no one got killed— then you'd be looking at murder, not robbery.

Do you understand?

JUVENILE: Yes sir.

JUDGE: Work with us. We'll work with you.

JUVENILE: Yes, sir.

Although court personnel consider referrals for sale of drugs or possession of drugs as serious offenses, including felony possession of marijuana, it is common for the court to take a less severe course of action when a juvenile has no prior referrals and the family and school situations are adjudged to be beneficial to the juvenile. When decision-makers feel the offense does not indicate a pattern of delinquency, they may recommend that the case be taken under advisement or given a conditional dismissal. Thus, the juvenile is not put on formal probation, nor placed outside the home; and, if no additional referrals are received, the petition will be dismissed.

A major consideration in these cases is the age of a juvenile, for many of those charged with major drug activity are nearing the age of majority. In such cases court placements are limited or virtually non-existent. Likewise, such placement outside the home is deemed necessary only when the behavior is viewed as part of a general pattern of delinquency. Similarly, probation is viewed as appropriate only when the home and school situations are evaluated negatively. When the juvenile's environment is perceived as stable and there have been few referrals, decision-makers may grant juveniles the opportunity to demonstrate that the offense was an isolated incident.

Manslaughter charges resulting from automobile accidents also receive special consideration from court personnel. If the juvenile has no prior referrals and there was no drug or alcohol involvement in the incident, court personnel may view continued court supervision as unnecessary. Decision-makers have the option of ordering or recommending psychological assistance if the accident caused serious psychological problems for the juvenile; they may also revoke a juvenile's driving license if carelessness is considered a major factor in the mishap.

If, in the period of time between the alleged incident and a juvenile's hearing, the family and juvenile take independent action to deal with the situation, court personnel may take this into consideration when choosing between dispositional alternatives. When parents are viewed as concerned with their child's misbehavior and attempting to deal with the problems, the juvenile and family may be praised for making progress unassisted. Likewise, court workers may view further court involvement as unnecessary. The following case involves major allegations, but the juvenile had only two prior referrals and the family had evidenced concern over the situation.

#96: Initial Hearing [21 minutes]

Hearing Officer
Court Worker
Mother
Father
Juvenile ("Howard")
Court Clerk
White Male, 16 years old
Referral #3:   Burglary and stealing

HEARING OFFICER: [Reads the allegations and explains the hearsay evidence.] You have three choices: admit, deny or make a statement. For example, the usual statement is something like, "I was just with the others." What do you want to do?

JUVENILE: Admit.

HEARING OFFICER: The allegations are true by consent.

FATHER: They're basically the same as the police report.

HEARING OFFICER: Now I'd like to ask Mr. Simms (court worker) for an evaluation.

COURT WORKER: I met with Howard and his parents one evening. He dropped out of school in March and has gone to work full time for Father. We've discussed G.E.D. [Graduate Equivalency Diploma.] He doesn't have any involvement with these boys, and there are no problems at home.

JUVENILE: I just did something really stupid.

COURT WORKER: He's been making good progress on his own.

HEARING OFFICER: How'd this all happen? Now, I'm talking with you today.

JUVENILE: We just decided to do it. There were two other guys, neighborhood friends.

HEARING OFFICER: Restitution? What did you take?

FATHER: Money, cameras, radios. I have no idea where they went. Probably sold them, the money was probably spent.

HEARING OFFICER: Do you have a home owner policy?

FATHER: Yes.

HEARING OFFICER: They sometimes cover juvenile acts.

FATHER: Not if they were done purposely, not an accident.

HEARING OFFICER: How'd it happen?

JUVENILE: We just sold them, split the money.

HEARING OFFICER: Was anyone over [the age of majority?]

JUVENILE: One.

HEARING OFFICER: Who was the prime mover?

JUVENILE: I don't know whose idea it really was.

HEARING OFFICER: Do you know the difference between a misdemeanor and felony?

JUVENILE: I don't exactly understand.

HEARING OFFICER: These four are all felonies. If you were an adult, tried and convicted, you could get no less than a total six years up to 20 years. I want you to understand the seriousness of this. You're making decisions on your own now. Your parents can't be with you 24 hours a day.

JUVENILE: I could be spending a lot of time in prison?

HEARING OFFICER: Right. The juvenile court can certify you. We believe in giving you one mistake. You've gotten everyone's attention. I don't have the words to tell you how much mental pain you've given your parents. They're the only two people who really care you're on this earth.

[To court worker.] What is your recommendation?

COURT WORKER: A conditional dismissal until "age of majority" [two months].

HEARING OFFICER: That'll be the order. Court costs will be assessed. Now I want you [to juvenile] to work out some way to pay your parents back for the court costs.

If you come back with another felony it could mean certification or placement. I urge you to complete G.E.D. You'll never get this period of your life back. One hundred years ago they'd take you out in the public square and cut off your hands. Now we've gotten civilized; we take persons involved in crime and lock them up. Do you wish to have a rehearing on this?

JUVENILE, MOTHER, AND FATHER: No [sign waiver of right of rehearing].

HEARING OFFICER: Do you have other children?

FATHER: Two others. Howard's in the middle.

HEARING OFFICER: How are the others doing?

FATHER: Fine. Thank goodness this has been the only time.

HEARING OFFICER: Good luck. Court's adjourned.

In making an analysis of the impact of the number of referrals on the disposition of cases, it is important to recognize a phenomenon which may be called "positive recidivism." If a juvenile returns to court with an additional referral, but the new referral is *less serious than the original referral,* court personnel, although displeased, may view the juvenile as making progress. As one probation officer explained, if a juvenile was originally referred to court for burglary and returns for running away, the overall situation is getting better. One hearing officer remarked to a juvenile referred on a runaway, "This is Mickey Mouse compared to the three felonies you've been involved in earlier. I'm glad to know you're not into that."

Although juveniles who have been called before the courts, ten or more times are generally considered candidates for extensive court involvement, there is one situation in which a large number of referrals may be interpreted by court personnel as indication that court involvement should be terminated. This may happen especially when all or the majority of the referrals have involved status offenses. Particularly if a juvenile has a long history of status referrals, has been placed in several court facilities, and the family situation fails to improve, court personnel may decide they have no further services to provide a family. Although there is a general reluctance to "give up on a case," there are instances in which decision-makers feel that they can have no impact on a situation and insist that parents deal with the problem unassisted.

In one controversial case, a 15½-year old girl had been under the court's jurisdiction for over two years. Although the majority of her many referrals to court were status offenses (incorrigibility, runaway, curfew, truancy), she had been held in detention several times, occasionally at the request of her mother. She also had been placed in several facilities, in a foster home, and sent to live with relatives. None of these efforts were successful in resolving the family conflicts. Court personnel viewed the inability of the mother and daughter to resolve their conflicts as the major source of the difficulties.

The juvenile returned to the court on a curfew violation, and the court worker recommended she be committed to the Department of Corrections. Both the juvenile and her parents adamantly opposed such action, and the public defender suggested that the juvenile be sent to live with her father in another county. After 45 minutes of testimony, which brought out the fact that intervention and placement by the court had not brought about any change, the judge poignantly expressed his frustration regarding the court's lack of success in the case.

Do you have any idea what this case has cost us? I shouldn't ask that. When I look around this room and figure up the services, it's kind of a shocking thing. And at the end, things are no better than what we started with. With all due respect to the court workers, but I have to disagree.

I think this family is rotten spoiled. I'm getting. . . . People give their heart and souls to help and all they get is kicked in the behind. You're all spoiled. You can always come and get help. Well, I think you've taken your toll on the taxpayers. When are you going to wake up? I just wonder when.

If I close the case, you'll be back. Can you put something together? Tell me. It's probably not right for me to offer you to another county. As recent as Christmas, you spent a week in a foster home. . . . Can you put something together and save the taxpayers a couple of bucks? I don't think anything we do will help. If you come up with a plan, I'll go with it.

I'm being as mean as I can be. I don't want you bugging the police, the probation officer. I don't want it. We've wasted enough time and energy. . . .

PUBLIC DEFENDER: It's my understanding the father owns a farm, and the entire family is planning to move.

JUDGE: Who are you going to call when you get there? How long before you move?

FATHER: How am I going to know when this is in effect?

PUBLIC DEFENDER: He's there already.

JUDGE: How long until the whole family wakes up and tries to solve this? I feel sorry for the people in that county. I'm being mean. I want to wake someone up. You, Candy, you're laughing. You don't care.

JUVENILE: Sir, can I say something?

JUDGE: Say it with actions. It goes up into thousands and thousands of dollars that have been spent on this case. I want a plan. How soon?

FATHER: Next week.

MOTHER: We'll take her up tonight if necessary.

FATHER: I had the idea she could spend the week with me and the weekend here.

JUDGE: It'll never work. I want her out of the county. I want you all out of the county. Either that or wake up and solve your own problems.

PUBLIC DEFENDER: She'll go immediately.

JUDGE: If you come back to the county, you're going to. . . .

[Juvenile talks with Mother.]

JUDGE: See, you're fussing already. Dad, I want you to be the one to say you'll do it, because they can't do it.

I don't want her back in the county. You're going to be picked up whether . . .

MOTHER: I own property. I can't just dispose of it over night. She has friends. Can't she even come back to visit? Are you excommunicating her?

JUDGE: Yes, I'm excommunicating you. This only happened 21 times by accident!

MOTHER: She's not allowed to come back?

JUDGE: Not at the present time.

MOTHER: We have relatives, how can . . . ?

JUDGE: If you come back, she'll end up in detention.

MOTHER: It's not all of it. You don't know.

FATHER: We'll take care of it.

JUDGE: I'll release her to Father. This is against the recommendation of my people; they'll have to bear with me. . . . I don't know how I'll do the order.

"Number of Referrals": An Ambiguous Variable

Although a consideration of the "number of referrals" appears to be rather straightforward, such is not the case. There are numerous contingencies and considerations which must be taken into account. First, as noted in Chapter 5, the number of referrals to court is due largely to the exercise of discretion by outside forces: law enforcement officials, parents, schools, community agencies.

But court personnel also have a direct impact on the number of referrals recorded for a juvenile. Each referral does not necessarily indicate a single offense: Several alleged incidents of delinquent activity may be grouped together in one referral. For example, a juvenile charged with 44 burglaries had only 13 referrals; he returned to court on four new burglaries which were recorded as one additional referral.

Thus, "a referral" to court may indicate a single allegation, several allegations which occurred on a single date, or several allegations encompassing several days. It is also possible for one incident to be recorded as several allegations. For example, one encounter with law enforcement officials may result in charges for several offenses; these may be counted as one referral or several. Court workers make this decision based on their preferences and habits.[1]

Thus, unless all decision-makers, including the court workers, legal department members, and the presiding officer carefully review all referrals rather than merely noting the number, "number of referrals" may be a misleading criterion upon which to base decisions. Some court workers are sensitive to this and attempt to determine the nature of past referrals as well as the findings regarding those allegations in order to present a more accurate picture of the juvenile's past experience with the court. But hectic schedules, heavy caseloads, and crowded dockets rarely permit such in-depth analysis. Thus, a juvenile's past record may be reduced to a number which, when taken at face value, is extremely misleading.

Degree of Involvement

The nature and extent of a juvenile's involvement in the alleged incident is often a crucial factor in the decision-making process. When a juvenile has acted with others who are viewed as more culpable, sophisticated, or streetwise, partial vindication may be afforded the juvenile. This is particularly true when juveniles commit offenses with adults or when they are seen as less involved in the crime than their companions. For example, when three juveniles participated in an armed robbery, the juvenile who procured the gun and the one who actually fired it were considered prime movers in the incident, accorded more responsibility for what transpired, and given more severe dispositions than the third who "went along" with the wishes of the other two. When a juvenile is viewed as easily influenced by other wrongdoers, that juvenile's participation may be viewed as the result of indiscretion or poor judgment, rather than intentional, hard-core delinquency.

The following case provides an example of the consideration by court personnel of the nature and involvement of a juvenile in a crime. A 16-year old girl was involved in an armed robbery with her adult boyfriend; the boyfriend attacked a gas station attendant with a crescent wrench. *Any* juvenile involvement in such an offense is viewed as extremely serious by court personnel, but the fact that the juvenile only acted as a lookout and did not personally attack the attendant had a considerable influence on decision-makers. The case illustrates other factors which influence court personnel. The intake worker stressed her belief that the juvenile was underprivileged, had never been given a break, and was overly influenced by her adult male companion; and the judge stressed the fact that, in his view, the juvenile justice system has little to offer a teenage mother. Other variables which influenced the decision included the fact that the juvenile lived in another state, had done well while in detention, and was not considered to be likely to participate in any further misbehavior.

#244: Pretrial Conference and Hearing

Judge
Prosecuting Attorney
Public Defender
Court Worker (Intake)
Supervisor of Court Worker
White Female, 16 years old
Referral #1: Armed robbery, assault with intent to rob, and stealing over $50

Pretrial Conference [20 minutes]

COURT WORKER: Her friend has had an arraignment [in adult court].

PUBLIC DEFENDER: Did Mother and her boyfriend show up?

COURT WORKER: Yes. Father's sick, an alcoholic. He gave me the phone number of Nick's Tavern. Said to call him there after 10 A.M.

[Official beginning of conference.]

PROSECUTING ATTORNEY: Just looked at the allegations. It should be "in consort"—allegedly with male adult.

COURT WORKER: It was a vicious act, not patterned. She's not a vicious person, Your Honor. She has an illegitimate child. She went through the state mental process and was found to be all right.

She thought she was pregnant and didn't want to go through one alone again. I can't excuse the act. She was good in detention, but is anxious to get back to her 15-month old son. Ms. Snowden [a social worker from another state] says she has potential; their chief social worker is willing to accept her. We talked with the interstate compact. She can go back to Mother's home through it. Another alternative is commitment to our Department of Corrections, go through their program, then return home.

JUDGE: How is the victim?

COURT WORKER: Treated and released.

JUDGE: What'd she hit him with?

PUBLIC DEFENDER: She didn't hit him.

PROSECUTING ATTORNEY: She was a look-out for her friend. The boy hit him with a crescent wrench.

COURT WORKER: She's a little river rat. Her natural father worked on the river. She has a poor self-concept. I told her I'll have to teach her how to pick a man. She was involved with a 28-year old guy, heavy into the drug world. She got out of that; didn't want to raise a baby like that. I don't think certification [to adult court] would help her. She'd just sit up there two months. Her accomplice has one month to go.

PROSECUTING ATTORNEY: The Chief Juvenile Officer will agree not to certify her. There's a problem with the [interstate] compact. We don't belong to the part for interstate transfer in institutions.

JUDGE: Was she under jurisdiction in the other state?

COURT WORKER: She was never adjudicated delinquent there.

PROSECUTING ATTORNEY: If we went with courtesy supervision and she didn't obey, we could file an order as violation of supervision, then take jurisdiction. This is a possible free felony, but she has a son.

JUDGE: What do you think?

SUPERVISOR OF COURT WORKER: Jane [court worker] has been on the phone to the interstate compact, the social worker, and prosecuting attorney. They're quite unusually interested in the girl.

JUDGE: Why can't we keep it [her case] open and send her back?

PROSECUTING ATTORNEY: I asked, but they said no.

PUBLIC DEFENDER: They go to 18 there [juvenile court jurisdiction extends to 18 years].

JUDGE: For all practical purposes, if we sent her there with it marked open 'til January, we don't do anything. What the hell is probation to a 17-year old with a 15-month old child living with her mother? What are they going to do, look at her and say?

COURT WORKER: If she violates probation, they can send her to their state training school. If she violates it, they won't send her back here.

PROSECUTING ATTORNEY: What if something happens, and they find this is open. Say she's out shooting pheasants and. . . .

JUDGE: Good thing you said that instead of "out shooting peasants." . . . I don't know. They take a crescent wrench and. . . .

PROSECUTING ATTORNEY: That's a nasty thing.

JUDGE: Let's adjudicate delinquent and send her back. How will she get from here to there?

COURT WORKER: Mother and Stepfather are here.

JUDGE: We'll take jurisdiction. . . .

COURT WORKER: It gets tricky. If we take jurisdiction, it must go through the interstate compact.

SUPERVISOR OF COURT WORKER: We don't belong to the amendment for transfer from our institution to theirs. We can't send to DOC and transfer.

COURT WORKER: . . . might take a week after the hearing.

JUDGE: She's been with us a month.

COURT WORKER: Now that we get right down to it, we didn't have the petition signed on time. We didn't. . . .

PROSECUTING ATTORNEY: Shhh. Shhh. That's all water under a bridge.

JUDGE: How'd they catch them?

COURT WORKER: The boy took off in a stolen auto. She was in her father's. . . .

PUBLIC DEFENDER: You can type up a regular order.

[Supervisor of court worker goes to get packet regarding interstate compact.]

PUBLIC DEFENDER: Does this make all this legal?

PROSECUTING ATTORNEY: I'm surprised they even bothered to put periods in the interstate compact. Have you ever tried to read that?

SUPERVISOR OF COURT WORKER: We don't have all the forms.

PUBLIC DEFENDER: Make up a regular order; the judge won't sign it. . . .

Hearing [13 minutes]

[Juvenile, Mother, and Mother's boyfriend join others]

PROSECUTING ATTORNEY: The public defender and I have agreed to amend the petition to read "in consort with others as a lookout."

The juvenile officer had filed a motion to certify [to adult court]. The juvenile officer will withdraw that motion.

[Takes appearances of individuals present.]

JUDGE: It is my understanding through our discussion, as per the suggestion of Mr. Reynolds [prosecuting attorney], the court will permit the juvenile officer to withdraw the motion to dismiss the petition which would allow the circuit court to treat you as an adult.

It's my understanding intake is recommending that we take jurisdiction and request courtesy supervision.

Are you willing to admit to the allegations as amended?

PROSECUTING ATTORNEY: Assault made on person, juvenile was a lookout rather than the perpetrator. Stealing of currency by means of a gun, also as lookout.

PUBLIC DEFENDER: We admit to the allegations as amended.

JUDGE: Let's review. We could've sent you to the adult court. It has not been our decision to certify you. I understand you will cooperate with courtesy supervision. Is that correct?

JUVENILE: Yes.

JUDGE: What it amounts to is you, with a companion, stole about $250.
. . . The recommendation of intake is that we take jurisdiction and
request courtesy supervision. We'll send you home with Mother and
ask the juvenile authorities in your home county to render courtesy
supervision. Does that sound like something you want to do?
JUVENILE: Oh, yes.
JUDGE: I'm doing this because I feel it is in your best interests. I understand you have a child.
JUVENILE: Yes.
JUDGE: Mom, I'm going to send her back with you. I want you to work
with the juvenile authorities.
MOTHER: I will, Your Honor.
JUDGE: Linda, you need some help. I don't know what possessed you
to take a weapon and hit someone; he could've been killed. It's no
excuse that you were just standing by. If the person you were with
did something, it's the same as if you did it. The sentence in the adult
court would be five years to life. That's the way this state looks at this
offense. Just being there as a lookout, you're guilty. I want you to take
a pretty good look at where you're going, young lady. We'll make
this as an alternative to detention. You've been with us 30 days.
JUVENILE: To the day.
MOTHER: Thank you, Your Honor.
JUDGE: Good luck to you.

In addition to the nature of the offense and the number of past
referrals, two other major factors in the outcome of cases are the
orientation of the presiding officer and the issue of legal representation, that is, whether or not the juvenile was represented by
legal counsel and whether the attorney was a representative of
the public defender's office or a privately retained attorney. Little
emphasis has been placed on these two issues, but the present
inquiry demonstrates that these are crucial and complex factors.

Legal Representation

The role of the defense counsel greatly influences juveniles'
experiences within the court system, but presently that role is
ambiguous and ill-defined. Juveniles have the right to legal representation during formal court proceedings, but they often mis-
understand their rights and frequently fail to exercise them. Equally
important, court personnel have varying opinions regarding the

appropriateness of defense counsel participation in decision-making. Although some court personnel welcome and support the participation of defense counsel, attorneys may encounter hostility and suspicion. They often receive the subtle or direct message that they will not be encouraged to pursue the strict advocacy role to which they are accustomed. Likewise, the treatment orientation of the court implies that resisting adjudication or disposition would hinder efforts to help the child and attempting to "get juveniles off" through "technicalities" is not the responsible, adult course of action (Hufnagel and Davidson, 1974; Emerson, 1969).

Attorneys may also be uncertain regarding their function within the juvenile system, for they are confronted with numerous dilemmas, none of which have been resolved conclusively. In particular, private attorneys are often unfamiliar with juvenile law and the procedures of juvenile courts, for they rarely practice in that setting. They often experience contradictory expectations and desires from court personnel, parents, and juveniles, and must balance these competing interests in their relationships and interactions with these three parties.

In addition to the danger of court personnel attempting to limit the effectiveness of defense counsel, there is an equally important possibility that the defense counsel will inadvertently curtail their own effectiveness. Although there is increasing participation by private attorneys, the bulk of juvenile cases are represented by members of the public defender's office. Public defenders who are assigned to a juvenile court on a regular basis have the distinct advantage of experience within the juvenile court and a familiarity with court personnel. In such situations the defense counsel is in a better position to establish rapport with decision-makers, bargain more effectively for juvenile desires, and perhaps gain occasional concessions for clients because of personal or working relationships with court personnel.

However, when public defenders are regularly assigned to a court, or perhaps employed by the court, there is great risk that their effectiveness may be limited because they may become so well integrated into the court system that they adopt the philosophy and orientation of the court, becoming more an appendage of the court than representative for the child (Platt, 1977; Duffee and Siegel, 1971). Similarities between defense attorneys and court personnel in social background, education, and lifestyles create the possibility that the defense counsel's relationship with court personnel may take precedence over the obligation to the juvenile.

In addition to potential difficulties in working with social workers, court attorneys, and judges, defense attorneys must be prepared to deal with parents. In doing so, they often find themselves in the awkward position of being caught between conflicting parental and juvenile desires. Those attorneys retained by parents to represent their child may experience extreme confusion regarding which party is the client. When conflicts arise, attorneys often pursue the course of action favored by parents. Even when the attorney is appointed by the court and financed by the state, there is a strong tendency to support parental wishes over those of juveniles. Despite the frequent conflict in parental and juvenile interests, only rarely do parents retain separate counsel to advance their opinions. Most commonly the court assumes that the interests and desires of parent and child coincide.

In addition, attorneys often experience role disjuncture when their clients are adolescents. They must decide whether they should act as a strict advocate of juvenile desires or to act as a guardian making decisions regarding "the best interest of the child," irrespective of juvenile wishes. Many choose the guardian role advanced by court personnel, some become interpreters of court proceedings, and others attempt to be both a guardian and advocate, often finding it a difficult or impossible task. A minority of attorneys interpret their role as the traditional adversary, arguing for juvenile desires regardless of their own opinions. The public defender acknowledges that she sometimes plays both roles of guardian and advocate, but on the whole she interprets her role as the traditional adversary, attempting to provide juveniles with the benefit of her experience but arguing for their desires despite her opinion.

. . . You find yourself sometimes being an advocate, pure and simple. Sometimes you find yourself being a guardian, almost solely, and sometimes you try and balance them. I'd say, on balance, I'm more an advocate because where the guardian comes in is my trying to help them understand why the social worker and I have the best idea here, and they don't have the best idea. I will try and make them see that, and I will say, "Look, I'm being, trying to be objective, and I will fight for what you want, but let me say that if I were the judge and trying to be impartial, I would think the worker has some very good arguments. This is why." So I do try and do that as a guardian, but I do believe that the only person who's going to be an advocate for them is me. And therefore, since they've got a lot of guardians—they've got the judge as basically a guardian, the attorneys here like to think of themselves that way, the social workers are, the psychologists, psychiatrists, the parents, you know—that by the time everyone figures out what they think's best for the child . . . the child frequently has some real good insights into what's best for themselves, and so that's why I feel like I should be an advocate for them.

The Impact on Decisions

At the present court, all juveniles whose cases are heard before the juvenile judge (a representative of the state circuit court) are assigned counsel; the majority of them are represented by the public defender. To the contrary, in the courtrooms presided over by the three hearing officers, approximately 78 percent of the juveniles are *not* represented by counsel. As will be discussed shortly, juveniles have the right to legal representation, but the clarity with which they are informed regarding this right varies.

Although such information is not available for all of the juveniles referred during the year, the relationship between the severity of the final disposition and legal representation can be explored through the 250 cases observed.[2] Over half (58.2 percent) were not represented by an attorney. Those juveniles were more likely to be placed on probation than were juveniles who were represented by attorneys (36.3 percent compared to 19.8 percent). But when the possibility of receiving the most severe dispositions (placement outside the home in either group homes or institutions) is examined, those juveniles who were represented by attorneys were more likely to receive these dispositions than were juveniles not represented (35.8 percent compared to 9.6 percent).[3] Further statistical analysis reveals that, *regardless of the*

types of offenses with which they are charged, juveniles represented by attorneys receive more severe dispositions.

Observation of court activities indicates that legal representation is most successful during the early stages of a juvenile's involvement with the court. Defense counsel is often successful in
preventing the court from taking jurisdiction over juveniles and
placing them on probation, especially when the juveniles have
had no prior referrals to court. However, defense counsel is less
effective in preventing placement of juveniles outside the home,
the more serious disposition.

To understand why juveniles represented by attorneys are more
likely to be placed outside their homes than those who are not
represented, it is important to scrutinize court policy. Whenever
a probation officer or intake worker plans to recommend that a
juvenile be placed outside the home they routinely request that
defense counsel be appointed for the juvenile. This policy, coupled with the fact that in the vast majority of cases the recommendations of court personnel are followed by the judge and
hearings officers, results in a direct link between legal representation and the severity of disposition recommended by court personnel and imposed by presiding officers. Primarily, the assignment of defense counsel represents a ceremonial act taken by
the court prior to imposing a severe sentence.

A separate issue relating to legal representation pertains to
whether a juvenile has a privately retained attorney or the public
defender. Three-fourths of the juveniles represented in the cases
observed were represented by the public defender assigned to
the court; one-fourth were represented by private attorneys. Juveniles represented by private attorneys are likely to receive *less
severe dispositions* than are those represented by the public defender.

The public defender assigned to the court enjoys widespread
respect and friendship with court personnel. She is considered
hardworking by most staff members and has considerable working knowledge of the manner in which the juvenile court operates and the alternatives available, including placement options.
Although this familiarity is an advantage, the public defender is
less able or apt to severely challenge court personnel than are
private attorneys, for she must maintain ongoing relationships with

all court personnel. What is perceived by court workers as a vicious attack on one worker may have a detrimental effect on the public defender's relationships with other personnel. Likewise, the public defender is less likely to oppose the court placing a juvenile on probation than are private attorneys. Probation is less drastic when compared to the constant battles waged by the public defender to prevent court officials from taking juveniles out of their homes and placing them in group homes or institutions.

Equally important, the tremendous volume of cases (80 to 90 per month) handled by a single attorney limits the amount of time the public defender can spend in preparation for each case. Although when a juvenile is in detention (located in the same building as the courtrooms), the public defender has increased access and is thus aided significantly in the preparation of the defense, the majority of juveniles are not detained. Many of the public defender's actions are based on the "paper profile" of a juvenile and past experiences with court personnel, and an understanding of what general type of action will be viewed as appropriate. When a juvenile is not detained, the public defender usually has one prehearing conference with juveniles and their families, ranging from 30 minutes to an hour in duration.

In addition to handling a large volume of cases, the public defender must represent juveniles in four different courtrooms. It is not unusual for the public defender to be scheduled or needed in several courtrooms simultaneously. Although the public defender is regularly assisted by third-year law students doing practicums at the court, much of the public defender's association with them is spent familiarizing them with juvenile proceedings. Only toward the end of their stays at the court are they able to handle minor cases without the guidance and presence of the public defender, and often the student's tenure at the court terminates shortly after they have been sufficiently trained to provide genuine assistance for the public defender. The latter then embarks on yet another round of training assistants.

Private attorneys often have the advantage of being able to devote more time to a particular case; likewise they may take a personal interest in the case, particularly if they are family friends and know the family situation well. Although it is not always so, many private attorneys enjoy the advantage that their professional prestige affords. Likewise, because they have few cases at the juvenile court, private attorneys need not be overly concerned with maintaining constant rapport with court personnel.

Equally important, the link between social class and the private attorney must not be overlooked. The vast majority of juveniles are represented by the public defender. Those juveniles represented by privately retained attorneys are consistently more affluent than other juveniles before the court. As will be demonstrated in Chapter 14, the success of private attorneys may be more attributable to the affluence of their clients than to the private attorneys' legal prowess. More affluent families command more resources and are thus more successful in convincing court personnel that court involvement is unnecessary. This is accomplished by enlisting or procuring non-court assistance in dealing with juvenile problems. Subtly, the retention of a private attorney is yet another demonstration that a family is capable of resolving its problems on its own.

The Lack of Commitment

One of the most striking features of the court under consideration is its lack of commitment to the adversary process. Unlike many other metropolitan courts, it does not assign attorneys to all cases. Rather, the system relies upon individual presiding officers and court personnel to inform juveniles of this right, despite the fact that there is minimal accountability. Equally important, the court has assumed the stance that juveniles—even those who are held in secure custody—must request an attorney themselves.

Thus, while court personnel allow participation by defense attorneys and officially recognize juveniles' rights to legal representation, they limit the effectiveness of defense counsel through official policies as well as informal activities. The failure to insist that juveniles be informed of their rights in a specific and detailed manner, the failure to assign counsel to all cases, and the prevalence of informal decision-making sessions at which juveniles are not represented demonstrate the court's lack of support and enthusiasm for the adversary process. Clearly, the court does not view the provision of effective defense counsel as integral to fulfilling its mission of "protecting children."

The Presiding Officer

The ideological orientation, professional commitment, and personality of the presiding officer greatly influence the outcome of juvenile cases. The tremendous disparity in sentencing as well as the variety in courtroom activities are attributable directly to the presiding officer.

There are four presiding officers involved at the court under investigation.[4] As is widely recognized throughout the court, each represents a unique approach to judging juveniles. Equally important as the considerable diversity in styles and dispositions is the fact that court workers are able to request that their cases be docketed for a particular presiding officer. And although the request may be denied by the prosecuting attorney or changed if the presiding officer's docket is already full, in most instances court workers' requests and preferences are honored. Lower echelon decision-makers can anticipate a particular "brand of justice" and plan their recommendations and strategies accordingly. Thus, the individualization of justice within the juvenile court is linked inextricably to the personality and practices of individual judges.

Although theoretically all presiding officers must follow basic guidelines for the conduct of hearings, the manner in which the hearing proceeds, the type of questions asked by the officer, and the clarity with which legal matters are explained to juveniles and parents very with the personality, orientation, and effectiveness of the presiding officer. These distinctions are particularly significant among hearing officers, for most of their hearings involve a less formal atmosphere and many juveniles appear before them without attorneys. The judge's courtroom more closely approximates a trial situation in which prosecuting attorneys and defense counsel are responsible for much of the questioning and the direction of the proceedings. In contrast, there is considerably more direct interaction between juveniles (and their families) and the hearing officers.

Juvenile judges, of course, hold different views on the mission of the juvenile court and the manner in which they should conduct their proceedings. A major distinction can be made between those who are legalistic in orientation versus those who are more treatment-oriented. The former is an orientation in which due process is stressed and the presiding officer emphasizes the legal limitations and stipulations surrounding the juvenile court's power and purpose. One hearing officer closely approximates this model, giving strict adherence to legal procedure especially as it pertains to juvenile rights and due process.

This is particularly evident when they inform juveniles of their legal rights; the standard of proof they require before they judge a child; and the extent to which they consider the suggestions of court workers before passing sentence.

Hearing officer #3 refuses to discuss a case with the probation officer or intake worker prior to the open hearing unless the juvenile is represented by an attorney and that attorney is present during the informal discussions. Before judging a juvenile, he insists that charges against the juvenile be demonstrated beyond a reasonable doubt. Accordingly, he is hesitant to minimize the amount of time spent on adjudication, and in the disposition phase of the proceeding he studies the recommendations of court personnel more closely than do the other hearing officers.

This hearing officer also painstakingly details the right to an attorney, explains that an attorney would help present the case in the best light possible, and stresses the fact the juvenile has the right not to discuss the matter with the judge without an attorney. Unlike the proceedings conducted by the other two hearing officers, in which juveniles are informed of their rights through a rapid, mechanistic barrage of words, this hearing officer assumes the responsibility of clearly stating the rights. Not surprisingly, juveniles in this courtroom were more likely to request that an attorney be assigned to their case.

Hearing Officers #1 and #2 view the juvenile court more as a social institution, despite the fact they are lawyers by training. Accordingly, they tend to minimize the legal aspects of proceedings and emphasize the necessity of helping and treating juveniles. Generally speaking, they are more inclined for the court to become involved in a juvenile's life. In particular, Hearing Officer #1 is extremely treatment oriented, viewing court involvement as saving children. This individual is extremely well-liked, is frequently praised for embodying the "true spirit" of the juvenile court, and is very willing to accept recommendations that juveniles be put on probation or placed outside the home.

Hearing Officers #1 and #2 both permit, indeed encourage,

extensive prehearing discussions prior to the formal courtroom proceeding. Juveniles and their parents are not included in the discussions and the vast majority are not represented by attorneys. Thus, the prehearing conference becomes primarily a forum for court workers to demonstrate the appropriateness of the recommendations they will make in court. In the vast majority of these cases the original recommendation advanced by the court worker is transformed into the final disposition, despite the fact that the prehearing discussions took place *prior* to any adjudication or finding of guilt within the courtroom. Hearing Officer #2 is particularly notable for his overwhelming dependence upon court workers in the decision-making process. Almost without exception he follows the advice of the court workers assigned to the case and implements their recommendations regarding disposition. His lack of confidence in his own decision-making capability was a frequent topic of discussion among court personnel, including such staff members as court recorders and probation officers. He is also known for "homey" speeches to juveniles— speeches filled with homilies and fatherly advice. Such admonishments usually include discourses on the value of the family and hard work and are dispensed routinely, regardless of the particulars of the present case.

As will be discussed in subsequent chapters, the hearing officers also differ in the extent to which they are influenced by the juvenile's class, sex, or race. During hearings, as well as during informal discussions, Hearing Officer #2 frequently alludes to a juvenile's sex and race. He is the only presiding officer who routinely makes comments regarding racial conflicts.

The emphasis of the inquiry into a juvenile's situation varies with the hearing officers. One may stress educational endeavors and opportunities; another might inquire regarding extracurricular activities such as sports; another will emphasize juvenile attempts to seek employment. But even more important than the wide range in judicial styles is the tremendous disparity in the disposition of cases by the presiding officers. There is a significant difference in the percentages of cases in which they take jurisdiction and those in which they place juveniles outside their homes. Because the judge hears more serious offenses, it is important to control for the seriousness of offense when making comparisons, but even when this variable is controlled, there are significant distinctions between presiding officers in cases involving status offenders, felonies against persons, and other felonies. (Cases involving misdemeanors are the only type of allegation in which there is overall uniformity among presiding officers.)

In all types of cases, Hearing Officer #1 is more likely to take jurisdiction over juveniles and place them under the court's supervision; the juvenile judge is more likely than any of the hearing officers to give juveniles the most severe dispositions. In cases involving all types of offense, Hearing Officer #2 gives the least severe dispositions more often than any other presiding officer.

In multiple regression analysis in which several factors are taken into consideration, the influence of the presiding officer is equally evident. For all cases referred to the court throughout the year (10,500), the presiding officer is the second most important factor in explaining the disparity in sentences; only the number of prior referrals is more important. Consideration of whether or not the juvenile was detained prior to trial, age, sex, race, prior sibling involvement with the court, or whether the juvenile was referred by law enforcement officials or other community members is less important. (For complete statistics, see Chapter 14.)

In summary, although considerable attention is focused on the seriousness of the offense and the number of prior referrals, numerous other considerations must be recognized that influence decision-making within the juvenile court. The issues regarding legal representation are very crucial. Is the juvenile fully informed regarding legal rights? Is the juvenile represented by a lawyer? Is the lawyer a representative of the public defender's office or in private practice? Are there informal decision-making sessions at which juveniles are not represented? The answers to these questions greatly influence the fate of young people within the juvenile justice system. Furthermore, the identity and orientation of the presiding officer is an extremely crucial variable in the decision-making matrix. Although this dimension has often been overlooked and remains difficult to calculate, the final decision-maker in the juvenile process indelibly stamps justice with the imprints of her or his own personality, value system, and brand of justice.

The concept of individualized justice championed by traditional juvenile justice philosophy emphasizes the necessity of examining the behavior, attitudes, and propensities of juveniles. But to truly understand the process of individualized justice, as it is implemented within the modern juvenile court, it is necessary to examine the behavior, attitudes and propensities of those who administer juvenile justice. The philosophy of individualized justice stresses the characteristics of juveniles, but the *implementation* of that ideal is contingent upon the characteristics of decision-makers. "Individualized" refers as much to the interpreter of juvenile characteristics as it does to the juvenile.

Notes

1. If a juvenile has been involved in neglect proceedings (basically a "charge" against parents) that may also be counted in the total number of referrals.

There is also a computer designation "information record only" which, when entered in a juvenile's record, is coded as a referral and assigned a referral number. When queried regarding the meaning of such a designation, several staff members stated they never used it. Others stated that it did not signify a new allegation of delinquency against a juvenile, but merely indicated that there had been "an inquiry of some nature which involved the juvenile."

2. The percent of juveniles represented by counsel in the sample of observed cases is greater than it would be in a random sample. All cases before the judge are represented by counsel, and although the judge's cases comprise only 17 percent of the overall court cases, they comprise 21 percent of the cases observed. Because observations were designed to permit observation in all four courtrooms as well as participation in cases involving diverse types of offenses, a greater percent of felonies were observed than are in the year's total referrals. Thus, more juveniles were likely to be represented by counsel.

3. Duffee and Siegel (1971) suggest that juveniles who are represented by counsel receive more severe dispositions than those who waive the right to representation, but their study fails to provide insight into court policy regarding the appointment of counsel to cases.

4. The juvenile judge heard approximately 17.2 percent of the cases and the three hearing officers heard 31.6, 26.3 and 24.9 percent. Although the judge heard all certification cases and the most serious felonies such as manslaughter, forcible rape, and major armed robberies, the great majority of cases may be heard by any of the presiding officers.

CHAPTER 9

The Influence of Social Characteristics: The Issue of Race

A major debate in juvenile justice revolves around the question of whether juvenile court decisions are influenced most by legal factors (such as offense or number of referrals) or by a juvenile's social characteristics (such as race, sex, and social class). The rationale behind the social characteristics versus legal variables debate asserts that if "legal variables" are more highly correlated with decisions, juvenile court personnel are absolved of the charge that they have used their considerable discretion in a discriminatory manner. But, if the contrary is demonstrated, that is, if social characteristics account for more variation in decision-making, court personnel are condemned as discriminatory.

Those factors commonly categorized as legal variables such as the detention decision, screening decision, offense, and number of prior referrals are often portrayed as more appropriate, more objective criteria for decision-making. They are also taken as *ex post facto* indicators of the lack of racial, sexual, or class bias.

This distinction between legal and social factors is misleading and erroneous, one which does not aid in explaining the decision-making process. Firstly, as has been demonstrated in the previous chapters, the legal factors are not the "objective," bias-free factors researchers assume. Such variables as the detention decision, the screening decision, and even the offense and number of prior referrals have highly subjective dimensions. Rather than being factors untainted by human bias, they are "facts" which have evolved from decisions made by court personnel as well as community agencies. However, as is demonstrated by the statistical analysis of 10,500 referrals to the present court, a juvenile's race, sex, or social class influence the decision whether or not a juvenile should be detained prior to the hearing as well as the decision to process the case formally or informally. In turn, these decisions become labeled "legal" factors and are categorized as "objective" legal decisions. Accordingly, by the time a juvenile's case reaches the last juncture in decision-making, the final disposition (sentencing), these previous decisions (now viewed as legal factors) are more influential in explaining disposition than are the social characteristics. Thus, human interaction, replete with bias, becomes reified as legal decisions; those decisions become legal variables expurgated of any tinge of subjectivity. In a very subtle manner bias is transformed and deemed value-free, and those examining the decision-making process fail to recognize the full extent to which juvenile social characteristics influence juvenile court decisions.

Race and Discretion

The issue of racial discrimination within the juvenile justice system has been widely debated. Numerous theorists have asserted that the juvenile court metes out dispositions on the basis of a juvenile's race (Platt, 1977; Schur, 1971; Martin, 1970; Terry, 1967; Thornberry, 1973). Others have denied this contention, suggesting that courts have imposed sentences based on the seriousness of the offense and the number of previous referrals to the court (Berg, 1967; Polk, 1974; Gordon, 1976; Cohen and Kluegel, 1978).

Although only 4.8 percent of the county's population is black, 19.8 percent of the delinquency referrals involve black juveniles.[1] Consequently, at the very outset of the court process a disproportionate number of black juveniles are referred to court. As discussed previously, these referrals are beyond the purview of court personnel. Explanation therefore must be sought through examination of the referral practices of law enforcement officials, school personnel, and parents.

The racial composition of truancy referrals is a major indication of school practices: White juveniles comprise 76 percent of the cases and 24 percent are black juveniles. Thus, the percentage of black referrals to court by law enforcement officials (19.8 percent) and school officials (24 percent) is disproportionate to the black population of the country (4.8 percent). This may be due to the fact that a disproportionate number of blacks participate in delinquent behavior, or it may be due to racial bias on the part of the police and the schools. Research supports *both* contentions (Piliavin and Briar, Williams and Gold, 1972; Short and Nye, 1958; Empey and Erickson, 1966).

In addition to noting police and school policies, it is pertinent to consider whether parents of one race are more likely to view the court as the appropriate arena for the resolution of family conflicts, and subsequently refer their children to court more frequently. Two aspects of the present study suggest that black parents may be more likely to seek court assistance than are white parents. Of the 409 cases of incorrigibility referred to the court (mostly by parents), 30 percent involved black juveniles and 70 percent involved white juveniles. In the 250 cases observed, 39 were parent referrals; of those, 23 percent involved blacks and 77 percent involved whites. Thus, although they are inconclusive, these preliminary indicators suggest that the disproportionate number of black juveniles referred to court is due to parental attitude toward court involvement, as well as police and school referral policies.[2]

As will be discussed in Chapter 10, socioeconomic status may be a major factor in determining the extent to which parents view the court as the appropriate arena for resolving conflicts with their children. Many poorer families, a disproportionate number of them black, may seek court assistance because they lack the financial resources to explore other means of solving family problems. A lack of viable alternatives, rather than any desire on their part, forces the poor to turn to the courts.

Although it is important to note that the court becomes involved with a disproportionate number of black juveniles due to the referral practices of outside forces, the most pertinent inquiry for the present study is the juvenile court's decisions in processing black juveniles *after* this initial referral has taken place. As discussed in Chapter 3, black juveniles are more likely to be held in detention before their trials than are white juveniles and are slightly more likely to have their cases processed formally than are white juveniles (33 percent compared to 26.3 percent), which increases the possibility that they will be placed on probation or outside the home. The influence of race on final disposition is less obvious statistically, for as demonstrated in the Appendix, race is not a major statistical determinant of final disposition. Alleged offense, number of prior referrals, and the detention decision are more influential.

Although final disposition of a case, the dependent variable in the preceding discussion, is one of the major indices of any influence race may have upon court decisions, it is equally germane to examine the impact this variable has upon other aspects of everyday interactions between juveniles and court personnel. The nature of these relationships, the qualitative aspects of a child's experience within the juvenile justice system, and the court's ability to assist juveniles from varying subcultures have a definite, although less calculable, impact on the self-concepts and social identities of juveniles. The multitude of interactions between juveniles and decision-makers which precede and follow disposition are extremely crucial; racial identity influences the content and nature of these experiences.

Although it is an underlying theme that subtly influences court activities, racial conflict rarely becomes an overt issue during courtroom proceedings. Only once, in the 250 cases observed, did a participant openly charge the court with racism. A black father, angry with the court for placing his son outside the home, gestured toward the court worker and said this same man who tells Calvin he's his friend, will say, "He's just like all those other niggers," if he gets in trouble. The accusation went unanswered.

One hearing officer occasionally warned black males of possible consequences of continued crime on the adult level. The following comments illustrate his counsel regarding potential mistreatment by whites. The hearing officer was never observed issuing this warning to white males charged with similar offenses and thus exposed to the same possible fate.

Hearing

Black male 16 years old
Referral #5:   Operating an automobile without the consent of the owner
[felony] with no valid license and driving in an imprudent
manner

HEARING OFFICER: Whose car was it?

MOTHER: Someone he knew.

HEARING OFFICER: Did he let you drive it at some time? Why'd you take it?

JUVENILE: He let me drive it once, to park it.

HEARING OFFICER: You'd better apoligize. If I did the same thing, tried and convicted, I would get from two to four years in the state penitentiary. Even trying to get in a car is tampering; that's a felony, too. For the life of me you look like a fellow of above-average intelligence. You get up in the state pen—some big 22-year old white dude will have you going so fast you won't know black from white.

The same hearing officer made a similar comment to a 14-year old black male in court on a second referral of shoplifting under $50, a misdemeanor.

You appear to have a lot going for you. One hundred years ago they would've put your hand on a block and chopped it off. We've gotten civilized, we're not supposed to do that. Now we stick people in a jail cell. Some big white dude would have you upside down so fast it'd make your head swim.

Although 19.8 percent of the juveniles referred to court and 23 percent of those placed under the court's supervision are black, only 9 percent of the court's delinquency workers are black. (This figure includes delinquency intake workers, probation officers, and members of the short-term counseling unit.) The juvenile judge, hearing officers, and prosecuting attorneys are white; and 12 of 13 administrative or supervisory positions which deal directly with delinquency cases are staffed with white individuals.[3]

Several court personnel express concern that there are relatively few black workers or administrators. When questioned regarding what changes would benefit the court, a white probation officer states:

I'd like to see us, number one, get a black hearing officer. . . . It's partially, simply, because I think we should have a black person in a position of the higher authority. I've seen this in my area where it's helped to have a black principal come into the school where you're dealing with a fairly sizable black population. So often a black kid will see members of his race in every position except the one that's really got the control. That makes a real, I think it's a subtly, behind-the-scenes difference. When you're always second fiddle, you never feel quite right about it.

Court personnel vary in their assessment of the actual or potential difficulties in court relationships with minority juveniles. A few decision-makers deny that any significant distinctions exist between juveniles of different races.

[Are the blacks you come in contact with usually different than the whites?]
No, I wouldn't, can't say that they are really, you know, going back through my memory cells. . . . People are people regardless of their skin. Some of them you can't touch, whites, blacks, whatever. No, I wouldn't say that they're different in that respect. In fact, if anything, I'd say they've got a little more, the ones that I've seen, they've got a little bit more of a challenge. I'll put it that way. Which I think is healthy.

HEARING OFFICER

Other court personnel candidly acknowledge potential difficulties in the court's interaction with black juveniles; some express concern with the court's ability to meet the needs of such juveniles. When requested to discuss any differences between black and white clients, several white court workers acknowledged initial concern as to whether black juveniles would accept their supervision.[4] But as indicated by the following comments, most workers felt they had dealt successfully with such difficulties.

[Are the black kids you have different than the white kids?]
Not really. I don't think [so]. First I wondered if they'd come in here and act real nice, call me Miss Long, and just be real sweet. And I thought, well, they're just . . . but saying all these bad things like "white honkey," whatever. But they don't. I really, I mean I'm not saying they never say that, but I realize that they aren't thinking of me as a white person to make decisions for them and run their life. Maybe a couple do, but most of them react basically the same as white kids do. I don't even know if they talk to their friends that way. I don't think so. Because I know kids who know kids and they tell me about stuff.

PROBATION OFFICER

[Do you notice any difference in the black kids you might get, comparing them to the white kids?]

Yes. They're—it takes a while longer to warm up to them usually. I think especially the very, very poor, illiterate kid sees you as some sort of a somebody he can't reach. What do you know about it? And it takes a little longer to break down and really have him see you as a person, I think. I think just touching them is the quickest way to, especially the younger ones. If you just do them this way, or you just touch them, you know.

[Kind of put your arm around them?]

Yes. Once you touch them you seem to lose the barrier.

INTAKE WORKER

When queried regarding racial differences, numerous court staff members discussed the interrelationships between race and economic status, acknowledging the generally less affluent status of black juveniles.

[Do you think the black kids you see are different than the white kids?]

I don't know. I hate to generalize on that stuff, but I have a feeling that more of them have a poverty situation—come from the intercity type of situation than white children. I don't know. I can tell from the worker pretty well. But that will throw you off, too, 'cause we don't just necessarily have a black court worker for the black children, as you know, and so you can't tell by that. But it's just areas of the county that I can tell, that I know, for example, at my own end of the county up in Bedman, and I know the poverty that exists in that. And let's put it this way, I have an easier time understanding why a kid out of that intercity or intercounty, I guess you could call it, goes out and get in trouble than I do with a kid from Hightown or Logan [more affluent communities]. That's just a normal reaction, I'm sure.

[Do you think that influences your decision?]

No, not for disposition. There is the unfairness that goes with it. I have felt inadequate sometimes because an affluent family can come in and say, "We are able to take care of this problem. We can hire these people to counsel with our child and this and that and the other." And the poverty kid, be it black, or be it white, male, or female, can't do that. But I think in this court, by reason of our program, of the utilization of the LEAA, the Funding Act, and everything else, as well as county funds, we have provided, generally speaking, a fairness across the board. Because we do have programs for the affluent child as well as the poverty child and that's the goodness of this particular court. Now that's not true in every place in this state. I can guarantee you they just don't have the money, so they don't provide that. You get into some counties in this state, and it's just a matter of if the child doesn't have any money he may end up in D.O.C., whereas if he came from a doctor's family in town, he might end up in a high-falutin' boarding house, a boarding school.

JUDGE

[Are the black kids you have different than the white kids?]
    Not always, but probably the majority of blacks we get are probably in some of the lower economic situations. That is, as I say, not a hundred percent true, because we have some black families who are certainly economically doing quite well. But probably the majority of black kids are from the lower-class, more deprived families. That would be one difference perhaps. Other than that, they all pretty much have the same type of problems.

HEARING OFFICER

Other court personnel feel that black juveniles frequently have more school and family problems than other juveniles.

[Are the black kids you see different than the white kids?]
    Well, I think we see more black children who are having school problems and family problems. Without a study on it, I suppose it would be just speculation, but sometimes I think that many of the black families aren't pushing education, or it's not as important to them as it is to the families of some of the white kids. And if it isn't important to the parents, then it isn't going to be as important to the youngster. And quite often I think we do see more black families where there is not a father in the home. . . . I'm not just thinking in terms of numbers; I see that, black kids without fathers in the home who are doing just as well as white kids with fathers. We see a few more problems in the school situation with some of these black kids. I guess more on an individual basis.

HEARING OFFICER

The public defender disagrees that black juveniles are more likely to come from inadequate family situations. In the following comments she also discusses what she views as the court's inability to adequately deal with the needs of black juveniles.

[Do you think that the black kids you deal with are different than the white kids in any way?]

There's definitely a problem in their trusting me. There are all kinds of racial problems. I don't think they think of me as a racist. I think they think of me as one person they can trust, but they have so limited trust always for any white person, especially with this system. So, that's one of my problems; they don't really open up to me that much. They don't look to me for any kind of symbiotic relationship at all, and some white kids do. So closeness is not there with most of them, only a very few. . . .

I think they're skeptical of everybody who's white, and I really think it is a racial thing. Or just skeptical of everybody, period. But since so many people in power here are white, it looks like a racial kind of thing. They know they don't—from what I can see, the options here for black kids are so very limited. We either send you home to the same awful situations that you were in that caused you to steal whatever, or we send you to D.O.C. And no one really thinks that sending them to D.O.C. is really to change them for the better. And it might work for some, but it's nothing like sending a white kid who's got school problems and family problems to Sunrise [group home]. It really is nothing comparable at all.

[Most black kids don't go to Sunrise?]

Hardly any. They just don't want to take any. They'll take a couple, but they'll always use the IQ as a reason, and they'll use the fact that there's not a real solid family to work with. All the things that a black kid has a problem with, every single black kid has a problem with. So, in other words, instead of saying we don't want black kids, they use other criteria, but it's the same thing. And, yes, you have Comptom for blacks. You find that there's a real racial thing, Comptom for blacks, Ranchton for blacks, Sunrise for whites, Valley View for whites, and that kind of thing right down the line.

I don't think black kids really think that we understand what they need, and I don't think we do. Because what most of them need is not a loving family. I've really found that most blacks come from loving families. I have to generalize a lot, but I've really found that most of them do; that their mothers really are concerned, and they've got loving family situations, brothers and sisters. And you can see them sitting around and really into each other as a family out in the hallways. Much more than white kids. You'll see many more white kids sitting apart from their families and their mothers and fathers, not even talking. So that's not what they need. . . . I don't see their families as inadequate. I see what society had given them as inadequate. I see their education, and I see the fact that they don't get enough stimuli, maybe, to help them get along as inadequate perhaps, but certainly not the love and affection and all that, the nurture. They get that.

And the stealing I just think is almost a logical consequence of their situation. So, you know, it's hard. I can see why they look at us. . . . I've said to little black kids before, "Well, now as long as you're stealing, you know they're going to have to take you out of the community and put you in D.O.C." And you stop, and they'll say, "Well, why should I? Everybody else is doing it. We got our TV ripped off; we got our stereo ripped off." And they're talking about their inner-community thing that's going on, and their attitude is you're a schmuck if you stop. And I'll just look at them and think, of course . . . you know, what do you say? There's really no answer to that. So they do think this whole place is a farce, and I don't think there's any real understanding of what they need.

I'm firmly convinced that what you need for black communities is a black family court run by a black judge, black social workers, black everybody. And they may be more strict in some ways. I'm not saying blacks would be easy on blacks. But, they'd understand each other so much better. They'd know what they need, and they'd know when they have a problem and when they don't have one. I think a lot of what we do here with black families is just put our own values on them and try and figure out what to do. And sometimes it's the wrong choice. So, black kids in that way, yes, they are different. Black kids will be more likely to say they didn't do it. They're much more sophisticated that way. White kids almost invariably tell me they did it; even when they want to go to trial on it, they'll treat me like a big sister or mother or something.

PUBLIC DEFENDER

A major contention among court critics is that the cultural differences between black juveniles and white decision-makers inevitably generates an atmosphere of mistrust, but equally crucial, that many court staff members are uncomprehending and unsympathetic to the life situations and value systems of minority children. Court personnel discussed the cultural contrasts between black juveniles and the larger white society, including their association with the court.

[Would you make any observations as to whether the black children who come in are any different than the whites?]

Yes, they're, in the main, much more deprived. They have a lot less experiential background to perform from. They're more alienated from the general culture of the people that dominate the society and make the decisions on how the society's going to be run. They're much more dependent; they don't have the wherewithall

to make their own decisions, and they therefore tend to come under the gun over here, either being charged or being told what to
do. . . . Maybe that's all, maybe it's not true, I don't know. But
that's the way I generally look at it. They're behind the eight-ball
because they're not fully integrated members of the majority group.
[Most people in decision-making here share that culture. . . .]
    Right. They expect certain behavior and expectations out of black
people which just shouldn't be possibly demanded of them. On the
other hand, we all have to live together, and somebody's going to
have to say what the culture's going to be like. The law is as much
a reflection of the culture as it is many a time of natural law or
anything else. That's what it generally is. It reflects the way the majority thinks things ought to be run. So the blacks are expected to
run their behavior in accordance with the way we think they ought
to be run. If they don't, they transgress the law.

                                              PROSECUTING ATTORNEY

A probation officer discusses the differences in dealing with
black juveniles and suggests that the court is "harder on" blacks
than whites.

[Are the black kids you come in contact with different than white
kids?]
    The environmental issue, everything's different. I mean, is there a
significant difference between black and white? Is that what you're
asking? I've already established that there's a difference in every kid
and . . . .
[Do you have very many black kids on your caseload?]
    Yes. I'm the only worker in this area that does. . . . Black kids.
. . . there are some things, a number of things, that are different.
And I think that if you're going to be a worker, you've got to bring
to it an understanding of basically things not to do. Not things that
you need to do. There are some don't's; there aren't that many do's
because then it just relates to any other case. But there are some
basic don't's. . . . The basic don't's, schools have a big problem
with black kids when they misbehave, and if you're going to try and
get a black kid physically to do what you want them to do, you
don't do it tentatively. . . . You know too many times. . . . people
say, "Come with me, come with me." If you're going to put a hand
on a kid, you put hour hand on them, boom, "You come with me."
and, "You get your black ass over there." Or something like that,
and do it. You have to be firm. More so than you would be with, I
guess, all the other kids. That's just the way I function. Now some-

one else might do it a different way. But that doesn't happen that often. That's a big problem with the schools, you know. I try to talk with the teachers and counselors about stuff like that. Look, if you're going to do it, do it in the right way. You shouldn't have to do it at all, and I only remember one time I had to do it in the last year or so.

Yes, there are differences, and a lot of it's intuitive. A lot of it's intuitive. I don't think statements about other workers, whether they're. . . . I'll say somewhat too good; I won't say it's somewhat too bad. On any given day and any particular case, anybody can be bad. Who am I to say what's a good worker and what's bad? I don't know. But I would think that those who are the best workers don't have preconceptions or notions of what they should do or what they're going to do. Ninety percent of what they do is on instinct. That's what I do. So, I wouldn't know how else to handle it, 'cause if you go into it thinking one way, and that might be inappropriate, and you still go ahead and do it, well, that's stupid. You're setting yourself up for something. So, black kids, yeh, black clients are different. Sure, they're different than any other kid.

[Have you ever had a black kid show resentment toward you because you're white, or the staff at the court is white?]

Oh, yes. No particular magic cure on how to handle it. I mean you can't overcome it, that's the way it is. Sure it's true. I mean that's the way society is. Sure we're harder on black people than we are on white people. Of course. I don't care how liberal the court thinks it is, it ain't. No way.

[Why do you think that is?]

Well, as far as the court is concerned, I think the problems sometimes are easier to identify. The behaviors are easily seen as being negative. Sometimes when it comes to a black child, but I don't know if that's true. I don't get a whole cross-sectional view of the court. I don't know. These are tough questions; I can only say with some degree of certainty with my own caseload.

[What were you thinking when you said sometimes it's easier to identify the problem?]

Well, most of the time, I have very few, if any, black status offenders. I mean, mainly it's a delinquent act. It's a shoplifting, it will be a burglary, it will be stealing something, a bicycle or something like that. I mean it's there. It's a theft or something. It might be penny-anti, but it's theft or something like that. Or, that's prejudicial right there. Not all blacks are thieves. All right, I don't mean to say that. But usually it's something that's more readily identified as being negative. I guess the white kids, just 'cause there are more white kids, these other negative behaviors are kind of filtered down by all the hoards of runaways, status offenders, stuff like that. I mean the wandering hoards of kids running around the county on the run.

The Black Dialect

One potential source of misunderstanding and difficulty is the black dialect spoken by many juveniles and their parents. The majority of court personnel acknowledge that they encounter difficulty in understanding what a black juvenile or parent is attempting to express.

[In a hearing, have you ever had difficulty understanding or communicating with a child or parents who spoke in a decidedly ethnic or racial accent?]

I think sometimes you do with black children. But I just tell them to repeat it. If they're testifying and I'm not hearing it, I'll stop them or I might ask a few questions of my own to make sure I understand what they're saying. As far as other ethnic groups, I can't recall any.

JUDGE

[Have you ever had an instance where you had difficulty communicating with or understanding someone who had a definite ethnic or black accent?]

Oh, yes.

[Does that happen very often?]

Not so much any more. Probably more so years ago than today.

[How did you handle it when it happened?]

Well, it's, it is difficult. You have to, I guess, just ask him to repeat it. But it can be a problem because, you know, they're running together words or slurring and hard to grasp. But I would depend upon, as I say, continually asking them to restate the question or perhaps, sometimes the parents can sort of interpret, too, what Johnny said and this is what he means.

HEARING OFFICER

Although not personally experiencing difficulties with the black dialect, one prosecuting attorney suggests that most court personnel underestimate the seriousness of the communication problems and proceed without actually understanding what the black individual has said.

[Have you ever been in a situation where there was some difficulty in a hearing communicating with a family or juvenile because they had a decidedly ethnic or racial accent?]

I particularly have very little problem with that. I have traveled a good bit. I almost never am unable to understand. I don't think, maybe one or two people in the last three years I haven't been able to understand. I pick it up very quickly because I notice I've been in a lot of hearings where people can't understand them and I understand them perfectly, and I'm really surprised people can't understand them.

A lot of people don't listen to other people closely enough. I like to. I can think of today; there was this black boy talking, and I could pick up every word he said. . . . You have to listen up, and a lot of people don't listen up around here. They really don't try to catch what the juvenile is saying. They kind of know what they want to hear, so they just ask questions. . . . (get) a non-verbal sense and go on. I think it's a bigger problem than people know.

PROSECUTING ATTORNEY

When attempting to assess the impact a juvenile's race, sex, or social status have upon the interaction process, it is necessary to explore the manner in which those factors influence individual decision-makers. In addition to exploring institutional policies or trends, it is crucial to explore the feelings and attitudes of individual staff members. For this is the essence of individualized justice: The outcome of the court process is as dependent upon the characteristics and attitudes of the decision-makers as it is upon the characteristics and attitudes of juveniles and their parents. If an individual decision-maker reflects racist, sexist, or class prejudices, then, consciously or unconsciously, these attitudes influence their interactions with juveniles. If decision-makers informally comment negatively on interracial marriages among parents or interracial sexual relationships between juveniles, if a court staff member tells jokes with racial overtones, it may not mean that black juveniles automatically receive severe dispositions. But it does indicate that these predelections influence, perhaps subtly, the juvenile's relationship with court personnel, the manner in which decision-makers view minority juveniles, and ultimately, the nature of the juvenile's experience.

And although we may question decision-makers regarding their attitudes toward the poor, girls, and minorities, such interviews often fail to reach the heart of the matter. One decision-maker candidly expressed the problems of dealing with his own prejudices and his attempts to filter out such predispositions when dealing with juveniles.

[Are you the type of person who's concerned with greater social issues?]

I used to be. I really don't hassle with them any more. I've become very middle-class. . . . I'm going to live my own life and I'm going to try to be as happy as I possibly can and do whatever pleases me as long as I don't hurt other people in the process. Yes, one time I was very concerned, very, very concerned and spent a lot of time. I don't, and I don't intend to.

[Has your work here influenced that or have other external . . . ?]

My work. I have become—when I started here I was a bleeding-heart liberal, and that's how I would title myself—wishy-washy liberal revisionist. . . . Now I'm to the point where I'm still liberal, still vote Democratic, and, you know, I was still for (political candidate) and all that entailed and so forth. . . . But I've become slightly prejudiced, whereas I think that I wasn't at all before.

[From this job?]

Perhaps. I can't really put a finger on it. Perhaps. And I've become a lot more conservative, and I've become a lot more concerned with victims' rights, you know.

[I see.]

A *lot* more concerned with victims' rights and maintaining the community and maintaining community standards, high standards. Not necessarily moral standards, but standards as they relate to crime, etc., etc. So I've changed a lot, an awful lot. Incredibly so.

[When you say that you feel you've become a little more prejudiced, is this something that you're aware of or that you can give examples of?]

Um, no. No, I really think it's a difference in dealing with mostly a college academic community as opposed to dealing with, I don't mean this the way it sounds, the real world, the world as such.

[You mean in the past you were dealing mainly in the college environment?]

Sure. Sure.

[Now you deal with a total urban, metropolitan area?]

Yeh. Yeh, no specific examples. Like, prejudice. Not meaning that I will send a black kid to D.O.C. before I'll send a white kid to D.O.C. That's not what I mean at all.

Oh, just that when I see a black person now, my thoughts are as much negative as positive when I see a white person. You know, I do the same thing with what I would consider a hoozier, you know, a redneck. My thoughts are exactly the same. So I guess, prejudice doesn't cut racelines entirely. To a certain extent, of course, it does, but not entirely. It's more as to economic class, intelligence, education. I really don't have any tolerance for poorly educated, it's kind of contradictory but, uh, bigoted people.
[You don't think that influences your work here?]
I honest to God don't. I really don't. I've thought about it, and I've been conscious of it, but I try to make myself conscious of it. [Right.]
No, I don't. Because I don't deal with that sort of community so, you know, my dealings are. . . . Very seldom do I deal with uneducated people. I'm usually dealing with at least a high school graduate, the parent and, generally speaking, a kid who is on his way to finishing high school or at least. I would say my general range of IQ, just as a general thing, I would say is between 90 and 120. I have two kids that were tested at 85 and very few that test below 90. If they do it's like 89. I have two kids in Special School District. They're both LD [learning disabilities] not retarded . . . EMR [educable mentally retarded].
[Do you think that bias or that sentiment is present in the court then?]
I don't know. I honestly can't answer. I honestly can't answer.
. . . I would say generally speaking, generally speaking, no. At least the people that I know, but my friends are not in that type of court.

Although individual decision-makers may candidly acknowledge personal propensities or tendencies, they often, simultaneously, feel that as professionals they are able to screen out any or most biases when dealing with juveniles. The degree to which anyone can successfully "screen out" or "hold in abeyance" personal values is an extremely important question which defies easy resolution. And to do so within the juvenile justice system is particularly difficult, for the decision-makers' role is to use themselves as purveyors of a child's situation and needs, a task which requires utilization of the entire individual, not merely counseling or administrative skills. It is not sufficient to assert that the juvenile court is not any more racially prejudiced than the general society; it is not enough for court personnel to merely reflect societal trends and shortcomings, for the juvenile court is charged with the awesome task of guiding and protecting juveniles without prejudice or discrimination on the basis of race, sex, or social class. For the juvenile court to merely reflect societal biases is to fail to realize the goal of individualized justice.

Notes

1. An additional .4 percent of the county's population is not white (other than black), and .1 percent of delinquency referrals are for juveniles whose racial identity is classified as "other nonwhites." Because of the extremely small number of other ethnic groups, the present discussion emphasizes court interaction with black juveniles.

2. It is important to note that the vast majority of referrals to court are from law-enforcement officials, rather than schools or parents. The number of referrals to the court may be based on racial discrimination as much as participation in delinquent behavior. For if police are predisposed to refer black juveniles to court, this will directly influence the number of referrals. Likewise, since court workers exercise discretion in grouping and recording the number of referrals, discrimination may conceivably occur at these stages.

3. These positions include the director of court services, chief juvenile officer, detention supervisor, director of clinical services, director of special services, delinquency intake supervisor, supervisors of probation units (four units), the director of the short-term counseling unit, the director of learning disabilities program, and the director of intensive treatment unit.

4. A court worker's assignment to a particular geographic area of the county is not based on the actual composition of that region or the racial identity of the court worker. Thus, in addition to the common situation of white workers supervising black juveniles, black court workers must also confront any difficulties they encounter in supervising white juveniles. Also, because of the predominantly white population of the county, several court workers have caseloads that involve white juveniles only.

CHAPTER 10

The Influence of Juveniles' Sexual Identity and Social Class on Decision-Making

The Response to Female and Male Delinquency

The expectations of decision-makers and their responses to children are greatly influenced by the sexual identity of the child. It is a factor which influences numerous subtle dimensions of the interaction as well as more obvious decisions. The great majority (74 percent) of all delinquency referrals involve males: 84 percent of all felony referrals and 80 percent of all misdemeanor referrals. Females only account for 26 percent of the overall delinquency referrals, but they are involved in 41 percent of all referrals for status offenses (58 percent of runaways; 43 percent of incorrigibles; 33 percent of truancies; 25 percent of possession or consumption of alcohol; and 21 percent of curfew violations).

As discussed previously, females are more likely to be detained prior to their trials, despite the fact they are commonly involved in less serious offenses. The influence of sex on final disposition is less obvious: without controlling for the type of offense, there is no relationship between the severity of the disposition of a case and the sex of the defendant, despite the fact boys commit more serious crimes and are referred to court more frequently than girls. When a distinction is made between status offenses and adult-like offenses, the consideration of sex has a slight influence on the severity of the disposition. Males are more likely to receive the most severe dispositions when they are involved in felonies and misdemeanors, and females are more likely to receive the most severe dispositions for particular status offenses.

The fact that the court's response to juveniles varies with sex and type of offense reflects both referral trends and common conceptions based on sexual identity. Males are referred to court much more frequently for adult-like offenses and, as such, are viewed as requiring severe treatment to curtail future infractions of the law. In contrast, most females are referred for status offenses, and although such behavior is undesirable in males, it is generally considered more detrimental to females. Running away or incorrigibility is seen as far more consequential for females than males, for the former are viewed as more vulnerable, easily influenced by older males, and requiring greater protection. Pragmatic considerations, such as the possibility of pregnancy, enter into the court's response to female status offenders, but their decisions also reflect the general society's depiction of females as less able to care for themselves and as requiring close supervision.

When dealing with females, court personnel frequently stress the importance of maintaining a "good reputation," as well as avoiding the possible dangers of unsupervised activity.

> We'd all agree you're a very attractive young lady. You can have a lot of problems if you go looking for them. You need to obey your mother.
>
> HEARING OFFICER
> (to a 15-year old,
> referral #1, curfew, runaway).

> The most important person around is you. You should be concerned with your most valuable possession, your reputation. I know that boys can run around, steal or whatever and it won't affect their reputation, but it's different with a girl. You'll be living at home with your parents until you get married and you have to be concerned with yourself and your reputation.
>
> HEARING OFFICER
> (to a 15-year old,
> referral #1, incorrigibility)

Sexual identity subtly influences the court's assessment of juvenile activities; it affects the types of questions asked as well as the expectations of decision-makers. For example, participation in sports is regarded positively and frequently evokes praise from court personnel, but such inquiries and discussions are generally confined to males. Males are more frequently questioned regarding their employment opportunities and are expected to have afterschool and summer jobs. They are routinely advised of the necessity of education in order to support future families. And, although females are also admonished to take advantage of educational opportunities, advice regarding the job market is sometimes given in the form of a warning that employment may be necessary *if* they don't have someone to support them.

Troublesome Female Status Offenders

As mentioned previously, most females referred to court are involved in status offenses, one-third of all female referrals are runaways. Although a few female court workers expressed a preference for dealing with such cases, the vast majority of court personnel, males and females, assert that female status offenders are the most difficult cases to handle.

> . . . . when I look at the status offender thing [I] know that it's going to be more than a regular law violator.
> [Oh, really?]
> Status offenders take more time. They always do.
> [Why do you say that?]
> Experience. They do take more time, particularly the girls. They're incredibly hard to deal with. No, really. A female status offender about 14-years old is the hardest case that you'll have to work, period.
>
> COURT WORKER

> [Do you find girls easier to deal with than boys?]
> No. I think they're difficult, very difficult. I would say the most difficult and that's why I have been really against, you know, removing the status offenders from the juvenile court because the girls that I see simply would not, I would say 99 percent of them would not, voluntarily go any place and try to get help. You have to almost cram it down their throats but even then it doesn't always work, but at least you've tried. No, I think they're very difficult.
>
> HEARING OFFICER

Court personnel suggest two major reasons for the complexity and difficulty in attempting to deal with female status offenders. They suggest that there are difficulties inherent in attempting to deal with any status offender, but there are special problems stemming from the personality traits of young girls. Status offenders are commonly regarded as more difficult to help than are juveniles who have participated in adult-like crimes. Decision-makers suggest that the underlying causes of status offenses are difficult to assess, that status offenses often arise from family conflicts, and that long-term court involvement is often necessary before any change can be affected. As graphically stated by the following court worker, relationships with status offenders are often seen as more demanding and less rewarding than those with other clients.

[Do you think there are different types of kids you see?]
   Different types—what do you mean?
[Different kinds of kids?]
   Oh, sure. Every kid's different. Every single kid is different. I've never had two kids alike. There might be similar circumstances and stuff like that but no two kids are alike. I don't know how many kids I've worked with in these years, but that's how many kinds of kids I've worked with.
[Are the girls different than the boys?]
   I hate working with girls. I just hate it! I can't tell you how much I hate working with girls.
[Why?]
   They're more difficult, let me count the ways. They're more demanding, they're more difficult, they're more needful, they're more exasperating, they're more everything. I mean, just keep going. And they are a pain in the ass! I hate working. . . . Give me a felon! I got so excited the other day when I heard I was getting a felon. Five burglaries in three days and, oh, I can deal with that! I mean, I really like dealing with that. I can sit here and I can pound on the desk and that's great. I love that. Oh no, I hate working with girls. I hate working with status offenders because it's a no-win kind of situation. You're damned if you do and you're damned if you don't. Girls, I tend to be more, how do I function? I told one of my kids this and she threw it up to me later. . . . I think I told her, I said I tend to be, let's see, [either] more patient or less patient. I tend to be less patient with girls, because, number one I'm chauvinistic as hell, and two, I recognize I don't like working with girls. I mean I

really don't. I get along with them fine and they usually go goo-goo over me and all that kind of stuff. . . . But I hate working with girls. They're just more time-consuming. I've had, I'm this adamant about it because within the last nine months over half of my caseload has been girls and I'm sick of it, just sick of it. I'm in the process now. I closed out three of them last week just 'cause I was tired of looking at them. Get them away from me. So, I don't like girls.

PROBATION OFFICER

In addition to the problems encountered when dealing with status offenders, court personnel suggest that personalities of girls are more exasperating. In the following comments the public defender acknowledges difficulties in representing girls, and a court worker suggests general personality distinctions between boys and girls.

[Do you think that the girls you deal with are different than the boys in any way?]

They're a lot less tolerable. [Laughter.] They really are. Yeh, it's too bad. I mean, I'm usually a very woman-prone woman. I like women. But most of the girls are frequently hard to take. They're very, very self-centered and spoiled, sort of the traditional woman stuff that I don't like too much. You know, they don't have strength of character at all, and a lot of these boys really do. You know, they're acting out of hurt sometimes, but they tend to have a certain strength of character. They've been cut off by their families a lot of times, but most of them are not whimpering in the corner, "My mommy doesn't love me, my daddy doesn't love me." You see that somewhat, but not that much. Among girls, girls are always expecting to be pampered no matter who they are and from what background. And that's really what they're asking for from me, and as I say, that's sort of what I was alluding to. I don't pamper people and I don't like it and don't like to be pampered. And so I guess that's why I don't get along as well with girls.

PUBLIC DEFENDER

[Are most of the girls that you have status offenders?]

Yes.

[Are they more difficult to deal with than the boys?]

They're very different. I think they're more difficult because they're usually more devious. They'll make firm commitments to the rules and lay out a complicated action plan and then we'll find them sneaking out in the middle of the night or running away, or cutting class, saying, "Oh, I want to go to school and I want to finish and that's exactly what I want to do." And then they'll go to school and cut classes. So, the boys we haven't had that problem with.

COURT WORKER

Thus, court interactions with juveniles are influenced by the sex of the juvenile because boys and girls are commonly referred for different types of delinquent behavior, but also because court personnel have varying expectations for girls and boys and perceive general attitudinal and behavioral distinctions based on the sexual roles for which juveniles are socialized.

The Influence of Social Class

It also was becoming impossible to ignore the fact that the broad discretionary powers the court officials had been granted were resulting in flagrant discriminations against girls in some cases, boys in others, racial and ethnic minorities, and poor families. (Flicker, 1978:32.)

The issue of social class has been extremely controversial in the juvenile court, with numerous commentators suggesting that court personnel systematically discriminate against juveniles from lower-class backgrounds (Martin, 1970; Schur, 1973; Platt, 1977; Thomas and Cage, 1977; Flicker, 1978).

The philosophy of the juvenile court—with its thoroughgoing social investigation of the alleged delinquent, and its relative lack of concern with the particular offense—virtually ensures that stereotypes will influence judicial dispositions. . . .

In our society, lower-class children more than middle-class ones, black children more than white ones, and boys more than girls, face high probabilities (i.e., run a special "categorical risk" in the actuarial sense) not only of engaging in rule-violation in the first place, but also of becoming enmeshed in official negative labeling processes (Schur, 1973:121, 125–6).

But opinions on this issue are not unanimous, nor is the "empirical evidence" conclusive, for various researchers have suggested the contrary, asserting that legal factors such as the seriousness of the offense and the number of referrals to court are more consequential in the decision-making process (Terry, 1967; Arnold, 1971; Cohen and Kluegel, 1978). In turn, other writers suggest that these more legalistic variables are influenced by class bias among referral sources, particularly among law enforcement officials (Williams and Gold, 1972; Piliavin and Briar, 1964).

At the present court, the possibility of class bias is not an acknowledged or openly discussed issue. Rather, the manner in which social class impacts upon decision-making is multidimensional and, most frequently, obscured from public view. Nevertheless, social class does exert a tremendous influence over the workings of the court and its meting out of "individualized" justice.

Foremost among these factors is the ability of middle or upper class families to mobilize private resources on behalf of the juvenile.[1] In addition to the availability of personal monies, middle and upper-class parents often have insurance policies which cover psychiatric and other treatment services. Because court funds are limited, family efforts to provide private treatment resources are viewed positively and encouraged by court decision-makers. Such action is interpreted as an indication of parental concern regarding their child's behavior and problems. Also, when more affluent families either provide their own services or pay most of the cost of court-ordered services, court personnel consider it an economically expedient arrangement which permits the court to utilize its limited funds to aid juveniles whose families are unable to provide services.

Likewise, although court personnel generally praise those treatment facilities regularly employed by the court, decision-makers recognize that the "better," more innovative programs are beyond the price range of those facilities which the court can afford. Thus, these more costly programs may be seen as specifically designed to meet a juvenile's needs, and therefore as more closely approximating the ideal of individualized treatment espoused by the juvenile justice system. Also, more affluent families may already be in contact with private psychiatrists, psychologists or treatment facilities. As stated by a court attorney, ". . . . You often see prior involvement with some fairly highpriced help which tends to denigrate what the court could possibly offer."

Social Status and the Private Attorney

Regardless of their parents' financial status, the majority of juveniles who are represented by an attorney are handled by the public defender. The immediate accessibility of this attorney, combined with the fact that court workers may recommend the public defender to families because of her familiarity with the court, influences the choices of even affluent families.[2]

Virtually all juveniles represented by private attorneys are middle or upper class. Although court personnel disagree on the influence of a private attorney within the juvenile system, several suggest that these attorneys are more likely to resist further court involvement in the form of supervision, and are more likely to utilize "stall tactics" in delaying final disposition of a case.

In the following comments, a court worker discusses the potential effects of social status, as well as the contention that more affluent juveniles may be prevented from receiving needed help due to the interference of a private attorney.

[Would you say when you make your recommendation that the family's financial situation influences what you recommend?]

It influences it a lot. Although, you know, there's two schools of thought to that. One, you're saying do you want the child who can afford an attorney (to have one). And I'm convinced that if you're in trouble you need a good attorney. I mean if you want to get out of the trouble. You know, that's our democratic system. It doesn't mean a poor person can't have a good attorney too if they get a good public defender who's on their side, but there's two ways to look at that.

Sometimes poor kids get more help because their parents don't kick up a fuss, they just sort of go along or the kid does get jurisdiction [is placed under the court's jurisdiction] fast. He doesn't have an attorney and so they get involved in the system and get some help and the rich kid can have a real good attorney who can say, "Don't go in," and "Don't co-operate," and "Stay away." And the kid can be in all sorts of trouble, you know, for theirselves. So there's two ways to look at that. But I'm thinking of a case that I just had where the kid came into detention. The parents were very wealthy and from a very prominent family. And he—they were saying help. He came into detention because he had written a whole bunch of checks on his mother's account over a period of six months before she ever found out about it. She was just so busy with all her social things that she didn't keep her bank [account] that close. And she didn't realize he had written them and they were $20 at a time. I don't know how he got them cashed. I can't get one cashed!

But he had, and it had totalled two hundred and something dollars in six months. There had been a big fight and they had brought him to detention, incorrigible application on their own. We were working, boy, we were working with the situation. Got a contract made, the mother and stepfather and the boy. The mother was terribly high and we got her and the boy to see a private psychiatrist and we really were making some progress, I guess.

We weren't making a lot or he wouldn't have gotten into more trouble. Then he came in for armed robbery, $2500 from a friend's home. Well, they got scared and got an attorney, and the attorney says don't spoil things, so we stopped everything. We didn't see him. He didn't come in.

. . . . Then his attorney started the old stall. Three or four months passed, another stall and then a reset [rescheduling of the hearing], another reset. Meantime about three or four referrals came in and by this time, the family's—the mother's—calling me again saying, "Can't I?" I said, "Come in my office. Let's talk." So we started another program, completely independent of the armed robbery that we know he's going to beat because the people are friends and they're going to withdraw the charges and all. The attorney's telling them that they're going to say he was home in bed that night and. . . .

[The robbery was dismissed?]

Yes.

[But the parents had filed the incorrigible?]

That was still open so they did get some help.

[They wanted to be involved?]

By this time they were in with their attorney and were saying, because her father was a friend of the judge's, that they were getting a little paranoid and then begin to think, you know, get angry with their attorney, saying, "Hey, we could have gotten some help." It was just crazy and then they came into court [the hearing] saying, "We got to get this kid out of the house and we got to have some help." And all the time I'm saying, "Well, the kid's been to military school; he's been everywhere." And I think a lot of it was they did need the kid out of their hair. He was a terrible problem, a really hyper kid, just drove everybody crazy. . . .

INTAKE WORKER

Although court personnel view the attempts of more affluent families to avoid court involvement as regrettable because juvenile needs go undiagnosed and untreated, the most significant consequence of a family's ability to provide outside treatment is that, in doing so, they are able to minimize the stigma placed upon their children. For, those children placed in court-operated group homes or state institutions are officially categorized as "delinquents" and immersed in the legal system. If the only available facilities are those affiliated with the court, the court must take jurisdiction and enter a legal order placing custody with that facility.

To the contrary, if the family has provided alternative facilities—a private treatment center, private psychiatric counseling, a private boarding school—further court involvement may not be necessary. The court does not deem it necessary to take jurisdiction and is not legally involved in the juvenile or family situation at that time. The case may be placed on an informal standby basis, but heavy caseloads pressure court personnel to limit involvement and allow the family to deal with the situation.

Thus, although the rationale commonly expressed by court personnel, that is, permitting more affluent families to provide their own treatment services increases the funds which can be expended on behalf of poorer juveniles, is an economically sound argument, it also functions to allow more affluent families to avoid any stigma that results from involvement with the juvenile justice system. And although court workers (to varying degrees) defend the quality of care provided by state facilities, the vast majority of families resist placements. The vast majority of juveniles do not want to be placed in state institutions, but the ability to avoid such action successfully is often directly correlated with the family's ability to provide other alternatives.

In the following case a middle-class family is able to prevent certain placement with the Department of Corrections by financing an expensive alternative.

#115 Pretrial Conference #1

Judge
Prosecuting Attorney
Public Defender

Chief Juvenile Officer
Court Worker
White Male, 16-years old
Referral #6:   Sale of drugs

COURT WORKER: He was in detention, but release was recommended. Mother and Father are divorced. He's living with Mother. Mother says, "Mike's secretive, hard to handle." And he's had trouble with alcohol and drugs.

I'm recommending against certification [to the adult court] because of the extent of his involvement as a middle man.

The repetitive nature is important. I don't think just formal supervision [probation] would help. He has no goals. A group home placement isn't sufficient. My recommendation is D.O.C. [Department of Corrections].

JUDGE: [To Public Defender.] What do you think?

PUBLIC DEFENDER: I have a real problem with this one. He doesn't have a bad record and he's less culpable than most of the kids we have on sales (of drugs). He was befriended by an undercover agent. He didn't have the drugs in his home, he sought them out for his friend.

JUDGE: Did the agent look like Serpico?

PUBLIC DEFENDER: Yes.

JUDGE: If I were a kid and some guy with a beard and long hair asked me [to get drugs], I'd get as far away as possible!

PUBLIC DEFENDER: Right! He's working regularly. Wants to show the court he can do it in the next six months. When I talked to the mother she didn't understand D.O.C. completely. She didn't understand they could keep control 'til he's 18 if he goes to a group home in the city.

I asked [the mother] what the problems are. Curfew's the major thing.

PROSECUTING ATTORNEY: What about the drinking?

PUBLIC DEFENDER: I asked her, "Can you control him?" She says after he's been out after curfew he seems extremely up-tight. She says she doesn't think he's into drugs. After I explained D.O.C. she said she could make it.

CHIEF JUVENILE OFFICER: I'm recommending against taking it under advisement. Mike can profit from an authority situation. His involvement somewhat mitigates against commitment but his age pushes for it. D.O.C. aftercare could be extended. We could do it in our own group home but there exists a limit. He'd only have effective supervision [for a short time].

JUDGE: Does he have contact with Father?

COURT WORKER: He did live with Father. He's [Father's] concerned.

PUBLIC DEFENDER: Would you elaborate what in his history shows he needs this kind of. . . .

CHIEF JUVENILE OFFICER: The history shows that he's not under the solid control of his mother.

PUBLIC DEFENDER: Most 16-year olds are like that.

CHIEF JUVENILE OFFICER: Most are not out arranging $1000 drug deals.

PUBLIC DEFENDER: He doesn't have a delinquency pattern. Why not give him a chance to show the court he can make it?

PROSECUTING ATTORNEY: The report shows a lot of problems at home. No effective parenting, no goals. . . .

PUBLIC DEFENDER: [Starts to speak.]

PROSECUTING ATTORNEY: Can I just finish? Mother has not told our worker that there's no trouble. She hasn't told us what she told you.

PUBLIC DEFENDER: I thought you were finished.

COURT WORKER: Father doesn't feel he can help control him, therefore he's refusing custody.

JUDGE: Did they both agree he could drop out of school at 15?

COURT WORKER: Mother agreed. I don't know why.

JUDGE: If I take it under advisement, we might be leading into more trouble.

CHIEF JUVENILE OFFICER: What we may be seeing, referrals may have altered his behavior, perhaps he's more responsive and responsible. Prior to his apprehension he was not under control.

PUBLIC DEFENDER: My whole point is that there could be conditions for not placing him with D.O.C., like G.E.D. [General Equivalency Diploma] participation, holding down a job, and no community trouble.

PROSECUTING ATTORNEY: But the kid can't make it at home.

PUBLIC DEFENDER: I wouldn't have come in here and said he would make it at home if I hadn't talked with the mother and him.

JUDGE: We better set it down. Let me hear it. I kind of think we shouldn't hear it as a certification. There's an odor of entrapment. We're going to keep him [in the juvenile justice system]. A group home's a possibility.

CHIEF JUVENILE OFFICER: The only limitation is there are 120 days 'til he [reaches the age of majority].

JUDGE: If he got involved in another one like this he'd be gone. Certification. He'd have to know this. Would a group home help or hinder? I don't think he can stay at home.

COURT WORKER: We've discussed group homes. There's not one really. Sunrise has no openings and the others are not appropriate. D.O.C. offers direction.

JUDGE: If we had Stress Challenge [outdoors program]. . . . We have a program to send him to, but no resources.

PUBLIC DEFENDER: How much does it cost?

COURT WORKER: For about 40 days, $600 to $800.

JUDGE: That's a choice. . . . Should we try the referrals [have an adjudicatory hearing] or as dispositional?

PUBLIC DEFENDER: What are the allegations?

JUDGE: Consorting to sell two pounds of marijuana, one gram of PCB, and hashish. If he'll admit to one, that'll be sufficient.

PUBLIC DEFENDER: You can pick a date. He's admitting to consorting to sell. I don't know what the hell that is.

PROSECUTING ATTORNEY: I can amend it. "Consorting to sell" means to aid and abett. Go talk to him.

PUBLIC DEFENDER: I have talked to him. I'll check out the father's finances and get a statement.

Pretrial Conference #2 [Nine days later; three minutes]

CHIEF JUVENILE OFFICER: He doesn't have any disability that would qualify him for aid for vocational training. We'll have to use the economic resources of the family.

PROSECUTING ATTORNEY: They tried to get him in on a psychological (have him come to be tested psychologically), but he wouldn't come. He said it was because of work.

PUBLIC DEFENDER: I'd have to get his side on that. I'd like to re-emphasize that the offenses are not the ordinary: he didn't have it in his home to sell. He just acted as a facilitator. The family supports him going to Stress Challenge.

JUDGE: They'll take him?

CHIEF JUVENILE OFFICER: He was interviewed and they'll take him. The limitation of that is that it necessitates the expenditure of family funds. I'm not sure if they have more for further expenses. But from our experience this is the kind of kid that would do well [at Stress Challenge].

JUDGE: Aren't we sort of at the end of the rope?

PROSECUTING ATTORNEY: The father had custody, but couldn't handle him. The mother was unable to handle him. They're not able to control this kid.

JUDGE: If the family's willing to spend that kind of money that's where he ought to go. I'm not sure D.O.C. would be any better. If they'll spend the dough, this would be a program that would be equal to D.O.C., better than it. Even if he went to Pinetop [D.O.C.'s outdoor program]. If it were me, I'd go to Pinetop and just walk around in the woods.

Do you disagree, Gary [chief juvenile officer]?

CHIEF JUVENILE OFFICER: I've shared the limitations and relative strengths of Stress Challenge. We'll still have some time to make an evaluation after he comes back from Stress Challenge. He'd still have about three months under jurisdiction. We could use "career planning program" for him.

PROSECUTING ATTORNEY: What I'd like to do. . . .

PUBLIC DEFENDER: That's really unfair. They're [parents] not sending him there because they want to, but rather as an alternative to him being sent to the Department of Corrections.

PROSECUTING ATTORNEY: I think the kid needs some kind of control.

JUDGE: I can still put him at D.O.C. if it's necessary later.

CHIEF JUVENILE OFFICER: Would he take a commitment with a stay?

PUBLIC DEFENDER: I don't know that it makes any difference. He knows this is it.

JUDGE: I like the idea when the family comes in and says they'll dig down in their jeans and come up with the money. Then he has a commitment to them *and* the court.

CHIEF JUVENILE OFFICER: We could get the control with a commitment [to D.O.C.] with a stay.

JUDGE: I vacillate on stays. They don't mean too much. I say, "If you blow this, you'll go to D.O.C."

PROSECUTING ATTORNEY: We could make the stay conditional upon completion of this program.

JUDGE: I'm not going to send him there under those conditions. I'm not going to say he has to make it. That's a tough course. He could fall out of a tree or something. It's a hell of a physical course. I couldn't make it, not even when I was his age. Certainly not now.

CHIEF JUVENILE OFFICER: Maybe there's some logic to control through a commitment with a stay.

JUDGE: But jurisdiction is the key. If he messes up, he'll be looking at me. If he came in on subsequent offenses I might certify him. I just don't write it. . . .

CHIEF JUVENILE OFFICER: But if he sees it in the order it might mean something.

JUDGE: I'll do it either way. If it makes you feel better, I'll put it in the order.

Courtroom [16 minutes]

[Father and juvenile join court personnel in courtroom. Mother is not present, is at work.]

PROSECUTING ATTORNEY: [Takes appearances, verifies juvenile's birthdate.]

I'd like the record to reflect that the mother, although duly served, is not present. I'd like the bailiff to call "Mrs. Clara Sampson."

[The bailiff goes to the courtroom door and calls "Mrs. Clara Sampson" three times.]

BAILIFF: Your Honor, she answers not.

PROSECUTING ATTORNEY: The record should reflect the pretrial conference and that the juvenile admits to the allegations.

JUDGE: Let me review. On January 17 you consorted to sell a controlled substance, marijuana, two pounds, valued at $810. On January 31 you consorted to sell PCB, one gram, valued at $90.

On February 2 you consorted to sell a controlled substance, hashish, one pound valued at $100. Tell me what happened.

JUVENILE: One police officer got ahold of me. He was friendly to me, bought me beers and things like that. He asked me if I knew where he could get drugs.

I went to a big party and heard some guy talking. . . . I set it up.

JUDGE: These were the only occasions on which this happened? Of course, you didn't know then that he was a police officer.

JUVENILE: Yes.

JUDGE: On that record I'll take jurisdiction. Although we talked about this in the pretrial conference, it's a good thing to have you tell me. I've pretty well indicated to your attorney what I'm inclined to do, but I'd like to have the chief juvenile officer testify.

[The Prosecuting Attorney calls the chief juvenile officer. He is sworn in and sits in the witness chair.]

PROSECUTING ATTORNEY: Please state your name and occupation.

CHIEF JUVENILE OFFICER: Gary Holcum, chief juvenile officer.

PROSECUTING ATTORNEY: Can we admit to his qualifications?

[The public defender agrees to admit to the witness's qualifications.]

PROSECUTING ATTORNEY: Have you reviewed the file?

CHIEF JUVENILE OFFICER: Yes.

PROSECUTING ATTORNEY: What is your recommendation?

CHIEF JUVENILE OFFICER: That the court should order the juvenile to participate in Stress Challenge at family expense. We also recommend a commitment with a stay in order to have ongoing control.

PROSECUTING ATTORNEY: Please explain what it means.

CHIEF JUVENILE OFFICER: Custody is with the Department of Corrections. It is stayed while he is in the program [Stress Challenge]. It could be lifted in the event of another offense or violation of probation conditions. If he successfully completes the program the stay will be dropped.

PROSECUTING ATTORNEY: No further questions.

PUBLIC DEFENDER: No questions.

[Chief Juvenile Officer steps down from the witness stand.]

JUDGE: Let me review so we all understand. Mike's going to [reach the age of majority] in three-and-a-half months. We discussed in chambers and have two possibilities: Number one, commitment now to the Department of Corrections. I understand you were screened and would go to Pinetop [outdoor facility]. D.O.C. isn't just Crockertown [the main facility and a secure institution].

Number two, Stress Challenge. It's an expensive program. Court funds for it have been cut. There are two things you should realize. Number one, your folks are undergoing a severe financial hardship to make this possible. And, number two, if you mess up and blow it, you'll be back here. You have something to show to your parents and the court. I happen to think it's an excellent program. It's up to you to decide if you'll make it or not.

PROSECUTING ATTORNEY: You and your mother must make the arrangement. You'll have to do something today.

PUBLIC DEFENDER: I'd like to point out that since the court is ordering this, even though the parents are financing it, it wouldn't be too much for the court to help with the arrangements.

JUDGE: What's needed?

CHIEF JUVENILE OFFICER: I think they need to be contacted by the court to let them know the court has okayed it.

[The Prosecuting Attorney comments to the Chief Juvenile Officer in a low voice.]

CHIEF JUVENILE OFFICER: There's probably one further thing, the financial part.

PROSECUTING ATTORNEY: A contract has to be signed.

PUBLIC DEFENDER: Can I clear something up? This man should not be put on the spot at all. He was handed a financial statement the last time he was here and met with the court financial officer. We were all mystified because the family is paying.

JUDGE: That was my doing. We often have them fill out statements even when the court can't supply the funds.

The key to this is for us to get the job done—so he doesn't miss going Monday [in four days].

FATHER: May I ask a question? Where do they want the money and when?

JUDGE: [To Court Worker] Can you help us?

COURT WORKER: Yes, we'll call there right after this.

PROSECUTING ATTORNEY: I want you to wait on a copy of this order. You'll need to take it to Stress Challenge.

PUBLIC DEFENDER: They're not thinking of running away.

Posthearing

The Chief Juvenile Officer asks the prosecutor why she is upset. The prosecuting attorney replies she has a suspicion about it because the family has a pattern of not controlling the kid.

Cultural Contrasts

Numerous theorists have suggested that the predominantly middle-class backgrounds and orientations of decision-makers decrease their ability to appreciate and relate to the worldview of lower-class children. Accordingly, court personnel are depicted as predisposed to viewing the lower-class family as "unstable," "inadequate," or "unable to provide appropriate supervision for juveniles." Critics also suggest that the life experiences of poorer juveniles limit their ability to interact with court personnel in a manner which will be positively evaluated by decision-makers, that is, that they are less educated, less articulate, and less verbal than juveniles from middle- or upper-class backgrounds. Likewise, parents with middle- or upper-class backgrounds are seen as more prepared to communicate with decision-makers, more able to articulate their opinions, and thus, more successful in conveying the "appropriate" attitude and degree of concern.

Although their cultural affinity with decision-makers provide middle-class children with an advantage in demonstrating that further court involvement is unnecessary, it is erroneous to suggest that this is always the case. The court worker's negative evaluation of the family's and juvenile's attitude and demeanor may outweigh their cultural affinity and level of education, for middle- or upper-class status alone is not sufficient to convince decision-makers that court intervention is unnecessary. To the contrary, decision-makers may view affluence as detrimental to a juvenile's development.

[Are there any kids that you just don't like?]
   Some I feel so stymied about what to do, but there are none I actively dislike. For instance, one juvenile from an extremely wealthy family—great future as a surgeon which is what he wants to be.

He's a very likeable boy that I want to shake because his life situation is so protected that there are lot of things he'll be able to get away with, even legal things, that most kids can't, because his parents have a lot of money and can buy good attorneys. So I have some negative feelings against him which has nothing to do with his personality.

COURT WORKER

Thus, although middle- and upper-class families and juveniles may enjoy the advantage of sharing in the worldview and life experiences of most court personnel, these similarities are not foremost in the decision-making process. Although their problems may be categorized differently, middle- and upper-class juveniles are often seen as needing court intervention.

[Have the black juveniles you have contact with been different from the whites in any way?]

Well, in this setting they run such a gamut of race and social class that the distinction between black and white is really more, I think, pretty minor. There's definitely social class distinctions between the blacks who live in a poor community and the ones who are upwardly mobile or the ones who are attempting to be upwardly mobile. It's a different group. But, if I were to talk about distinguishing characteristics I'd relate more to class and area of the county rather than race.

[What are some of the class . . . ?]

Well, we see some upper class kids in this setting who are materially very affluent, but emotionally very deprived. You see a lot of status offenders in that respect and some felony offenders. We see the middle-class suburban child who is isolated from a community. You know, a kid who lives out in a subdivision and has very little in terms of community support, neighborhood peer group support, and any kind of recreation is a long way from their home. They wind up roaming around shopping centers and get into shoplifting and, a kid who's been uprooted and isolated in terms of a support system. We see, and we see more blacks than whites in this category, the upwardly mobile families who move into their area where the parents really feel that they're doing something worthwhile for the kids. But the kids have a hard time adapting. Or a kid who moves from the inner-city and has a hard time being accepted by a peer group, adapting into new expectations and a lot of times these kids will get into trouble. And then we see some poverty families who are just making ends meet. You know, one-parent families, tons of kids, the mother's working, making ends meet takes every energy that she has and it's a neglect situation. . . .

COURT WORKER

The following discussion by a court worker highlights attitudinal differences between juveniles as perceived by a decision-maker, as well as the disadvantage experienced by less articulate juveniles in their interaction with court personnel.

> I see kids here who come the way you would go to the dentist. They expect to come in, their brothers come in, their cousins come in. I tell them, "I don't want to see you here again." The hearing officer tells them. And I know they're going to be back. I know it's just a matter of time. . . .
>
> The attitude that the lower-middle-class kids, kids whose fathers are in construction, mothers are nurses or hostesses, receptionists, whatever, those kids take it much more as a matter of course. It's just something they do like they go to school. Whereas the more middle-class or upper-class family gets scared, they're the ones who call. . . .
>
> They're [lower class] less frightened and in an odd way much more realistic. You can't bluff them. You can't say, "If you violate this or that we may have to send you . . ." because they know kids who've gone to the Department of Corrections and they know it takes a hell of a lot before that happens. Or they know their probation officer's not going to be right on top of everything all the time. They're streetwise and courtwise. They have a sense.
>
> I may get less info from them. It's more, they're less verbal, less aware, less able to take responsibility for themselves. They need to be asked. They need a structured interview in which I say to them, "What grade do you get in this class? What do you do Mondays after school?" And I don't conduct that type of interview. So from that type of talk I get less info than other workers may.

Many court personnel freely acknowledge and express concern regarding the material deprivation of many juveniles, but these decision-makers vary in their assessment of the implications of such poverty. Some equate financial disadvantages with emotional poverty, others do not. And as is illustrated by the following comments, many court personnel see a child's contact with the juvenile justice system as a means of providing opportunities, rather than punishing or stigmatizing.

[Are you a person who's concerned with social issues or social problems in the larger society?]

Not actively, but I think very much so personally. I think I'm affected very much by things that go on, but I'm not an active go-getter. I think I feel for it and I keep it more to myself and do the little things I can. I don't get involved in the big system.

[What issues are you interested in?]

Well, general inequality, the things that make me sick, you know, when you see the kids that I deal with who come from very low incomes and no fathers around. Just their plight and how they're so disadvantaged. It's very aggravating and it gives me a lot of guilt feelings thinking I've had it so easy. It makes me want to say, "Okay, I want to have a socialist system here. I don't want to worry about all this crap. And nobody's going to have anything—we'll start from the bottom up. All little kids are going to have food in their stomachs and everyone's going to have a mother who loves them." And that type of thing. It's more of a personal thing with me than getting really involved in the social issues. It's more of the just downright injustice of life, I guess.

[A lot of the kids you see here make that evident?]

Yeh, it's pitiful sometimes and it's very upsetting to see rejection in these kids. These kids are rejected so much and so very few material things they have in just the way of a decent, clean home, decent, clean clothes to wear, a mother who's home and cares about them.

[Do you think the court system works against those kids more than the kids who are middle class or affluent?]

Works against them did you say?

[Right.]

No, I think sometimes it's the only hope they've got. A number of the kids I've placed [outside the home], I think if they weren't placed and removed from that situation, at least temporarily, and had a chance to experience a little bit better. Going to school, somebody concerned about them, somebody getting their breakfast for them in the morning, helping them decide. You know, how getting around other kids from different social backgrounds, they might never have gotten out of that. They wouldn't survive, so, I think, in a way, it offers them a whole lot. I think that I treat the kids I have, in fact, I probably treat them with more concern than the kids from affluent homes. I spend more time with my kids with who I know there's no other services available.

[So you see the benefits to those kids, especially the poor kids, as outweighing any disadvantages or stigma they might get from being there?]

Well, I don't know about the stigma. I think all kids are stigmatized by it. Sometimes we tend to forget about that because the court's where we work every day, you know. Why are you stigmatized with that? You don't realize that. In fact, I was sending a court order for an alternative to detention over to a foster mother. This girl has been living in a foster home, you know, so she enrolls in school tomorrow. They have to have proof of custody. So here I'm thinking, wait a minute, they're going to go in and look at a detention order or alternative to detention. The kid's going to have a bad point on her record right there, 'cause they're going to think, "Oh, this kid's really. . . ." But there's not really any way to avoid it. They have to have a copy of the order, they have to know the situation. But you tend to forget about all that stuff—you're so used to it, it's part of life. You don't realize that some people think, "Oh, my God!" Because I don't tend to think of these kids as any different than any other kid that I see on the street. It just happens that they come to me because they've got a few problems that have been caught or that people are aware of. I don't think of them as any different, or bad kids, or, you know, any different than the other kids. 'Cause I know a lot of things that I did when I was a kid and my brothers and sisters did, and people they hang around with. So I mean, I just never got caught for anything. I never ended up in the court system.

[But do you think other people would communicate that. . . . ?]

Yeh. But, see, I tend to forget that sometimes unless I'm really conscious of it. I tend to forget that people do judge them differently. It's hard to be careful under certain situations. . . .

PROBATION OFFICER

Thus, although the impact of social class upon the decision-making process is difficult to assess, there are major areas in which this factor plays a crucial role. The social class of a family may influence the decision-makers' perceptions of the family's ability to provide adequate supervision for a juvenile, the juvenile's and family's ability to communicate with court personnel successfully, and the family's ability to mobilize alternative resources for treatment to avoid undesired court involvement.

Notes

1. Both Emerson (1969:98) and Cicourel (1968:273ff) have commented upon this factor, but their studies were conducted at courts which served predomi-

nantly lower-class juveniles, and therefore, such mobilization of resources was rare. The contrary is true in the present inquiry.

2. Officially, court workers are instructed not to become involved in a family's decision whether or not to retain an attorney, but their opinions are frequently sought by their clients. Court policy stipulates that parents will contribute to the expense of the public defender according to their financial ability.

CHAPTER 11

The Crucial Variable of Home Environment: The Court's Appraisal

> . . . I think, obviously, you've got to think about the break-
> down of families. That's a tremendous social problem, and no
> one will ever be able to convince me that that isn't a great deal
> responsible for the problems the kids have today—'just see too
> many of them; it's just got to be a big factor.
>
> Hearing Officer

Although social scientists vary greatly in their evaluation of the
extent to which the family should be viewed as a cause of delinquency (Hirschi, 1969; Rodman and Grams, 1967; Wilkinson,
1974), the juvenile court emphasizes the role of the family in the
creation, treatment, and prevention of delinquency. In accordance with the juvenile justice system's concern with the offender
rather than the offense, a juvenile's home situation and character
are foremost in importance when decision-makers choose between dispositional alternatives. The court's perception of a juvenile's personal attitude and demeanor is intertwined with it's
assessment of the overall family situation.

> Well, it's a team effort, really, I feel. Well, if you have parents
> that really don't seem concerned, I think you're looking at some-
> thing that the kid doesn't develop into a more serious problem down
> the line because a lot of our referrals stem from a lack of concern
> by parents.
>
> **HEARING OFFICER**
>
> [In those initial hearings when you don't have a recommendation
> from the court worker, what factors influence your dispositional de-
> cisions?]

All right. I will question the parent and the child on first of all, the school situation, what kind of grades the child is making, what he's capable of making—if he's making D's, if he's capable of making A's. I will ask the parents about the observance of rules in the home. Does the child observe the parents' rules, are there problems with that, does the child generally help out with the chores at home, do the parents approve of the child's friends? Let's see, that probably pretty well—school, home, and community.

HEARING OFFICER

When evaluating the home environment, decision-makers are primarily concerned with the parents' ability to provide adequate supervision for the juvenile and to maintain control over the youngster's activities. In the following cases involving three siblings, the court worker considers the mother's supervision to be inadequate, asserts that the disheveled condition of the home is indicative of a lack of parental concern, and recommends that the court take immediate steps to intervene in the situation. Despite the fact the juveniles have never been to court previously and the present referrals are minor, the intake worker recommends that the juveniles be detained immediately and placed outside their home as soon as possible. The hearing officer rejects this proposal in favor of a probation officer's recommendation that he be permitted to work with the mother and children within the family setting.

Prehearing Discussion

[Hearing officer and court workers.]

Intake worker recommends that the court place all three juveniles outside the home (two brothers and a sister). He also wants the court to hold all three in detention until placement can be made.

The hearing officer says that the court can do that, but wants to know if there are any alternatives. She doesn't want to hold them unless it's absolutely necessary, especially when their cases involve status offenses.

The intake worker suggests that the sister go to "Shelter Care" and perhaps the boys could be put in foster homes. He states that the house was "absolutely filthy" when he and the probation officer visited and that the mother provides no supervision for the children. The children are not attending school.

The probation officer joins the prehearing discussion. He agrees with the first court worker that the house was very dirty when they visited and that the mother wasn't home. But he disagrees with the recommendation for immediate placement outside the home. He asks the hearing officer to let him try to work with the mother and kids at home.

The hearing officer says she will let the probation officer try to work it out without placing the kids outside their home because he's had a lot of success in situations like this.

The intake worker says he'll go along with the recommendations of the probation officer because of his greater experience, but he's not certain it will work.

#23: Initial Hearing [15 minutes]

Hearing Officer
Intake Worker
Probation Officer
Mother
Juvenile ("Paul")
Court Clerk
White Male, 14-years old
Referral #1: Stealing under $50 (misdemeanor)

The hearing officer reads the allegation in which the juvenile is accused of taking a tape deck player with a friend.

The juvenile denies the allegation. He says that when it happened the other boy was staying all night with him and that he found out later that his friend had run away from home. The friend said he wanted to go home and get some of his things for the night. No one was home at the friend's house, so the friend took the tape deck.

The hearing officer asks Paul why he has not gone to school lately, says she understands that he usually goes pretty regularly but has stopped.

Paul states that he went to school with his sister, but someone beat him up and took his notebook. He's afraid to go back.

Paul's mother says that it was *his* notebook, too, because she bought it for him. She says the school is terrible, and that she was hoping to move away, and that's why the kids weren't enrolled on time.

Paul states that the kids who beat him up don't go to the junior high school; they just come in and roam around the halls. He says the school only has one guard, and that these kids tell him they're looking for someone, so he lets them in. The guard was at school when the juvenile was beaten.

The hearing officer asks the probation officer if he is familiar with the school situation.

The probation officer says he knows the situation, knows the guard, and will see what he can do to help.

The hearing officer says that this is one reason why the court worker will be assigned to the juvenile—to help at school. The hearing officer instructs Paul to be sure to tell the probation officer if he has any more problems at school, but he must go to school. She warns Paul that if he does not start to go to school regularly, the court may have to place him outside his home.

Paul promises he will start going again.

The hearing officer rules the allegations of the petition to be true, takes jurisdiction over the juvenile, and places him under the supervision of the probation officer. A review hearing is scheduled.

#24: Initial Hearing [10 minutes]

Hearing Officer
Intake Worker
Probation Officer
Mother
Juvenile ("Marcie")
Court Clerk
White Female, 15-years old
Referral #1:   Truancy

The hearing officer asks Marcie why she doesn't go to school.

Marcie says she does not like school because of all the fights and problems there.

The hearing officer says that Marcie did not go to school regularly where she used to live either, so it could not just be the school. She asks her what she does not like about school.

Marcie says she just does not like it.

The hearing officer asks what she does when she is at home during the day.

Marcie says she just watches television.

The hearing officer says there are two alternatives. The juvenile can start going to school regularly while living at home, or the court will have to place her outside her home to go to school. She says the state provides the opportunity for everyone to get an education, and the court must enforce the law.

Marcie says she understands what the hearing officer is saying, and that she will start to go to school from home.

Marcie's mother begins to cry softly during the hearing and continues throughout.

The hearing officer rules the allegation to be true, takes jurisdiction over the juvenile, and places her under the probation officer's supervision. A review hearing is set.

#25: *Initial Hearing* [20 minutes]

Hearing Officer
Intake Worker
Probation Officer
Mother
Juvenile ("Billy")
Court Clerk
White Male, 15-years old
Referral #1:   Truancy and Tampering with an auto (felony)

The hearing officer states that, according to the records, Billy never registered at his new school after the family moved, and that he has attended school only two to four days in the last four months.

Billy says he does not like the school with all the fights.

The hearing officer says she can understand that he would not like the fights at school, but the truancy referral is from the school he was supposed to go to last year too. Why didn't he go then?

Billy's mother says he just does not like to go to school. He is going to quit when he turns 16 soon. He likes to do things with his hands and wants to join the army.

The hearing officer says maybe the Job Corps would be a good possibility.

The intake worker says that the Job Corps is only taking kids 17-years old because there is such a demand.

The probation officer says he will try to work something out.

The intake worker says he is very concerned because Billy's mother did not enroll the kids in school when they moved, and the house was very unkept when he and the probation officer visited. Mother wasn't at home then either.

Billy's mother begins to cry again and continues to do so throughout the remainder of the hearing.

Both the mother and Billy deny that the house is dirty all the time and say that that was the one time when the court workers visited. Mother says she did not enroll the kids in school when they moved because she was hoping to move out of the district, but she could not. She says she was not at home when the court workers visited because she was out trying to find a job.

The hearing officer asks Billy what happened in the car incident in which gasoline was reportedly taken out of the car.

Billy says he didn't do it, but he was with the kid who did.

The hearing officer explains that legally he is as responsible as the boy who did it because he was there and did not get away. Therefore he is as guilty as the person who did it, according to the law.

The probation officer says he will try to work on getting the juvenile into the Jobs Corps and perhaps some vocational schooling could be found.

The hearing officer says she hopes that things will be going better by the time the review hearing is held. All three juveniles must go to school regularly. She stresses to Billy that it is his responsibility, as well as that of his brother and sister, to help their mother clean house. Everyone in the family must cooperate. She stresses that Billy must avoid any future situations like the auto incident. The hearing officer takes jurisdiction, places the juvenile under the probation officer's supervision, and schedules a review hearing.

Billy's mother thanks the hearing officer. The probation officer goes with the mother and juvenile to meet with family.

In addition to an assessment of the overall "stability" and structure of a family, court personnel focus on the parental reaction to their child's involvement in delinquent activity. If, in the opinion of decision-makers, the parents evidence concern, discipline their child, or seek outside help in controlling the juvenile, the family situation is regarded positively as one which offers structure and support for the juvenile.

[In what type of situation do you feel that jurisdiction and supervision is *not* necessary?]

Well, sometimes what seems like a fairly serious offense may be well handled by the parents, and so I don't really base it on the offense. I really feel it's based on the offense, plus what the people have done about it since it occurred, and usually there's a month and quite often more than a month between the time it occurred and the hearing. In many cases I've found . . . that the so-called delinquency offenses, the serious offenses, are handled better by the parents than status kind of offenses. They may have allowed the youngster certain freedoms and responsibilities and then found out that the youngster's been breaking into the neighbor's home with the kids or something. They crack down, and they find out where he is and when he's coming home, who he's with, and make him pay it back and make him do something. They're on top of the situation and they let the youngster know he's made a mistake and he's going to have more restrictions on his freedoms than he previously had.

And so, quite often in those cases, even though it might involve what would be a felony offense if committed by an adult, by the time they come to court there's not too much the court has to do in many of these cases. The parents are really quite shocked and upset that the youngster would be involved in that sort of thing and they want to do something about it.

HEARING OFFICER

In the following cases, court intervention is deemed unnecessary due to parental disciplinary action, despite the fact the action is relatively minor, that is, denying use of the telephone for two weeks, assigning chores at home, and not permitting the juvenile to take a friend along on the family vacation. Although the juvenile admits to a felony and reportedly is not doing well in school, the case is dismissed, and the court does not become involved in the situation. The family's more affluent social status and the involvement of a private attorney are also important considerations in the case.

#51: Initial Hearing [25 minutes]

Hearing Officer
Private Attorney (Defense Counsel)
Mother
Father
Juvenile ("Martin")
Court Clerk
White male, 15-years old
Referral #1:   Auto theft (felony) and driving without license

Pretrial Discussion

[Hearing officer and attorney.]
   The private attorney tells the hearing officer that Martin was involved but is very contrite and has learned his lesson. He states that his parents have already placed restrictions on him, and he does not feel the family needs the court's supervision. They are a very good family. They are longtime friends of his. The parents are his daughter's godparents.
   The hearing officer says he is pleased to hear the parents have taken action, and if they are already dealing with the situation, perhaps court involvement is not necessary.

Hearing

The hearing officer reads the allegations in the petition. Martin admits he was involved, and the hearing officer rules the allegations to be true by consent and asks him to discuss what happened.

Martin says he and a friend were out at midnight, saw a Jeep, pushed it out, then drove it. They were stopped by the police shortly. He says it was a stupid thing to do, and that he did it without thinking.

The hearing officer asks Martin what he's learned from this experience.

Martin lists the lessons he has learned, "I've learned you can't just go out and take other people's things like that. I've learned I have to shape up, stop doing what's wrong and do what's right. I have to think things through before I do them."

The hearing officer states that the last statement is an especially good idea. He asks how Martin is doing in school.

Martin says he goes to a parochial high school and is a freshman. Says he gets C's and D's.

Martin's mother says he can do better than that if he tries.

The hearing officer discusses the importance of doing the best one can in school, and instructs Martin that he should try even in the hard subjects, not just the things he likes. He tells Martin that he must get an education to learn to support himself in the future and to care for the family which he will probably have in a manner he wants to. He points out that his parents will not be able to take care of him then.

The hearing officer then asks the lawyer if he wants to discuss anything.

The lawyer states that Martin's parents have already taken action to discipline the juvenile.

Martin's mother states that the action they have taken for Martin includes making him stay away from the other boy involved, not allowing him to use the telephone for two weeks, giving him chores at home that he does not like, and not allowing him to take a friend along when the family goes on vacation next month. Originally, Martin and his brother each were allowed to take a friend along.

The hearing officer assesses court costs and tells Martin he is to work out an arrangement to pay his parents back. He explains to Martin that this type of act in the adult court is a felony and, if convicted, he could go to the state penitentiary. He also explains that any juvenile over 14 years of age could be certified to adult court to stand trial as an adult. He says that he wants Martin to be aware of how serious an act it was.

Petition dismissed.

A family's ability to demonstrate that they have taken appropriate disciplinary action is particularly crucial when the offense is not a major, person-to-person crime, and the juvenile has few referrals to court. In the following case parental discipline and the juvenile's regular employment mitigate against court supervision.

#193: Initial Hearing: [14 minutes]

Hearing Officer
Private Attorney
Mother
Father
Juvenile ("Greg")
Court Clerk
White male, 16-years old
Referral #1:   Possession of 16.5 grams of marijuana

At the prehearing discussion between the hearing officer and the defendant's attorney, the attorney tells the hearing officer that Greg is "very contrite, scared as hell, frightened as hell" and that his parents have already taken extensive action to deal with problem. They have given him 30 days of very restricted activities and have not permitted him to drive since (two months). (Greg has a regular job at Grand Amusement Park.)

The hearing officer asks if the attorney thinks the family needs court involvement and if Greg needs to be brought under the court's jurisdiction.

The attorney says he does not think the family needs the court to be involved, that the parents have everything under control.

Hearing

HEARING OFFICER: I understand you wish to make a statement about the incident.
ATTORNEY: Yes, we do.
HEARING OFFICER (TO GREG):   The petition states that you had in your possession sixteen and a half grams of marijuana.
JUVENILE: Yes, sir, I did.
HEARING OFFICER: Can you tell me what happened?
JUVENILE: Well, we were on a small alleyway near school, and I had the bag [of marijuana] in my hand. The police drove down the alley and stopped us.
HEARING OFFICER: Where did you get it?
JUVENILE: At school.

HEARING OFFICER: From another student?

JUVENILE: Yes.

HEARING OFFICER: Did you tell the officers where you got it?

JUVENILE: Yes.

HEARING OFFICER: Having sixteen and a half grams is enough to the police and court to assume you had it in your possession to sell. I don't know if that's true or not, but if you or the other youngster come back to court with a second possession you may not be before the juvenile court. You may be certified to go before the adult court.

A problem that the court has is that a lot of placements will not take a juvenile who's 16. The Department of Corrections is one of the few who will.

This is different than having a couple of marijuana cigarettes. The law may presume you intend to sell it, the judge may presume that. You want to stay out of anything like this.

ATTORNEY: Greg has been and is still under continuing punishment for this. He can't drive the car and has other penalties imposed. He has a steady job. I would suggest a suspended type of disposition.

HEARING OFFICER: Where do you work?

JUVENILE: At Grand's in the clean up and good preparation part.

HEARING OFFICER: Do you work every day?

JUVENILE: Six days a week.

HEARING OFFICER: Parents, what would you like to tell the court?

FATHER: I would like to say about the young man that many times he's double-shifting at work. He's been hoping to get an automobile and putting in a tremendous amount of time. He works all winter. The boy isn't lazy. He's not afraid of hard work. He goes all the time trying to make a dollar. If he was lazy or indifferent to work, I'd have a different outlook. I am prejudiced; he is my son. But I'd also like to say many of his employers have commented on the quality and sincerity of his endeavors.

HEARING OFFICER: Do you feel any need for the court to be involved?

FATHER: I think he's learned a pretty good lesson. He is on supervision. He checks in and out. We want to be able to tell anyone where and what he's doing.

MOTHER: All his life he's been taught the dignity of work. He's not unaware of work. He's a very good boy, and I hope he's learned his lesson.

HEARING OFFICER: Are you a good student?

JUVENILE: Pretty well in most subjects. I don't like science.

HEARING OFFICER: You're only short-changing yourself; if you put something into a subject, you're preparing yourself for your own future. You can get a better job if you put something into school. I know many youngsters are experimenting with drugs and alcohol. I'm not going to sit here and say it's harmful or not. Studies go both ways. But I do know it's against the law. If other things are more important to you, you'd better stay away from this.

I think you've learned something. I'm glad to hear penalties and sanctions have been imposed. We each have to learn responsibility, but we don't get freedoms and responsibilities automatically. We have to earn what we get. You may want to stay away from this; it isn't worth the risk.

JUVENILE: I'm being kept pretty busy. The law's got the upper hand. It's not something to mess with.

HEARING OFFICER: I don't expect you to agree, but you need to know the law. The allegations are true by consent. I'm going to order a conditional dismissal for December [three months]. If you don't come back to court, this will be dismissed. I'm going to tax court costs, and I want you to pay them back. Good luck to you.

As has been discussed, a family's social status may greatly influence the court's initial impression of its viability, for, more affluent families may be more able to effectively demonstrate their concern for their child by seeking treatment on their own. If these services are sought in the interim between the referral to court and the actual hearing, decision-makers may feel court involvement is unnecessary. Likewise, middle- or upper-class families may be more able to provide supervision, in the form of paid help, when parents are absent from the home. In less affluent families in which both parents or a single parent work, juveniles may be unsupervised, causing court personnel to view the family situation unfavorably.

However, as Cicourel (1968) and Emerson (1969) have observed, poorer families often have an extensive network of relatives who contribute to the supervision of juveniles. And although costly private treatment facilities are accessible only to the affluent, families of all social backgrounds may provide an alternative to decision-makers by offering to send the juvenile to live with relatives for a period of time. This option may be exercised by the court personnel when the offense is not a major, person-to-person offense and decision-makers feel an immediate change in the living environment will remove the juvenile from harmful influences.

The Right of Total Review

The state's Juvenile Code empowers the court to order a social study be made, including "an investigation and evaluation of the habits, surroundings, conditions, and tendencies of the juvenile." The court's perception of the family situation plays a major role in this investigation. The evaluation is based on impressions received by decision-makers during interviews with juveniles and their parents, as well as interaction during the courtroom proceeding. If the juvenile or a sibling is under the court's jurisdiction, the decision-maker's evaluation is based on a series of impressions and interactions with the family.

When queried regarding the manner in which they evaluate the stability and effectiveness of a family, decision-makers list numerous factors which influence the final assessment.

> . . . . how they spoke about one another, the attitudes and manner with which they talked about each other, you can tell a lot from that. . . . Try to find out if the parents are in the home. If they both work, if there's only one parent, how often they are home, how much time do they spend with the kids, how much time do they spend supervising them. You don't have to ask those kind of things directly because you probably would get, "Oh, I spend (time), I adequately supervise" that kind of thing. So you kind of get (that) from what their activities and attitudes are, how much time—how much do they know about the school situation.
>
> HEARING OFFICER

Court personnel also are greatly influenced by their perceptions of the manner in which juveniles and parents relate to each other, whether they evidence respect and concern for each other, the interaction between siblings, the extent to which parents allow juveniles to express themselves, and the extent to which conflicts exist. Although decision-makers have numerous divergent approaches to exploring the viability of a family, the vast majority agree that this is the crucial issue when deciding between dispositional alternatives. Placement outside the home is frequently recommended when the home situation is viewed as unstable, unhealthy, or exerting a negative influence on the child's development. A probation officer offered the following explanation for a recommendation that a juvenile with numerous status offenses be committed to the Department of Corrections (after repeated failures in other placements).

[Why did you feel she should go to D.O.C.?]
Because I think the kid doesn't have a chance at home. . . . The whole situation at home was just so sick for that child, and Mother had, they were both such manipulators. Susan was one. I really liked that kid; she was one of the kids I felt had a lot of potential and was just being murdered in that situation. Mom would just screw up everything and was terribly inconsistent at home. There was a love-hate relationship between mother and daughter. The kid changed. She is not going to make it if she stays with her.

PROBATION OFFICER

Families have the right to resist this total review of their home situation, but such resistance is rare, and would most often be regarded as evidence of the family's lack of concern or failure to seek resolution of their problems. One intake worker expressed concern over the potential invasion of family privacy, especially when investigations are conducted prior to adjudication.

[Now, if you're doing a PI (preliminary investigation) and they're not in detention, you have to contact the family and ask them to come in?]
Right. And some of the families are resistive. They think it's none of our business to know all their personal life, and they'll stall. And I can see their point, I mean. And really I'm not sure we have the legal right if they don't want to give us this, at that point [prior to adjudication] to get all involved and ask them how much they make and how many times they've been married. I mean, I have some strong feelings about that, whether we have the right to do that.
[Have you ever had any families just absolutely refuse to discuss this with you?]
A couple of times, but not often. I mean, usually you can break that down by telling them, you know, that it is so that we can know the whole situation and make a plan and that we are here, we're on the juvenile's side, and we are here to try to work with the whole situation, and to try to help.

The intake worker expressed reservations about conducting inquiries, especially when the juvenile has been referred for status offenses.

. . . . There's a lot of talk about that [runaways] and about status offenses, and I certainly feel that when a parent first comes in for preliminary investigation. But there's many times that I feel like I'm infringing on their rights. I don't like asking them about their personal life. I don't like asking them how much money they make if they're resistive. I don't know if we have that right. I really don't, if they refuse.

[Until the judge orders them?]

   Right.

[So you are sensitive that you may be invading their privacy. . . .]

   Right. Sometimes I thought I really was invading their privacy, and when I've done a PI on a status offense, which I have many times— you approach it from a help standpoint. So what in the hell right have we got to bring them in here and do all that?

Despite the decision-maker's reservations, expressed above, this juvenile court routinely investigates the entire family situation prior to adjudication (the determination of a juvenile's "guilt" or "innocence") as well as after the court takes jurisdiction. Even when juveniles are processed informally through the short-term counseling unit, the family situation is examined closely. Regardless of the alleged behavior which initiates the juvenile's interaction with the court, evaluations of the family situation are seen as crucial to the court's analysis of the needs of juveniles. In addition to considering income, marital status, number of children, and the nature of family relationships, decision-makers probe whatever aspects of a family's circumstances they consider germane to the case. Likewise, each decision-maker employs her or his own standards and methods for assessing the stability or inadequacy of the family.

Because complete evaluations of the family situation are most often presented during official or unofficial prehearing discussions, families usually do not hear the court worker's blunt appraisal of their home life. But even when they listen to the decision-maker's abbreviated comments in the courtroom, parents occasionally express disagreement with the evaluation, questioning the extent of the court worker's insight into the situation. In the following case the court worker evaluates the family situation negatively; the mother questions the court worker's understanding of the family problems, and the juvenile fears that court workers will force him to be disloyal to his parents.

#94: Initial Hearing [26 minutes]

Hearing Officer
Court Worker
Mother
Father
Juvenile ("Lynn")
Court Clerk
White Male, 16-years old
Referral #3:   Curfew

Prehearing Discussion

HEARING OFFICER: I have the juvenile referred for a curfew and only a
third referral. I can't figure out why it's scheduled for an initial [hear-
ing].

COURT WORKER: There's a fourth referral coming in, a runaway. The
family's a mess. They've been calm today, and I hope it carries over
to the hearing.

Hearing

HEARING OFFICER: I understand there's another referral coming in, a runaway. We'll include it and discuss it, too. Now, today, we're here on
what's called an initial hearing. We don't have any witnesses, just a
report. It says you were in violation of the curfew on March 13. You
have three choices today: admit, deny, or make a statement. Which
do you want to do?

JUVENILE: I admit.

HEARING OFFICER: The allegations are true by consent. Now we go into
the disposition where the court inquires how the youngster is doing.
I'll ask Ms. Angelo for a report.

COURT WORKER: My involvement began [two years previously] on a
truancy. I met with the juvenile and his father. There were numerous
problems at that time, flare-ups. I recommended family counseling and
Lynn was willing. Father was not. Part of the problem was connected
with drinking. The parents were and still are going through a divorce.
The juvenile is being pulled apart. . . . I later closed the case but met
with Lynn informally, and Father called me on the phone. On [year
later] we received a second referral for possession of liquor, but there
was no lab report. With my knowledge of the family background I

decided on the option of a hearing. Lynn was living with Mother and nervous problems developed. A doctor recommended he [Lynn] live with Father. Flare-ups still happen.

Two years ago Lynn's grades and attendance were good. Now he's missing. Father works late and, in my opinion, there's not proper supervision.

HEARING OFFICER: How many children?

FATHER: This is my only one.

COURT WORKER: I feel neither one [parent] is more capable than the other.

HEARING OFFICER: What you've been charged with, there isn't a felony in four violations. Just this controlled substance. All the others are status offenses. [To worker] What are you recommending?

COURT WORKER: I'm recommending the court take jurisdiction and place Lynn under its supervision [probation].

HEARING OFFICER: How long were you gone when you left home?

JUVENILE: About one and a half weeks.

HEARING OFFICER: Why did you split? Problems at home?

JUVENILE: It's hard to explain, sort of.

HEARING OFFICER: I'm trying to find out what kind of a man you're going to be.

JUVENILE: I wasn't going to let my girlfriend run away alone. She's 15.

HEARING OFFICER: Do you know what kind of legal problems you're getting into? That's chivalrous trying to protect her, but you'd better not do it again. How's school?

JUVENILE: I'm thinking of going back in the fall.

HEARING OFFICER: What are you doing now?

JUVENILE: Maintenance for apartments.

HEARING OFFICER: You're going to work all your life. You need to get an education. Your mind's only three-fourths developed. It doesn't have the smarts it will when fully developed.

The court will take jurisdiction, and you'll be under supervision. Counselor will try and help. You need to get an education. Unfortunately, the court has to remove some from home and they don't like it. It's advantageous to have a third party who can be totally objective about the situation and give some guidance.

Do you follow me? How do you feel about this?

JUVENILE: I'm not sure. They might be trying to get me to say something against my mother or father.

HEARING OFFICER: They don't work that way.

FATHER: If it's going to help him, I'm willing to go along with it.

HEARING OFFICER: On the curfew, were you with your girlfriend? I'm mentally waiving between a conditional dismissal and jurisdiction.

COURT WORKER: If I can add something, I'm really concerned with the lack of consistency on the part of the parents.

MOTHER: What do you mean?

COURT WORKER: He's been pulled apart for two years. He's very nervous and immature. I've seen changes in his appearance and attitude, and his comments to me that he's involved in marijuana and alcohol and activities with his girlfriend and friends.

You [parents] tell me all sorts of things. Lynn has told me about conflicts between the two of you. It's the same with the divorce. You can't make a decision.

MOTHER: It goes into a lot more than that. There's a lot you don't understand.

COURT WORKER: I know there are. . . .

HEARING OFFICER: Let's swing this around to the major concern. Lynn only has a few months until he reaches the age of majority. I believe it's in the best interests of the child for the court to take jurisdiction.

Now, you'll be under the court's supervision. It's Ms. Angelo's responsibility to help you. And if you don't do what she says, she can have you brought to detention. The juvenile court has the authority to keep someone 'til they're 21, but that's very rare.

FATHER: May I say that most of the trouble is staying out after curfew.

HEARING OFFICER: After he [reaches the age of majority] that won't apply any more.

FATHER: That's what most of my hollering, chewing him out, is about. Even after he was picked up, he'd stay out.

HEARING OFFICER: We'll have to work on that. Now, are you satisfied with what we've done here, or do you want to have a hearing before the judge?

FATHER, JUVENILE: Satisfied. [Sign waiver of right to rehearing.]

HEARING OFFICER: Good luck to you. Court's adjourned.

Most court personnel assert that investigation of the entire family situation is imperative if the court is to achieve its goal of treating juvenile needs. But at least one decision-maker suggested that the preoccupation with examining the overall family situation may deter the court from successfully dealing with the problem for which the juvenile was originally referred to court. This individual suggested that the policy of assigning a worker to each juvenile creates a situation in which probation officers become overly concerned with resolving all familiar problems, and, in fact, seek out family problems to justify court involvement.

[Are you convinced that the court is doing an excellent job at treating?]

Oh, yeh. I think we're probably ahead of the game, but you ask me can we improve. Absolutely. If you ask me, can we work with everybody, I have to say no. I would think that our success rate is probably a heck of a lot higher than most people because of the kind of services that we've got here and the kind of results we've been getting, our willingness to research what we do and look at it objectively, you know. I think it's helped us in this respect because we've thrown out certain kinds of services.

I think there's some other kinds of changes just on a social work basis that I'd just like to see. I don't like the process of assigning a kid to a worker when you take him under supervision because there's a certain amount of illogic behind that, or lack of logic. Why does every kid need a worker? Why can't a kid be assigned to a program? If he commits a traffic offense, we assign him to a traffic school. Why can't we take a kid who is having a school problem at 15 and 11 months and assign him to the GED [Graduate Equivalency Diploma] and have the director of the GED program report back to the hearing officer and keep him only for the period of time that it takes to get him to GED and get him out.

Why do we have to continue finding problems in the family? I could come into your house and find problems, and if you and I sit down and talk long enough, I'd find some problems with you. Anybody, me, the janitor, you know. When you get involved in the life of a child on a one-to-one [basis], does that entitle you to keep on digging, or do you deal with the problem that presents itself to the court? Work on that problem, get it under control and close the case out. My feeling is that we inappropriately place kids under individual supervision. We could just as easily put them into a group, put them into a program that we have, handle it on a short-term basis and close it. I'd like to see that kind of process.

[You don't see treatment as the whole child and all their problems?]

Nobody can do that. I have yet to see a person do that. You can't deal with all the problems. I've done family therapy and counseling, and one thing you learn real quick is to fragment the problem. . . . I've got a family where there's criminality involved. I've got a family with economic problems and health problems and a retarded kid. Now pray tell me, how are you going to handle it all at once? You can't. You fragment it; you begin to deal with one aspect of the problem at a time. What you see happening is that, if you can work with one, maybe one of the opposite side is beginning to diminish, that these things do relate to each other. So instead of working six problem areas you wind up only having to work three. But if you, as any kind of worker, try to deal with "the total family and its problems" you might as well leave town. There's also kind of an assumption that you can really do something about it—you can't. I can't make people richer or smarter or what have you. I can only open up the opportunity for that kind of thing. I'm a person who provides opportunities as a worker at this court for the kids. I try to get them turned on to that opportunity. The same thing with parents.

                                                                    COURT WORKER

Despite the fact that the juvenile court deals with ineffective, unhappy, and conflict-ridden families day after day, a basic assumption within the court's treatment ideology is the belief that the nuclear family can be restored to a functioning, positive influence in the lives of juveniles. Concomitant with the belief that family problems generate delinquency is the attempt to curtail delinquency through efforts aimed at buoying the family. Although the emphasis upon the family as a viable institution is dominant, it is an assumption that goes unchallenged or unquestioned by most court personnel.

[Is there an underlying assumption in family treatment that the American nuclear family is a successful institution, a good institution?]
   Gosh, that's a good question. I think so. I would think so. Your family is what fosters growth development, most valued character formation, where all that comes from. I would say that would be the assumption.
[The idea is that if the family is functioning as your group would see as healthy, then delinquency behavior would decrease?]
   Yes. Delinquency is an effect of an unhealthy family.

                                                                    COURT WORKER

One court worker specializing in family therapy acknowledged the lack of clearcut success in resolving family difficulties:

Hopefully, if you can help the family restructure itself, somehow they'll muddle through. Most families do today. I don't think any family's going to do terrific; they're rare. But most families manage to muddle through.

                                                                    COURT WORKER

Thus, a major assumption inherent in the juvenile court process is that the family structure not only contributes to the creation of delinquency, but that the structure can also be strengthened to minimize or eliminate delinquency. Accordingly, one of the primary concerns of decision-makers is the evaluation of the stability or viability of the family unit. Even when major allegations are involved, the court tends *not* to become involved in those family situations which they perceive as providing supervision and support for the juvenile. Conversely, even when the offense is minor, decision-makers tend to recommend court intervention if the families are perceived to be inadequate and unable to control juvenile behavior. A juvenile's alleged involvement in delinquency is sufficient reason, according to juvenile court philosophy, to turn a scrutinizing eye upon the entire family situation.

CHAPTER 12

The Impact of Juvenile Attitude and Demeanor

As Matza suggested (1964:3), the explanation for delinquent behavior is most commonly sought in the "character and background" of the juvenile. Accordingly, court personnel interpret attitude and demeanor as clues to the juvenile's history, and rely on these to make a prognosis of future behavior. The decision-maker's perception of a juvenile's attitude and demeanor forms the cornerstone for the evaluation of the juvenile's "moral character" (Emerson, 1969:192–5). These issues are foremost in the court's evaluation of the juvenile's situation, as well as in their decision whether the present referral represents a delinquent behavior pattern requiring court intervention.

When queried regarding their assessment of a juvenile's problems, decision-makers most frequently mentioned juvenile attitude and demeanor.

[In the initial hearing when you don't have any recommendations from court workers what factors help you make a decision?]

Well, I think looking at why the youngster is in court, first of all. In other words, the offense, and then you always check the number of referrals, if he's been here a few other times. . . . that definitely weighs your consideration of disposition, and I play attitude very much because how are we going to be effective in this echelon 'cause we have a short period, as you know, fifteen to twenty minutes. So, I'd say those three factors. . . .

[What sort of things, then, about attitude do you try to pick up in a hearing?]

Oh, for one thing, physical appearance, conversation, if he seems interested, if he's in here yawning, stretching and trying to put his head down on the table, why all those things I very definitely note. On the other hand, if he seems like he's apprehensive, responds, I feel that, you know, you've observed enough hearings not only in my courtroom but in other rooms. I think this is probably true of all hearing officers.

                                          HEARING OFFICER

[When you're getting ready for a hearing what factors are most important in deciding what your recommendation is going to be?]

The kid's attitude. That's probably the most important. The most important is the attitude because sometimes you can have a kid with a lot of referrals and still recommend, you know, continued supervision [probation] or a kid with one referral or two referrals you want to put in placement. How honest is a kid being with me, how willing is he to admit he made a mistake and wants to go to try to do better? And there's some definite empirical knowledge that he's doing better at home, you know, he's doing pretty well in school. Basically his attitude.

                                          COURT WORKER

Although the assessment of a juvenile's character is not a mechanistic, easily described process, there is generalized agreement among decision-makers regarding those characteristics which are indicative of a good attitude, and as such are evaluated positively. Remorse and an appreciation of the seriousness of one's delinquent activities are two extremely positive attributes according to court personnel. A willingness to discuss one's situation, potential problems, and future desires, as well as sincerity in attempting to prevent future mistakes are also extremely important.

[Do you get any clues from the juvenile's behavior, to help you decide disposition?]

Oh, sometimes. Obviously the kinds of responses you get. If they seem to understand what it's all about, seem concerned about it, upset maybe that they're in for it rather than not caring whether they're here or somewhere else at that particular time, whether they seem to realize that they made a mistake, that they've committed some delinquency act, or that they're causing themselves some future problems and understand that they have a need for an education. Yeah, you get a good insight from the youngster as to what his or her needs are.

                                          HEARING OFFICER

[Does the kid's attitude or whether they respond or not to what you're trying to do, does that influence your decision?]

Yes, that influences my decision greatly because if a kid shows me that he does not have a remorseful attitude regarding his behavior I have to look at that. We have a casework session and we're talking about the referral, what he was involved in, and he's glossing it over and denying it. And every time he gets into difficulty he's denying it, and he's not recognizing the fact that, I am involved, I should be taking a little bit myself. Sure, his attitude weighs heavily on my decision.

COURT WORKER

[All right, what clues are you looking for? Let's say you're looking to see if someone's going to be a repeater?]
I think it goes by intuition but I'm sure there are some recurrent ways that you can deal with it. I've never really sat down and thought about it, you know what sort of things I look for. It's, you just get that feeling. A lot of it has to do with attitude. Attitude, not necessarily toward me, but toward the parents and toward the court, whether or not the kid feels that it's serious, whether he feels very comfortable being in court, court workers, that sort of thing.

COURT WORKER

[Are some kids more cooperative than others as you see them in the hearing?]
Oh, Yes.
[Why do you think that is?]
I don't know, I suppose it's just the type of child involved, that come in I suppose basically with the right attitude that, you know, they have done something wrong, they're willing to talk to you about it. Some of them I think are willing to be helpful.

HEARING OFFICER

Those juveniles who are goal-oriented, who demonstrate that they have educational or vocational goals towards which they are striving, are viewed positively by decision-makers. Likewise, those who respond to court workers' suggestions for improvement, or "make progress" on their own, are viewed as honestly confronting their problems and making a realistic attempt to change their behavior. Because effecting attitudinal and behavioral changes is the major objective of the juvenile justice system, those juveniles who are appraised as working to improve their situations are regarded highly by decision-makers. As illustrated by the following case, even serious offenses can be outweighed by a decision-maker's conviction that a juvenile is mak-

ing an effort to avoid further delinquent activities and to plan for
the future.

#219: Pretrial Conference and Courtroom
[Approximately 15 minutes.]
Judge
Prosecuting Attorney
Court Worker
Public Defender
Mother
Juvenile ("David")
White Male, 16-years old
Referrals #2:   Burglary and stealing (felony)
          #3:   Burglary (felony)
          #4:   Stealing Over $50 (felony)
          #5:   Burglary and stealing (felony)
          #6:   Capias (issued for Juvenile to be brought to
          detention)
          #7:   Burglary and stealing (felony)

Pretrial Conference

   [Judge, Prosecuting Attorney, Court Worker, Public Defender.]
JUDGE: What do you want to tell me?
COURT WORKER: He volunteered a statement [to police] and returned
   [stolen goods]. I'm recommending D.O.C. [Department of Correc-
   tions] with a stay, combined with jurisdiction and supervision.
PUBLIC DEFENDER: I think it'd be good if you discussed your recommendation.
JUDGE: So many of them [allegations].
COURT WORKER: When he came to my attention he was not in the
   building [in detention]. He had been on the streets three weeks [after
   apprehension]. We issued a capias and he was in the building for a
   week.
       He's a different person. He has goals set up. He's talking about why
   he did what he did. He was needing the money. . . . He's in G.E.D.
   [high school diploma program] and the "Career Opportunities" Program.
       He only had one prior. [It was] counseled and closed. It was auto
   tampering.

He called me every other day. He's followed through with G.E.D.
. . . I feel he's amenable to treatment.

PUBLIC DEFENDER: It's a difficult home situation.

JUDGE: Why'd he deface all these buildings? Damaged a coin box at.
. . . boy, oh boy. Without getting into the burglary. I almost understand burglary more than defacing property. I don't know. I guess. [To
the Prosecuting Attorney.] What do you think?

[The prosecuting attorney doesn't have the opportunity to speak.]

PUBLIC DEFENDER: He's a different kid. I don't think you can look at the
offenses alone.

PROSECUTING ATTORNEY: The court worker agrees, the Chief Juvenile Officer agrees, the public defender wants it.

COURT WORKER: He knows if he's involved in anything else we'll lift the
stay [and send to D.O.C.].

JUDGE: I'll do it. I'm skeptical, but if it's your recommendation. . . .

COURT WORKER: My recommendation is based on the fact he's so dras-
tically different now. It's just like two completely different people. I'm
certain it can work in the community.

JUDGE: I'll do it on your recommendation.

Courtroom

[Pretrial participants are joined by Mother, Juvenile, Court Clerk, Bailiff.]

[The prosecuting attorney takes appearances of those in court.]

I'd like the record to show that Mr. Upton, juvenile's father, was
duly served by registered mail. I'd like the bailiff to call his name three
times.

[Bailiff calls "Mr. Upton" at courtroom door three times.]

BAILIFF: [To Judge.] Your Honor, he answers not.

JUDGE: As I understand through our discussion, there is agreement that
the juvenile admits to the allegations.

PUBLIC DEFENDER: All but "B" and "R" [portions of the referrals].

JUDGE: Is this correct, David?

JUVENILE: Yes.

JUDGE: Have you been over this with your lawyer and understand what
this means?

JUVENILE: Yes.

JUDGE: [To Court Worker.] You are recommending what?

COURT WORKER: Commitment to the Department of Corrections with a
stay and jurisdiction/supervision [probation].

JUDGE: The effect of the recommendation is that Mr. Josephs says he
believes you will work with us. I don't approve of your actions and

conduct. But they tell me, David, that you've learned a little bit from this series of events.

The court will take jurisdiction and you'll be under supervision with the view that this will never happen again. If it does, we'll come back here and you'll be off and running to D.O.C. We think you'll work with us, but we'll hold a little something over your head.

Even as certain characteristics are evaluated positively, others are viewed as general indicators of "a bad attitude." Attributes commonly mentioned as undesirable include "cocky," "surly," "rude," "whiny," "disrespectful," "no spunk," and "hard to mobilize." Generally, those juveniles who are reluctant or unwilling to cooperate with court personnel, disrespectful toward authority figures (including parents, school officials, police, and court personnel), or unwilling to attempt behavioral changes are viewed disparagingly. Those juveniles who are viewed as unresponsive to the attempts of the court to provide assistance, manipulative or devious in their relationships with court personnel are assessed negatively.

Some decision-makers reluctantly suggest that there are "unreachables," those juveniles who are totally unresponsive to court attempts to counsel or guide.

But, oh, the unreachables. The kind that will come sit in your office and will answer your questions but you know is not really getting anything out of it. Just answering your questions, not spilling their guts or anything like that, just going through the motions. I had one boy I really thought was unreachable in the sense that he, I didn't even know if he was bright enough to be reachable. He was that out of it most of the time. But now he's coming around and I think that sometimes it's just that—he had a lot harder shell and never really sat down and talked with anybody before. A lot of kids never sat down and talked with anybody on that level before. Parents don't do that with them, school doesn't bother doing that with them, the counselor doesn't bother doing that with them, and, of course, their peers don't do it. So their life is like one constant con game, you know, being cool and all that and when you sit down and say, "Okay, just be a person with me, just talk to me like a normal person" they don't know how to do it. They can't relate to that. It takes them a long time. They just sit there, you know, answer your question but not ever come out with their real feelings, or at least not for a long time.

COURT WORKER

One hearing officer frequently referred to "the 1 or 2 percent" of the population who are impervious to court efforts: juveniles who want to identify with and continue to participate in delinquent behaviors.

[Do you think there are different types of juveniles who come through the hearing room?]
   Yeah, there's no doubt about that. You get down to that bottom one percent that, as you heard me say, I could be Jesus Christ sitting here and talk like William Gentry [sic] Bryan and I don't think you're going to move them one iota. What do you do with those? Well, unfortunately, they're the ones you see behind bars and cells a couple of years down the road. I mean, you never stop trying, you never want them seated up there later on and think to themselves why wasn't I told or whatever. I feel not only for the workers but everyone involved in this court proceeding and that sums up my position—they've got no one but themselves to blame.
[What kind of kid would you say that is?]
   Uh, that is another good question.
[What makes them different from the other kids?]
   Well, they've got a short shot in regard to some part of the mental process, you know. You and I are adults. We all know, we all put it together during those three or four years of trying to find your own niche or whatever. I think the Big Man just put an off-breed in there, an off-grain or whatever, however you want to label it. This has been true for thousands of years. Not necessarily retarded either, there is that percentage.
[You mean that they don't understand what they're doing and what's wrong, is that it?]
   Oh, I think they understand but it's just their mode of operation, with the identity and the people they want to impress. Unfortunately they want to associate with losers. I think that's really about it.

                                                          HEARING OFFICER

The Art of Interpretation

The task of interpreting juveniles' behavior and attitudes to arrive at an evaluation of their character is an extremely complex process. Decision-makers readily acknowledge the necessity of distinguishing between appearances and genuine traits, but they also maintain that experience enables them to gather valuable clues by which to accurately assess a juvenile's attitude. These clues are gleaned from a juvenile's conversation, appearance, body language, and a multitude of subtle indicators as perceived by court personnel. Decision-makers must sort through the many signals emanating from a juvenile, unmask facades, and choose those authentic acts and statements which are truly representative of the juvenile's character.

[Are there any kids you don't like?]

Um, oh, the cocky kid who's cocky out of anti-social behavior as opposed to covering up insecurity or something. You know, the one who is just disrespectful, uses you, uses me like anybody else, just thinks they're here just to figure a way to get themselves what they want. I don't like the use of, you know, anybody else. And, I make that pretty clear pretty fast, that even though I am their advocate, I am their attorney, that I will not be used in that sense. I mean obviously, in some respect, you are just by virtue of being a lawyer. But I guess I demand respect as much as anybody else and that came after about a year of figuring all this out. I hadn't worked with kids all that much and I find every single one of them, every single one of them, no matter how bad it might have been, will really respect me for doing that and I do get the respect. They're almost asking you to do that.

PUBLIC DEFENDER

[Do you get any clues from unspoken behavior from the juvenile during the hearing that help you in your decision?]

Yeah, you have to be careful of it, because some children react differently than others. I've had a few where I felt that the reaction was disturbing to me. A surly attitude in the way they answer a question, in the way they conduct themselves, the way they seat themselves at the hearing, an unkempt look about them. You have to be careful though not to let something like that interfere with your judgment because sometimes the child is putting on a facade. This is the way they react to adults and it has nothing to do with their deep inner feelings. But we're all humans and, as a lawyer I used to instruct my juvenile clients to sit up straight and you say, "Yes, sir." you say, "No, sir." to the judge because it surely isn't going to hurt anything. And I'm sure that they're told that today but, it's hard not to let that affect you, and it has affected me in certain cases and I've told the lawyer and the juvenile that I felt the way the juvenile conducted themselves in the hearing was detrimental.

And, again, perhaps this answers a prior question, but one problem that a juvenile has in testifying in a juvenile proceeding, it's the same problem an adult has. If that juvenile is going to come in and swear, under oath, directly opposite to other witnesses there is the inherent power. I mean there is the inherent problem within that. Perhaps the court will become disturbed, not only about the instant referral but about the fact that the court believes the juvenile is testifying falsely and that's a risk that a lawyer takes whenever a juvenile gets on the stand so. . . . That's not a way they act in the courtroom but their conduct that is a risk. Now the lawyer sits there and says, "What do I do?" The juvenile says I want to testify. Well, you just make sure that the juvenile understands the risk involved and this is particularly so when you have a number of eye witnesses. You've got, as a lawyer, you've got to sit there and analyze a juvenile officer's case in a juvenile trial to see whether or not you really hurt your client sometimes by putting your client on and saying, "All of these people that have paraded in here are liars. I'm telling the truth. The world's all out of step but me." It's a tough burden to carry and you're not putting the burden of proof on them. Again, it's just, as I've told a lot of young lawyers, remember you're trying cases before human beings and they have human reactions so you must take that into consideration in everything you do in a trial.

JUDGE

[Are there some kids that you just really dislike?]
   Oh, yes.
[And what do you think that is?]
   Why?
[Yes, why?]
   Because they just act very obnoxious, you know. They're surly, they're rude, the whole gamut. Yes, and you just take an instant dislike to them. Now, I think sometimes you have to temper it a little bit, trying to decide maybe if the child really is nervous. And I think I've definitely had cases like that where I think they didn't know how to act, you know. They'd never been to court before and they were scared and maybe just had some sort of a facade that wasn't really them so I think you have to think about that too.

HEARING OFFICER

This task of assessing a juvenile's character is not a mechanistic process in which one assigns points to certain movements, mannerisms or comments to obtain a total score corresponding to a final estimation. Rather it is an "art" requiring the use of the decision-maker's total self and powers of discernment. It is not sufficient to observe behavior, one must also discover the motivation behind such behavior. As several court personnel have suggested, what may appear to be a surly or disrespectful attitude initially may be merely a superficial front used to mask anxiety or insecurity. But, although decision-makers acknowledge the intricacies of this art of interpreting juvenile behavior, the vast majority are confident in their abilities to do so. And so they must be, for this is the crux of their responsibility—to assess juvenile feelings and motivations. Decision-makers are not only required to evaluate juveniles, they frequently must do so within the confines of brief interviews and interactions, particularly during the juvenile's initial time to court.

In the following quotes court workers provide insight into the methods employed to evaluate a juvenile's behavior. In the first, a probation officer suggests that experience is the key to evaluating whether a juvenile is being honest. In the second, a probation officer explains that physical appearance may provide clues to attitudes; and in the third, a probation officer suggests a method for determining if a juvenile is attempting to manipulate the decision-maker.

[Are there times when someone who is under your supervision comes back into the building and you have to make a detention decision? What sort of factors influence whether or not you'd release. . . .]

Depends on status of offense, seriousness of offense, and whether or not he's a threat to the community. We use the three classics—threat to the community, threat to himself, apt to run away. And from that, again, I think you have to go partially on attitude, you know, where the kid's coming from. There are a lot of kids who will come in and get down on their hands and knees and say, "Oh, God, please Mr. Greene, let me go home. I'll never do it again." And you know damn well they're going to do it tomorrow. You know, so I don't necessarily think it's purely that but I think you have to use it, a little bit of intelligence for that sort of thing.

[All right, if a kid is saying, "Okay, let me out and I won't do it again." How do you know they are going to do it again?]

Usually through past experience.

[With that juvenile or with other juveniles?]

With that juvenile. Yeah, not necessarily because Joe Blow has done it but . . . the most recent case that I had, you know, the people came in and we had a detention hearing and I was asked, "Do you think that he will get in trouble again before the 19th?" which was when he had his formal court hearing and the recommendation was D.O.C. "Do you think he'll have another referral between now and then?" Yeah, I do and I think within the next week.

PROBATION OFFICER

[What kind of situation would you decide to use psychological or request a psychological?]

One of two situations. Placement if the situation required it. . . .
[Do a lot of them require it?]

Most of them, yeh. Or if I really thought this kid was potentially harmful to himself, talking suicide, talking crazy things, you know, wanting to hurt themselves or really had a very, very low self-esteem and felt badly about themselves. It's usually obvious when kids feel badly about themselves. You know, they carve. They put tattoos on themselves. Things like that. Then I usually do because I wonder how serious. . . .
[If they don't feel good about themselves they might tattoo . . . ?]

Yeah, tattoos, and when they feel good about themselves they want them off. Oh I know that, there's a correlation between tattoos and feeling good about yourself and not feeling good. I've seen so many of my kids. They all get tattoos when they're feeling bad and now that some of them are really coming around, working hard in placement or they're back at home and working hard, they all want those tattoos off, and they even try and get them off. So I, definitely to me, there's a correlation. Of course that's just in my head correlation, but I see it. I feel that's one thing that tells me a kid is feeling—if a kid is writing on himself or puts a new tattoo on you know they're not feeling good.
[What other signs do you look for?]

Well, usually you can just tell by the general body language of the kid, you know, the things they're projecting. Just their general behavior usually tells me too, so you can read them pretty well. I can look at them, or I can talk to them on the phone sometimes. This one girl I can just talk to her on the phone and just by the tone of her voice I can tell when she's really down, or when she's feeling real good, when things are going well. It's real obvious, some kids might carve on themselves, some are poking at themselves all the time. And a lot of my girls, which is really funny, they'll bite their fingernails and when they don't bite their fingernails they'll be so proud and they'll say, "Look, my fingernails are growing." And that's another sign. That's not to say that everyone. . . .

[Well, do they identify with you though because you have long nails?]

Possibly—I'm not saying everyone who bites their fingernails. . . . My husband bites his fingernails and I don't think it's because he's feeling bad about himself, but I think when they stop a lot of those habits which they consider as bad habits and they have control. What it is it's like self-control and taking, making a definite change because they want to change. And they got—they're the ones under control. They've got control over themselves now. That mind's not just going wild, you know, doing what it wants if they've got control. I think that's somewhat of a sign to me too. You know, little things like that.

PROBATION OFFICER

[Are there some of the kids that you just really like?]

Uh, huh. And there are some I really hate. I have a kid right now that I sincerely cannot stand. I mean I made no bones about it. Well, sometimes to her—I mean I just. . . .

[What is it? What is it about her?]

She's *nasty,* she's foul, she's . . . . She refuses to cooperate with anybody. She's extremely manipulative, she's *nasty.*

[How do you know when a kid's trying to manipulate?]

You heard a phone call this morning from Melissa in a group home and it took us five phone calls back and forth to one another on Friday about what this girl was telling her, her foster mother was telling her and what. Then she tried to come back to me. You get a pretty good idea that she's trying to manipulate somebody or manipulate a situation. And then I'll test it out sometimes too—I'll just finally say, "No." Now if a kid thinks they're right, particularly when you give them a "no" right away,—a "no" after you let them get half-way into it—you sort of cut them off and you say, "No." If a kid thinks they're right and they're not manipulating they'll keep going. They'll keep going. You've got to use that only at certain times because a timid kid or a kid that's at least not that assertive, he's going to stop. I mean you're going to intimidate him into taking "no" for an answer. But if it's a manipulative kid, and you tell them "no" and they think they're right, they'll keep going. If you tell them "no" and they stop, you're being manipulated. That's one of my guages.

There is a fine distinction between a juvenile who talks with court personnel freely and sincerely, attempting to cope with problems and willing to accept court assistance, and the juvenile who talks with court personnel freely in order to manipulate decision-makers and achieve selfish goals or desires. The former is laudible, the latter distainful. But the ability to distinguish between the two is an art which decision-makers insist they have mastered. They are confident in their ability to tell a charlatan or con artist from a sincere client, but the manner in which such expertise is obtained and practiced is elusive.

Because these decisions are such a crucial aspect of the juvenile justice process it is pertinent to ask if certain personality traits unduly influence decision-makers' final evaluations. Numerous decision-makers candidly acknowledge that verbal children, that is, those who converse readily with adults in authority positions, are easier to work with than juveniles who are unable or unwilling to articulate their feelings. The difficulty in determining whether reticence or a lack of cooperation stem from a scornful attitude, mistrust or a lack of social skills is an extremely important issue. Those juveniles who are able to express their feelings, as well as comprehend the concepts expressed by decision-makers, are more able to successfully participate in the decision-making process. Several decision-makers openly acknowledge that articulate, personable juveniles are those most commonly liked by court personnel.

[What kind of kids are the kids that you really like? What is it about them?]

Well—as far as the kids I like?

[Okay.]

Probably everybody likes a verbal kid. Everybody likes a verbal kid. It's easier for you. Anything that makes your job easier you're going to like. A kid that's successful, you're going to like the positive kids. I think anybody that tells you that they like a negative kid, a kid that keeps getting into trouble, you know, is ridiculous. Now true, some kids are verbal and get into trouble and you still like them. There are exceptions to every rule. Generally speaking, verbal kids that are successful you're going to like. And sometimes it's just—the literature suggests this, too—that you tend to hold onto your successes because they're so damned few and far between. You tend to hold onto cases that you really don't need to hold on to.

COURT WORKER

[Are there some of the kids that you really like?]

Yeah.

[What kind of kids are they?]

Oh, I don't know, I couldn't identify any particular type. But there's some kids who we've raised at the court, you know, who . . . and they say that in detention, they've been in detention and they really feel that detention's their home. They come back to see the staff or they'll come in to show us their Army uniform if they join the Army, or to talk about their new job or their new girl friend or their baby. And those kind of kids who usually are very deprived kids, but who've made an attachment to the people here, are the kids you really do feel like you've raised.

[Are there any kids that you really dislike or don't like?]

Yeah.

[What kind of kids, . . .]

Oh, I don't know. I guess the kind of kid that I really feel is hard to work is the passive, whiny kid and I've had a few girls like that who are just real apathetic, whiners. There's no gumption, you know; there's no spunk and it's so hard to mobilize anybody like that. They're kind of like the Carol Burnett character, you know— the whiny housewife. That's really hard for me to work with. I don't like them.

[Are there some kids who are a lot more cooperative than others?]

Yeah. I mean some kids refuse to talk to you. You know, and that's kind of a challenge, but makes it a little difficult. Yeah, some are real eager for help. Others—see another quality that is important for our work is the kid's ability to verbalize, you know. 'Cause a lot of these kids just don't have the verbal skills to tell you what's going on. A kid can verbalize and you can identify the problem for him and make them recognize that it's a conflict that they're having, internal conflict. It's not the conflict between me and my mother. You know, "My mother's a bitch and she won't let me stay out until 2:00 in the morning." but that it's a conflict in themselves. "I want my independence, and at the same time I'm not willing to assume responsibility for it." If you can get them to think in abstract—to think in oh, a psychological kind of way then it's a lot easier to work with then.

[What do you do with the nonverbal child?]

That's a good question. I don't know. I had one kid that what I wound up doing, this was an early case when I first came to the court, who I had for counseling, and he couldn't understand what counseling was any more than he could understand Newton's theory of physics. I would end up helping him study for the driving test and he was a borderline MR kid, that you know, it was real hard for him. . . .

[MR kid?]

Mentally retarded . . . borderline intelligence. Wasn't a good reader at all and on that basis we established a relationship. I went down with him to take the test. I took my own driving test at the same time, scored lower than he did, which just thrilled him. And that was a way of establishing a relationship. In others, in detention, of course, the token economy, the structure, the behavior is the way that they approach the kids.

INTAKE WORKER

Several decision-makers bluntly admit that, like most human beings, they tend to like those juveniles who like them. Likewise, they suggest that those juveniles who are responsive, "positive," and successful in the court process are those who offer the greatest reward for court personnel, and thus, are regarded highly.

[In dealing with your kids are there some that you really like, just really like?]

Naturally. Of course.

[Are there some that you dislike?]

Yeah, but you never, or at least I haven't, gotten to dislike a kid as much as I like them. You know what I mean?

[Yes]

There's only one right now that I can honestly say I don't like him and usually I will try to transfer in those cases.

[Well what kind of kid is this?]

I don't think it holds a pattern. It's just a kid that hits you wrong. You know, a kid that comes across wrong. I had another one not too long ago, he's at Crockertown right now and needs to be there. This is his second time his parole has been revoked. I guess, you know, if you want to be really honest about it, the kids that you don't like generally, not always, generally are those ones who are negative toward you.

[Who are not cooperative or responsive . . .?]

Well, no. Responsive is not the right word. Cooperative is not necessarily the right word. *Hostile* I think is the right word. I have a couple of those. I do and some of them I can get by and say well, you know, the kid's really got problems and I can understand that but there are other ones that you'd just like to punch out. Unfortunately you don't have the opportunity.

[What about the ones you really like. What is it about them?]

Turn it around. Somebody who has a great deal of potential, you know, and have shown potential, but are very repressed about that.

You try to bring out the potential. You know the kid that gets through, relying a little bit, you start to like. The ones who are at this point responsive to you, you'll find yourself liking.

COURT WORKER

Although court personnel list numerous characteristics which are desirable or undesirable, they also suggest a further dimension which influences their response to a juvenile. It is that dimension of all interpersonal relationships which defies explanation, that "chemistry" or indefinable attraction or tension which exists between two individuals.

The following comments poignantly illustrate the incalculable nature of the relationships between juveniles and court personnel. This decision-maker candidly asserts that those characteristics one finds pleasing in juveniles are identical to those by which one judges the worth of any individual. But even this does not explain fully the manner in which a final impression is imprinted upon the mind of the decision-maker. In addition to the identifiable, positive attributes juveniles should emulate, this court worker introduces an element of great significance. The court worker admits an appreciation of juveniles with spunk, spirit, intelligence, a sense of humor; but in addition to these traits, the decision-maker asserts that a subtle challenge is a positive thing in a relationship.

[Are there certain kids you really like?]
Oh, sure.
[What kind of kids?]
Oh, boy. That's hard to answer. It has more to do with my propensities, the kind of people I like. It's going to be really hard for me to give you an outline of a juvenile. If I give you a personality description I'm going to be describing the kind of people I seek out as friends and what they were like when they were 15-years old.
I tend to like kids who are responsive, kids who are verbal, kids who are bright . . . kids who have a sense of humor, kids who have some spunk. . . . I also, God help me, really like my sociopaths! One of my very first cases was a boy whom I liked very, very much and went out of my way for who is always going to be in trouble. He is very bright. . . . He has so many defenses that he's never going to make it as an adult, unfortunately. He has such a view of the world as owing him something. . . . but I really like him. . . . I liked him also because he was always trying to manip-

ulate me and I was always successful in thwarting him. And I like to think on some level that made an impression on him. So in some ways I like kids who are hard to work with—who are wilder. I am able to exercise my wits in term of standing up to them.

COURT WORKER

Although others may not share this individual's enthusiasm for a challenge, all decision-makers undoubtedly have qualities which they seek or appreciate and which influence their interactions with juveniles. For some it may be "honesty"; others may be attracted to those juveniles whom they feel have "never been given an opportunity in life"; still others may be attracted to juveniles in whom they see "future potential." The list of intangibles is endless and varies with the individual decision-maker, but they are, nevertheless, crucial in the evaluative process. It is this wide variation in personality, orientation, and propensities which makes the assessment of juvenile attitudes and behavior such an elusive art. Variation exists among juveniles, but perhaps more crucial is the variation which exists among decision-makers. For in the evaluation of attitude and demeanor, both the propensities of juveniles *and* decision-makers play a significant role.

CHAPTER 13

The Great Synthesis: Arriving at a Final Decision

[Does whether or not a juvenile's good for an allegation influence your recommendation?]
It can. Then again, you know, it's hard to say because there's
no. . . . When you approach this job, it's not if A's present
then you're going to do B, if C's then you're going to do, you
know. It's just hard to say. Each case is different, and it depends
on how you feel about it.

COURT WORKER

As the comment above indicates and the former chapters illustrate, decision-making within the juvenile court is not a mechanistic, calculable process. There are few unchangeable laws and
each decision-maker employs individual guidelines. The host of
variables discussed in the preceding sections are not considered
in isolation during the actual decision-making process: all are
considered simultaneously. Each may, and does, exert an influence on the final decision, but it would be erroneous to suggest
that the factors are weighted equally or that they constantly exert
the same influence. Such is not the case.

The alleged offense, number of past referrals, degree of involvement, court opinions whether the juvenile "is good for"
the offense, legal representation for the juvenile, orientation of
the presiding officer, as well as the juvenile's school performance, home environment, sexual and racial identity, social status, and perceived attitudes and demeanor all figure prominently
in the decision-making process. But, in addition to these many
factors which have discussed previously, there are innumerable

others which influence the interaction between juveniles and court personnel. The juvenile's "psychological portrait," physical appearance, or association with adult lawbreakers may influence the opinions and recommendations of court personnel. Court personnel may also be influenced by unofficial or extralegal considerations such as information regarding juvenile misbehavior which has not been officially labeled.

[Can you give me an example of a juvenile that could be let go but you decide that they should stay (in detention)? What sort of factors would influence that?]
Well, maybe a kid who—he's brought in for a runaway, and you know that he's been not only a runaway but into drugs and stealing and so on like that too. So, and you know that he's running away again. I remember last December I had a girl brought in, and I told them to hold her in the building [detention]. I was on vacation then, and they put her out to Shelter Care. And, of course, she ran away because I knew that she was very upset and very angry. And so there are times when the kids are in such a psychological state, and I know that they are, that we ask for something that's not the usual procedure.
[Now some of the things that you might know about, like drug involvement, there might not be any official allegations about that behavior; you might just be aware of it, or have heard about it, and that might influence your decision?]
Right. I can't, okay, I can't do anything legally as far as a person to be retained, and usually the parents and whoever would agree with this. You know, we talk this over, and if the parents want the kid released, there's not much I can do. Usually the parents are asking that something be done. Sometimes the child is, too.
COURT WORKER

Likewise, budgetary considerations, statutory guidelines, parental wishes, the policies of outside agencies, as well as the professional orientations and personal ideologies of decision-makers contribute to the final analysis. But the crux of the decision-making process is the complex matrix created by the interplay of these variables.

The interactions and relationships of court personnel are also significant, for although they are indirectly related to a particular case or juvenile, organizational dynamics may exert considerable influence on the final decision. Of particular interest in the man-

ner in which individuals with differing power or authority resolve
conflicts. As may be expected, lower-echelon decision-makers
such as intake workers and probation officers often defer to the
opinions of more powerful decision-makers such as the chief social worker, prosecuting attorneys, and presiding officers. A court
worker may recommend a more severe disposition than originally
intended following strong disagreement by the chief social worker
or prosecuting attorney. But because the present court permits
wide leeway to all decision-makers and places confidence in the
judgments of all personnel, the converse is often the case. It is
not unusual, and in some departments it is characteristic, for court
workers to steadfastly maintain their recommendations in spite of
opposition from other decision-makers. In these conflict situations (the minority of cases), the individual decision-maker has
the option of yielding to the opinions of others or "going on the
record" as favoring a disparate course of action.

Because of their authority, the judge and hearing officers mediate between differing opinions from court workers, resolving
such conflicts by making a final decision and issuing a court order. The manner in which they do so is determined by their evaluation of the individual making the recommendation, as well as
their own objective and subjective appraisal of the situation. And,
although the judgment of presiding officers is rarely, if ever,
questioned *openly*, it is not unknown for a "less powerful" decision-maker to recommend action contrary to the wishes of the
presiding officer.

In the following case, a probation officer resists a more severe
disposition, despite the fact that the judge is obviously convinced
of the youth's wrongdoing and the need for a severe sanction.
Likewise, the recommended disposition appears to defy the "objective" factors of the case: the juvenile has 23 referrals to court,
has failed in previous court placements, is perceived as having
an extremely bad attitude, and is found guilty of assaulting a police officer.

Despite his negative evaluation of the juvenile's attitude and
demeanor, and the past difficulty he has experienced in attempting to supervise the juvenile, the probation officer does not recommend the obvious, "normal" disposition for such a case, that
is, placement in a secure facility such as D.O.C. Instead he recommends that the juvenile be permitted to live with a relative in

the city and remain under the court's supervision. Perhaps the major variable in the probation officer's decision was what may best be termed "a sense of justice." For, despite his belief that the juvenile probably should be placed in DOC, the probation officer was not convinced regarding the juvenile's culpability in the incident which resulted in the charge for assaulting a police officer. Despite the judge's ruling, the probation officer was convinced that to commit the juvenile to the Department of Corrections *on that referral* would be unjust. And further, that such action would be interpreted thusly by the juvenile and any treatment potential of the placement would be destroyed.

#120: Full Contested Hearing

Black Male, 15-years old
Judge
Prosecuting Attorney
Public Defender
Probation Officer
Witness: Police Officer
Mother
Juvenile ("Norman")
Referral #23:   Assaulting a Police Officer; Stealing under $50

Pretrial Conference [3 minutes]

Agreement between court and public defender to dismiss stealing under $50 (wrist watch) allegation. Will hear the evidence on the assaulting a police officer (felony) charge.

Courtroom Hearing [10:50–12:13]

[The Prosecuting Attorney takes the appearances of individuals present in court, and validates the juvenile's date of birth. The police officer is called as the first witness, takes the stand, and is sworn in.]

PROSECUTING ATTORNEY: Please state your name and occupation.
POLICE OFFICER (WITNESS):   Mark Abers. Police officer in Chelsam.
PROSECUTING ATTORNEY: Were you on duty, on patrol, on October tenth at 4:30 p.m.?

POLICE OFFICER: Yes.
PROSECUTING ATTORNEY: What were you doing?
POLICE OFFICER: Responding to a call, a 10–10 in progress.
PROSECUTING ATTORNEY: What is a 10–10?
POLICE OFFICER: A fight.
PROSECUTING ATTORNEY: Were you alone at the time?
POLICE OFFICER: Yes.
PROSECUTING ATTORNEY: Were you uniformed?
POLICE OFFICER: Yes.
PROSECUTING ATTORNEY: What did you find?
POLICE OFFICER: I observed a crowd of several youths all gathered around. About 20 people. As I approached, the crowd broke up and began to run in all directions. I saw the juvenile and another subject engaging in something, some physical activity.
PROSECUTING ATTORNEY: Can you describe the activity? If not, please state so.
POLICE OFFICER: I don't really recall. It all happened so fast.
PROSECUTING ATTORNEY: How far away were you?
POLICE OFFICER: About 40 feet away.
PROSECUTING ATTORNEY: Did this juvenile run away?
POLICE OFFICER: Yes.
PUBLIC DEFENDER: Objection, leading the witness.
JUDGE: Objection sustained.
PROSECUTING ATTORNEY: Please continue your narrative.
POLICE OFFICER: As I approached, the crowd was thinning out. This juvenile and another ran until I hollered at him. He responded with, "What do you want me for?" He was verbally abusive, using obsenities. As I came closer, he wanted to fight, wanted me to get rid of my gun and fight him. As I tried to approach, he kept backing away. I observed another subject coming up on me this way, and the juvenile from that way. They noticed a police car coming to assist me, and they both split. I returned to the car and began searching.
PROSECUTING ATTORNEY: What was the reason for the search?
POLICE OFFICER: I was searching for the subjects in connection with the 10–10 I was investigating—the ones involved.
PROSECUTING ATTORNEY: Can you state that you saw them fighting?
POLICE OFFICER: Yes, definitely.
PROSECUTING ATTORNEY: Please continue.
POLICE OFFICER: Later on I saw the juvenile duck into a garage. Then he ran north, right to where I was located looking for them. I started chasing the juvenile. We went through a fence, somebody's yard. I wrestled him to the ground. Another police officer assisted me. We handcuffed him and took him to the station.
PROSECUTING ATTORNEY: Was there any struggle?

POLICE OFFICER: He didn't really strike at me, he just struggled as we were getting him handcuffed. He was very abusive. He told me his father killed a "pig", and I would be next. He wouldn't come out of the car and had to be physically taken into the station. He was placed in the interview room. The sergeant came out to see what the ruckus was about. The sergeant knows the juvenile. He kept getting out of the chair. Said he wanted to beat my ass. He kept using obscenities. The sergeant more or less gave up on the incident, said to leave him alone 'til he calmed down. I stayed there. Three times the sergeant came to check on us. I told him as soon as he calmed down, he'd be out of the handcuffs. The sergeant had to leave; it was two to three minutes. He left. On his way out, he said to take the cuffs off. I didn't feel he was ready to have the cuffs off. After he was taken out, I went into the room adjacent. I removed my gun belt, cuffs, etc. I looked in the mirror; the juvenile was in the sergeant's office. He was hitting his hand with a flashlight. I said, "Give it to me or use it." He gave it to me. I told him to go back in his chair and sit down.

The juvenile wanted to start sparring with me. He was in a boxer's stance, moving around the room. He wouldn't knock it off. I said, "It's your move. Either sit down or back up what you said." He took a swing at me. I decked him. I put him back in the cuffs. He picked up a chair and was going to use it. I picked up a chair. He calmed down. Shortly thereafter his mother came. I don't know how she knew her son was at the station. I didn't release him to the mother.

PROSECUTING ATTORNEY: What injuries were sustained?

POLICE OFFICER: I bruised a finger when I hit him and tore a muscle in my shoulder. The injuries were more or less self-inflicted while defending myself.

PROSECUTING ATTORNEY: Was any other officer present to see what was going on?

POLICE OFFICER: Officer Karloff was present. I'm not sure if he observed what was going on.

PROSECUTING ATTORNEY: Have you taken the juvenile into custody before?

POLICE OFFICER: No.

PROSECUTING ATTORNEY: Did you know him on the street?

POLICE OFFICER: No.

PROSECUTING ATTORNEY: No further questions.

PUBLIC DEFENDER: At any point was the juvenile booked for common assault?

POLICE OFFICER: No. I hadn't had a chance to book him.

PUBLIC DEFENDER: You had him at the station for some time?

POLICE OFFICER: I had him there for 10–15 minutes.

PUBLIC DEFENDER: Then what happened?

POLICE OFFICER: After the mother left, the sergeant told me to go back on the street. The juvenile was taken to detention [juvenile court detention].

PUBLIC DEFENDER: Did you inform the juvenile what he had been taken into custody for?

POLICE OFFICER: No. I didn't get a chance to.

PUBLIC DEFENDER: Was he ever booked for a 10–10?

POLICE OFFICER: I don't remember if I did that.

PUBLIC DEFENDER: You testified that you saw "some physical activity"? What was it?

POLICE OFFICER: What I meant was there was a crowd of people. I could definitely see two or three people in the middle of the crowd. It appeared they were fighting.

PUBLIC DEFENDER: Did you ever ask what was going on?

POLICE OFFICER: I tried to.

PUBLIC DEFENDER: What did you ask them?

POLICE OFFICER: I asked them to come over so I could talk to them.

PUBLIC DEFENDER: Is it not true that you never asked if they were fighting?

POLICE OFFICER: I don't remember. He wasn't being too cooperative. He called me "pig," "mother-fucker." He wanted me to take off my gun and fight him.

PUBLIC DEFENDER: Do you know the juvenile by name?

POLICE OFFICER: No.

PUBLIC DEFENDER: When did you find out who he was?

POLICE OFFICER: At the station.

PUBLIC DEFENDER: You injured yourself by hitting him?

POLICE OFFICER: Yes.

PUBLIC DEFENDER: Where did you hit him?

POLICE OFFICER: The forehead.

PUBLIC DEFENDER: A number of times?

POLICE OFFICER; I hit to knock him down. I hit him 'til he said he would quit it.

PUBLIC DEFENDER: Was anyone else there?

POLICE OFFICER: I can't say.

PUBLIC DEFENDER: During the time you were hitting him was he handcuffed?

POLICE OFFICER: No.

PUBLIC DEFENDER: Did he ever hit you?

POLICE OFFICER: He was fighting back at me, but he never landed any blows.

PUBLIC DEFENDER: During the period of time you had him at the station, did you tell him why you brought him into custody?

POLICE OFFICER: He didn't give me a chance.

PUBLIC DEFENDER: You did not try to?

POLICE OFFICER: Not that at all. He was out of control of his emotions.

PUBLIC DEFENDER: Could that have been because he wondered why he was there?

POLICE OFFICER: No, no.

PUBLIC DEFENDER: How do you know?

POLICE OFFICER: I know.

PUBLIC DEFENDER: You had him in custody for some time. Why didn't you tell him what he was being charged with?

POLICE OFFICER: He didn't give me a chance.

PUBLIC DEFENDER: That is all.

PUBLIC DEFENDER: Your Honor, I would like to request a brief recess.

JUDGE: The court is in temporary recess.

[The Public Defender takes the juvenile from the courtroom for a discussion.]

POLICE OFFICER [TO PROSECUTING ATTORNEY]: The main thing I want to instill on this kid is his nature, when he goes off, he goes off.

PROSECUTING ATTORNEY [TO POLICE OFFICER]:   If the judge would've had any questions [about your testimony] he would've asked before you left the stand. That's the pattern.

[The Public Defender and Prosecuting Attorney have a private conference.]

BAILIFF [TO THE PROBATION OFFICER]:   What type of kid is this?

PROBATION OFFICER: Hostile and aggressive.

BAILIFF: He's about due. [This is an obvious suggestion that the juvenile should be committed to the Department of Corrections.]

PROBATION OFFICER: Overdue.

BAILIFF: He's a big kid for 15.

COURT RECORDER: Does he have a brother? We had Peter Lockwood, 16, for murder. He was certified as an adult.

PROBATION OFFICER: No, he's no relation.

[Following a 19-minute recess the court resumes.]

BAILIFF: Order in the court. The court is now in session. The Honorable Jason Waletzko presiding. Please be seated.

PUBLIC DEFENDER: I would like to make a motion to dismiss because the police officer did not show reason for ever taking the juvenile into custody for a violation of the Juvenile Code, on the basis that one can resist an unlawful taking into custody.

JUDGE: Motion denied.

PUBLIC DEFENDER: I would like to call Mrs. Jennifer Lockwood. Please state your full name.

MOTHER: Jennifer Anne Lockwood.

PUBLIC DEFENDER: What is your relation to the juvenile?

MOTHER: Mother.

PUBLIC DEFENDER: On October tenth how did you find out your son had been taken to the police station?

MOTHER: I received a phone call from an unidentified person that the police were shooting at two juveniles. I asked them. The police said they were not shooting, but my son had been taken in for loitering.

PROSECUTING ATTORNEY: I object. That is hearsay evidence. Strike the remark about the police statement regarding loitering.

JUDGE: Sustained.

PUBLIC DEFENDER: Please continue.

MOTHER: Policeman met me at the door. He demanded $30 for his suit and said if I didn't get it he would take Norman to juvenile [juvenile court]. My son was in another room and told me not to leave. He had a big knot on his forehead and scratches.

PUBLIC DEFENDER: How long were you at the station?

MOTHER: Thirty to forty minutes.

PUBLIC DEFENDER: At any point were you informed why your son was taken into custody?

MOTHER: No.

PUBLIC DEFENDER: Thank you. No further questions.

PROSECUTING ATTORNEY: No questions.

[The Public Defender calls the juvenile to stand. He is sworn in.]

PUBLIC DEFENDER: Please state your name and age.

JUVENILE: Norman Lockwood. Fifteen.

PUBLIC DEFENDER: Have you been in court during the testimony of the police officer?

JUVENILE: Yes.

PUBLIC DEFENDER: On October 10 were you at the playground that afternoon?

JUVENILE: Yes, at about 4:30 p.m.

PUBLIC DEFENDER: What were you doing?

JUVENILE: We play football.

PUBLIC DEFENDER: How many were there?

JUVENILE: About 12.

PUBLIC DEFENDER: Were they friends?

JUVENILE: Yes.

PUBLIC DEFENDER: Did anyone get into a fight?

JUVENILE: We were wrestling, me and another boy.

PUBLIC DEFENDER: The boy mentioned before?

JUVENILE: No, another boy.

PUBLIC DEFENDER: What do you mean "wrestling?"

JUVENILE: Struggling for the football.

PUBLIC DEFENDER: When did you first see the police officer?

JUVENILE: We had broken up, he came up. He kept calling to me. Then he hopped in his car and took off. I was cutting through a lot, and he jumped me from the back.

PUBLIC DEFENDER: Did the officer ask you any questions?
JUVENILE: No.
PUBLIC DEFENDER: What did you say to him?
JUVENILE: I asked him what he wanted.
PUBLIC DEFENDER: You did not run from him?
JUVENILE: No.
PUBLIC DEFENDER: Where'd he go?
JUVENILE: He went up the street.
PUBLIC DEFENDER: What is the name of the street?
JUVENILE: Maple.
PUBLIC DEFENDER: Where did you go?
JUVENILE: Lansing Avenue.
PUBLIC DEFENDER: Were you on your way to work?
JUVENILE: Yes.
PUBLIC DEFENDER: Did you have to get a ride?
JUVENILE: Yes.
PUBLIC DEFENDER: What is the name of the place?
JUVENILE: Melvin's.
PUBLIC DEFENDER: What do you do there?
JUVENILE: Dishwasher.
PUBLIC DEFENDER: When did you next see him?
JUVENILE: In a lot. He jumped over the fence and grabbed me. He threw me on the ground and took me to his car and started smacking me. When we got to the station, the sergeant told him to take the cuffs off. He took me in a room and asked me if I wanted to fight. I said, "No." He said, "You did in the beginning." Then he hit me—hit me upside the head with the telephone.
PUBLIC DEFENDER: Did he tell you why you were there?
JUVENILE: Never.
PUBLIC DEFENDER: Did you use obscenities?
JUVENILE: Yes.
PUBLIC DEFENDER: Did you ever take a swing?
JUVENILE: No.
PUBLIC DEFENDER: Did you ever hit him in any way?
JUVENILE: No.
PUBLIC DEFENDER: Was there anyone else around?
JUVENILE: A lady said she heard.
PUBLIC DEFENDER: In that room?
JUVENILE: No, in another room.
PUBLIC DEFENDER: No further questions.
PROSECUTING ATTORNEY: You said you were wrestling? What was the reason?
JUVENILE: Just struggling for the ball.
PROSECUTING ATTORNEY: What was the number of people?
JUVENILE: Twelve.

PROSECUTING ATTORNEY: Why didn't you go to the officer when he called to you?

JUVENILE: I wanted to know what he wanted first.

PROSECUTING ATTORNEY: Did you have any reason to fear the officer?

JUVENILE: No.

PROSECUTING ATTORNEY: You never met or saw the officer before?

JUVENILE: No.

PROSECUTING ATTORNEY: Did you ever make the statement that your father killed a "pig" and that he was next?

JUVENILE: No.

PROSECUTING ATTORNEY: Do you know any reason why he'd say that in court?

JUVENILE: No.

PROSECUTING ATTORNEY: I understand the other police at the station know you.

PUBLIC DEFENDER: Objection. Irrelevant. . . .

JUDGE: Sustained.

PROSECUTING ATTORNEY: Were you brought over to juvenile court?

JUVENILE: Yes.

PROSECUTING ATTORNEY: Was anyone with you?

JUVENILE: Police officer.

PROSECUTING ATTORNEY: Your mother?

JUVENILE: No.

PROSECUTING ATTORNEY: Were you questioned over here?

JUVENILE: No.

PROSECUTING ATTORNEY: When did your mother first come?

JUVENILE: Detention hearing.

PROSECUTING ATTORNEY: When did you ask for a detention hearing?

JUVENILE: Monday.

PROSECUTING ATTORNEY: What day did this happen?

JUVENILE: Friday.

PROSECUTING ATTORNEY: Your mother didn't come over during the entire weekend?

JUVENILE: No.

PROSECUTING ATTORNEY: Did she come over when you asked for a detention hearing?

JUVENILE: Yes.

PROSECUTING ATTORNEY: No further questions.

PUBLIC DEFENDER: When you were brought to detention, were you taken to County Hospital and treated?

JUVENILE: Yes.

PUBLIC DEFENDER: Did you ask or did someone suggest it?

JUVENILE: Someone suggested it. The detention unit leader.

PUBLIC DEFENDER: Did you have X-rays?

JUVENILE: Yes.

JUDGE: Did they treat you?

JUVENILE: They looked at my head.

JUDGE: Was there a bandage?

JUVENILE: No.

JUDGE: Did you tell anyone downstairs that the officer hit you?

JUVENILE: Yes, the unit leader.

JUDGE: Were you bleeding?

JUVENILE: Yes.

JUDGE: He hit you with a telephone?

JUVENILE: Yes.

JUDGE: What number of times?

JUVENILE: Three.

JUDGE: What part of your head?

JUVENILE: Here [indicates forehead].

JUDGE: Did you see your mother at the station?

JUVENILE: Yes.

JUDGE: After you were hit?

JUVENILE: Yes.

JUDGE: Did you tell her?

JUVENILE: Yes.

JUDGE: That's all the questions I have.

[Juvenile leaves the witness stand.]

JUDGE: I'm trying to find the amendment to the supplemental petition. As I understand, we're dismissing the allegation regarding the wrist-watch. On the evidence presented, the court finds beyond a reasonable doubt that the juvenile did commit the allegation. To wit, did assault one police officer. In specific, his behavior was injurious to himself and injurious to others. [To the Prosecuting Attorney] Do you wish to present evidence for the disposition?

[The Prosecuting Attorney calls the Probation Officer to the stand, who is then sworn in.]

PROSECUTING ATTORNEY: Please state your name.

PROBATION OFFICER: Chester E. Snow.

PROSECUTING ATTORNEY: You are a probation officer?

PROBATION OFFICER: Correct.

PROSECUTING ATTORNEY: You have been supervising the juvenile since [date]?

PROBATION OFFICER: Yes.

PROSECUTING ATTORNEY: Did you have a chance to review the former worker's reports?

PROBATION OFFICER: Yes, I did.

PROSECUTING ATTORNEY: Was the juvenile placed twice?

PROBATION OFFICER: Yes.

PUBLIC DEFENDER: Objection, Your Honor, the legal officer [Prosecuting Attorney] is testifying.

JUDGE: Sustained.

PROSECUTING ATTORNEY: Please give us an account.

PROBATION OFFICER: The juvenile has been placed twice.

PROSECUTING ATTORNEY: Were they successful?

PROBATION OFFICER: When he was at Sunset Hills he left [ran away] one or two times. Then he was at Mercy.

PROSECUTING ATTORNEY: Why was he placed?

PROBATION OFFICER: Because we felt there would be further difficulty with him adjusting within the community.

PROSECUTING ATTORNEY: How often did you see him?

PROBATION OFFICER: Twice a week when he was in school.

PROSECUTING ATTORNEY: Was he in school during the last school year?

PROBATION OFFICER: He attended, but was suspended. There is litigation in progress. I haven't heard the disposition of the school board.

PROSECUTING ATTORNEY: When was the last day he attended regularly?

PROBATION OFFICER: In [four months previously], I believe.

PROSECUTING ATTORNEY: What steps have you taken?

PROBATION OFFICER: I haven't taken any recently.

PROSECUTING ATTORNEY: Why?

PROBATION OFFICER: Because of his hostility. He never wanted to co-operate with me. Mother is trying to find out about school.

PROSECUTING ATTORNEY: He hasn't been cooperative?

PROBATION OFFICER: I haven't seen him since he left here [detention].

PROSECUTING ATTORNEY: Why not?

PROBATION OFFICER: For one thing, I didn't want to get into the hostility.

PROSECUTING ATTORNEY: Is he employed?

PROBATION OFFICER: No. I talked with Mother about him trying to get his job back.

PROSECUTING ATTORNEY: What came of that?

PROBATION OFFICER: Nothing.

PROSECUTING ATTORNEY: How does the juvenile spend his waking hours?

PROBATION OFFICER: I don't know. I saw him sitting in the doorway once.

PROSECUTING ATTORNEY: Are there any outstanding referrals?

PROBATION OFFICER: No.

PROSECUTING ATTORNEY: There have been nine referrals in the past year?

PROBATION OFFICER: Yes.

PROSECUTING ATTORNEY: Why didn't you close the case when you didn't get cooperation?

PROBATION OFFICER: I couldn't answer that.

PROSECUTING ATTORNEY: What help does the court have for him?

PROBATION OFFICER: We don't have any more resources at this time.

PROSECUTING ATTORNEY: Is there a possibility he may return to school?

PROBATION OFFICER: Yes, he could, perhaps next year.

PROSECUTING ATTORNEY: Do you feel that the proper place for the juvenile is in his mother's home?

PROBATION OFFICER: Yes.

PROSECUTING ATTORNEY: Are you recommending that the court continue jurisdiction and that he be under your supervision?

PROBATION OFFICER: Yes.

PROSECUTING ATTORNEY: Would you explain?

PROBATION OFFICER: My position is that there don't exist any alternatives. I'm recommending DOC with a stay.

PROSECUTING ATTORNEY: Your reason?

PROBATION OFFICER: Maybe Mother might come up with a solution as far as school and a job are concerned.

PROSECUTING ATTORNEY: Would you attempt to work with the juvenile?

PROBATION OFFICER: Yes, if he'll work with me.

PROSECUTING ATTORNEY: Have you talked with him today?

PROBATION OFFICER: No.

PROSECUTING ATTORNEY: Do you have any reason to believe he will be cooperative?

PROBATION OFFICER: No.

PROSECUTING ATTORNEY: Do we have any program here for him?

PROBATION OFFICER: No.

PROSECUTING ATTORNEY: Have you considered a commitment without a stay?

PROBATION OFFICER: I had earlier.

PROSECUTING ATTORNEY: Why did you change?

PROBATION OFFICER: I think there might be a possibility he'll get a job, live with his aunt in the city.

PROSECUTING ATTORNEY: Would we request courtesy supervision in the city?

PROBATION OFFICER: Yes.

PROSECUTING ATTORNEY: Do you feel he is a danger to himself or the community?

PROBATION OFFICER: His peer delinquency relationships brought about this. If he stayed away from them, I'm not sure, but if he was out of the community, there might not be any more problems.

PROSECUTING ATTORNEY: No more questions.

PUBLIC DEFENDER: Is it not true that at the detention hearing the juvenile was sent to stay with a relative in the city?

PROBATION OFFICER: Yes.

PUBLIC DEFENDER: Did he have a job before this incident?

PROBATION OFFICER: Yes.

PUBLIC DEFENDER: In the problems with the school district, were you not assisting?

PROBATION OFFICER: No.

PUBLIC DEFENDER: Do you feel it might be wise to have somebody else help if there exists a problem between you two?

PROBATION OFFICER: Yes.

PUBLIC DEFENDER: Is part of the problem that you mentioned DOC, and then noticed the hostility?

PROBATION OFFICER: Well, yes.

PUBLIC DEFENDER: Has there been any difficulty since the last referral?

PROBATION OFFICER: Yes.

PUBLIC DEFENDER: Well, was that only a few months, had you had problems before?

PROBATION OFFICER: Yes, earlier.

PUBLIC DEFENDER: No further questions.

JUDGE: Has the juvenile been living in the city?

PROBATION OFFICER: I haven't been aware of where he was living. I've seen him in Chelsam [section of county where his Mother lives].

JUDGE: Has he ever actually lived in the city?

PROBATION OFFICER: I would not know.

JUDGE: You're recommending that I return him to his mother?

PROBATION OFFICER: Wherever he's living now.

JUDGE: Is there some question about where he's living?

PROBATION OFFICER: Yes.

JUDGE: I'll say right now I don't think he should go back into Chelsam. I sincerely believe the prosecution proved their case beyond a reasonable doubt. If he returns to the community, it's all downhill. I'd like to find out where he's living. We're kidding ourselves if we think he can go back. Whether he's in trouble or not, he'll appear to be. I'd like to continue the dispositional hearing. It's foolish to send him back.

PUBLIC DEFENDER: Why not question his mother?

JUDGE: I was trying, but, good suggestion.

MOTHER: Where Norman lives?

JUDGE: Yes.

MOTHER: In the city with his cousin; she's 26-years old.

JUDGE: What about the school problem?

MOTHER: They haven't showed me any proof that he's expelled. It wouldn't take a school board three months to expel someone.

JUDGE: He's apparently not in school.

MOTHER: I know he's not in school, but they won't let him back in. I don't have any help to find out.

JUDGE: I don't have any authority about the school. I'm not sure we're not delaying the inevitable. This is a serious matter we've been considering. I'm a little surprised at the lightness of the recommendation. I'd like to know more about placement in the city and courtesy supervision in the city. If that's not the case, we might want to look for a placement outside the home.

Get me a plan. What are the chances of school in the city?

We'll continue the dispositional hearing. I want to know more about the place where he's staying, getting him into school, and the possibility of courtesy supervision.

[Recess: Next hearing set for three weeks.]

Dispositional Hearing [continued three weeks later; 3 minutes]

Discussion in Judge's chambers: The Judge, Prosecuting Attorney, Public Defender, Probation Officer [mother, juvenile, and juvenile's cousin wait in hallway].

PROBATION OFFICER: I made an intensive study, and since the day he left here he's been working 5 to 9 p.m. and has increased it to 5 to 12 on weekends.

I talked with the cousin. She is cooperative. The juvenile communicates well with her. She'll get him into school in the fall. My feeling at this time is that he'll do all right. I'd like to supervise him and not request courtesy supervision from the city. And D.O.C. with a stay.

JUDGE: What's he say, Ms. Martindale?

PUBLIC DEFENDER: That's what he wants.

JUDGE: Let's write it up as a consent order.

PROSECUTING ATTORNEY: How do you want it?

JUDGE: What do you want [to court worker]?

PROBATION OFFICER: Physical custody with the cousin and legal custody with the court.

PUBLIC DEFENDER: Why do you want legal custody?

PROBATION OFFICER: I'd like legal [custody] in order to move with all deliberate speed.

JUDGE: As long as you're supervising, legal "with the court" doesn't really mean anything.

PROSECUTING ATTORNEY: His cousin may need it [legal custody].

JUDGE: Yes, for medical and school.

PROBATION OFFICER: Fine. All right. I didn't think of that. Fine.

JUDGE: Let's do it.

[No courtroom session. The Public Defender and Probation Officer discuss decision with the mother, her son, and cousin.]

The Subjective Element

One element which is frequently overlooked, especially when the decision-making process is portrayed as a predominantly rational process, is the subjective dimension of judicial decisions. Particularly when the goal of decision-making is total review of an individual's situation, as it is in the juvenile justice system, subjective evaluations play a crucial role in the final analysis and recommendation for a case. The decision-makers' experiences within the juvenile justice system do exert tremendous influence upon their decisions, but of equal import are their experiences as human beings, for it is impossible to separate the wielders of power from their personal beliefs and characteristics. The individual decision-maker's personal biases and propensities, as well as professional orientations, greatly influence the interaction with juveniles and families.

[When you're confronted with differing opinions from either two court workers or a court worker and someone from the clinical department or an outside psychiatrist, how do you decide which recommendation to accept?]

I think about, like I said earlier, you draw on your own experience as a lawyer and as a judge and as a human being, and you try to make what you believe is the right decision. In every case, as a judge, you're going to have a difference of opinion and, hopefully, after being in this profession for 30 years and as a judge for eight, I've got some insight to make decisions. That's just a part of the business of being a judge. I don't think any judge can say what he does or what she does. I think it's just a matter of a personal view drawn upon those factors.

JUDGE

Despite the belief of court founders that scientific social work would provide the knowledge and techniques necessary for accurate diagnosis and treatment of juvenile problems, such faith has not been rewarded. Many of the court's treatment orders are still experimental and quasi-scientific at best. Some decisions are made by attempting to choose the "least harmful" of several bad alternatives. And although, to varying degrees, court personnel express confidence and optimism about their treatment efforts, many recognize the tenuous nature of their task. They acknowledge that decision-making within the juvenile court is based as much upon insight and intuition as it is upon clearly defined, empirical evidence. As a quote from a former judge so eloquently states: "The sign of the juvenile court is the crossed fingers!"

Court personnel rely to a great extent upon their prowess as diviners of the truth, their ability to assess an entire situation by transcending superficial appearances to grasp the crucial dimensions of a situation. Accordingly, the recommendations and orders of court personnel are influenced greatly by an extremely subjective element, an aspect of decision-making which court personnel describe as "intuition" or "gut feeling."

> I rely on my sense of people, which is very amorphous. I work very intuitively.
>
> COURT WORKER

> No matter what anybody else tells you, I still think that 90 percent of it's *intuition,* and you know, trying to make some sort of reasonable decision as to whether or not the kid's going to do it again.
>
> COURT WORKER

> It's so difficult. These are all subjective things. Very seldom do we have the luxury of having something nice and firm like a school record or something like that to really sink your teeth into.
>
> COURT WORKER

> This really sounds unprofessional, but I think most of it boils down to your gut feeling about the situation. I don't see how you can remove that. . . . You've been seeing the kid on a regular basis for a long time, months. . . . [It's] almost my general reaction to all the information I've been getting on the kid. Mainly how the kid reacts to me, how open they are with me, how much sincerity I see there, how much work I see that needs to be done. It's so hard. I can't really pin it down. It's a gut feeling. . . . It is the accumulation of all your perceptions of all the information you've been given and all the people who are resources for you. But it all kind of comes together for you. And sometimes it doesn't. But sometimes it does strongly. Sometimes you just know this kid's got to be placed. It's not going to work at home. . . . You just know; it's hard sometimes to verbalize why.
>
> PROBATION OFFICER

The Great Synthesis is the essence of decision-making within the juvenile court. It is that complex process through which court personnel combine their own professional and personal judgments with the miniscule or vast amount of information they have received about a juvenile. The resulting matrix of facts, bias, experience, professional ideology, personal preference, and intuitive knowledge culminates in an assessment of the juvenile's life situation and produces a decision which will greatly influence that juvenile's future.

CHAPTER 14

Individualized Juvenile Justice: The Implementation of an Ideal

Inherent in traditional juvenile justice philosophy is the ideal of individualized justice, that is, the assertion that each juvenile should be appraised and treated according to individual needs. To implement this ideal, court personnel have been granted vast discretionary power in order to diagnose and meet the needs of juveniles. Court personnel are invested with this power, not by default, but by design; for they are charged with the awesome responsibility of evaluating a juvenile's entire life situation and offering a prognosis for the future.

This discretionary power is not unlimited: Statutory edicts and administrative decisions, as well as the actions of outside treatment agencies, do impinge upon the options of decision-makers. But, in the court under examination, extensive discretionary power still exists at all levels of decision-making, for even statutory guidelines and administrative policies are subject to reinterpretation and implementation by the individual decision-maker.

Court decisions are based on a multitude of considerations: the more identifiable factors such as alleged offense, a child's age, or number of prior referrals to court; decision-makers' evaluations of the juvenile's individual character and family situation; and the decision-makers' personal propensities and professional orientation. The manner in which decision-makers arrive at final decisions is a combination of the "facts" surrounding a case, an assessment of the family stability, a feeling for the juvenile's attitude, and intuitive knowledge. Much of the research suggests that the more subjective considerations frequently outweigh the more objective factors.

Court personnel make decisions in much the same manner as do countless individuals—incorporating an element of rationality and irrationality, experience and prejudice, knowledge and intuition. The distinguishing feature of court decisions and the reason why they are appropriate objects for concern is the far-reaching impact they exert on the lives of juveniles. Judges, probation officers, and intake workers are not just people making decisions; they are powerful people making decisions.

In rare situations, such as those in which major allegations of homicide or assault with intent to kill are found true, the options are extremely limited. Likewise, the availability of a placement facility for a particular juvenile, the juvenile's psychological profile, or the wishes of parents occasionally do intervene dramatically in a case to limit alternatives. But in the vast majority of cases, court personnel have a wide variety of options from which to choose, ranging from outright dismissal of the case to commitment to the Department of Corrections. There are tacitly agreed upon and loosely defined guidelines. Stable families do not require court intervention, status offenders involve extensive family problems, or recidivism indicates a commitment to delinquency. But none of these rules is immutable; the decision-makers' evaluation of the current situation is preeminent.

In those instances when lower-echelon decision-makers do not wish to take action usually considered appropriate for a particular type of case, it may be necessary to reconsider and advance the reasoning behind the recommendation, but the authority and confidence placed in each decision-maker minimizes the extent to which unusual recommendations must be justified. Even supervisory review depends upon the subjective evaluation of the individual decision-maker. Likewise, presiding officers have the right to override even the most carefully argued recommendation, due to both the authority of their positions and the confidence placed in their individualized judgments. Divergent recommendations or final decisions are not viewed as arbitrary or inappropriate; they are seen as integral to the administration of individualized justice.

The Lack of Uniformity

The range of orientations and personalities in decision-makers is tremendous: They employ various criteria and techniques to evaluate juveniles; they favor divergent "treatment modalities"; and they offer vastly divergent appraisals of the same treatment facilities. Accordingly, there is much variation in the responses of decision-makers to the same "objective conditions." The final outcome of this diversity may be viewed as individualized when it is based on juvenile characteristics, but risks being labeled inconsistent when it is based on the propensities and characteristics of decision-makers.

[Are there any improvements that you think would help the court?]
    Let's see. Well, the court's strength is the resources we have in the staff. . . . I'd like to see more consistency between decisions that are made. You know, it's not fair that one kid is sent to DOC for an activity and another kid who's done the same thing, because of the different court worker, the different hearing officer, (is) sent to supervision (probation). That's not fair . . . they (court workers) all work differently . . . this is a very subjective field and it depends on individual personalities and everybody sees things differently. . . .
                                                    COURT STAFF MEMBER

When an institution relies heavily upon the merits of the individual decision-maker, the strength of the system is equal to the strength or effectiveness of each individual decision-maker. At the present court, personnel vary in their assessments of the capabilities of other decision-makers: The judge has suggested overall quality, asserting, "I don't think we have any people that I have had any experience with who haven't done a good job, good to excellent. If we put it on a scale of one to ten, I think our people hit in around eight most of the time; some go to ten." However, other decision-makers disagree:

[Do you feel there are varying degrees of individual workers being prepared?]
    Some are very competent and some are completely incompetent. Very few of them do an excellent job.
[Very few?]
    I'd say very few do an excellent job. I don't know, I would maybe guess 10 percent did an excellent job; 80 percent do their 9 to 5; and 10 percent should not be social workers, maybe even 20 percent shouldn't be doing social work.
[Why?]
    Well, they don't treat a case on an individual level—they don't

seek placement when it's blatant on the record that that's what is necessary. They let things slide and it shows in their work in other areas . . . there's really very little you can do about it other than up and die. Most people are competent, it's just some are very good and some are very poor, just like anywhere else in life. But, unfortunately, unlike other places in life, the damage that the incompetence can do can't really be corrected by the exceptional people, like, if you're working in a business, the exceptional people carry the very unexceptional people. Here, however, since it's individualized social work, you can't do that. The people they work with, these bad workers, suffer accordingly.

COURT STAFF MEMBER

Preparation and Training for Decision-makers

The preparation and training which guide decision-makers in the exercise of authority is, to a great extent, an individualized concern. The bulk of one's "training" consists of the individual's own educational background, occupational experiences, and personal capabilities. Each court unit (intake, probation, legal department, presiding officers) provides indoctrination for a new decision-maker, but the thoroughness as well as the content of such training is dependent upon the individual charged with this instruction. Some workers have the opportunity to observe and question other decision-makers prior to assuming responsibilities themselves, but the demands of crowded schedules and waiting caseloads dictate that such opportunities will be limited. The vast majority of decision-makers learn the exigencies of their positions by assuming authority shortly after they are hired, perhaps immediately.

One of the major sources of the decision-maker's indoctrination into the court is a ten-week training session which meets biweekly. Because the sessions are conducted officially for volunteer workers, attendance is encouraged, but not required for full-time staff members. Equally important, these training sessions often are not held at the time an employee is first hired, so an individual may function within a decision-making capacity for weeks or months before receiving this official training.

In-service training sessions on such topics as family therapy or youth and drugs are sponsored by various professional organizations, the court's legal or clinical services departments may offer an occasional seminar, and state and national juvenile justice conferences are conducted annually. But attendance is optional and varies with the commitment and motivation of the individual decision-maker. Equally important, the funding for such training is frequently the responsibility of the individual decision-maker. Some decision-makers continually seek opportunities to gain additional knowledge and information to enable them to deal with the myriad of problems they confront daily. But many court personnel rely solely upon their present understanding, past experiences, and personal opinions. This situation is a function not only of individual indifference, but is also the result of a lack of officially-allotted time and resources for such activities.

In the main, court personnel learn to make decisions by doing so—the extent to which these decisions are based upon an ever-increasing store of knowledge and insight is largely an individual matter. Each staff member must assume the major responsibility of acquiring the capabilities necessary to merit the trust placed in them by the juvenile justice system.

When questioned regarding changes which would benefit the court, many decision-makers cited the lack of training opportunities, suggesting that more emphasis should be placed on the preparation of staff members to wield power.

> I guess what I'm saying, I'm saying that we need to have more in-service workshops to help our workers learn to relate to people, how to interview people, work in groups, kinds of questions to ask, time to listen, time to be direct, indirect, what have you—all of that. And I think this would make us a better professional staff . . . I think we have, you know, we have a little hit and miss, maybe we have one this week, maybe we won't have another one until maybe eight months later. . . .
>
> COURT STAFF MEMBER
>
> I think there needs to be better training. I don't think we train our people at all.
> [You mean in courtroom procedures?]
> I don't think we train our people period in this court because there's, I see too many people coming out of graduate school and what have you . . . they come in here, they're going to save the world. . . .
> [What training is there?]

Okay, you can train—you can put people in a training unit for four weeks before they ever start off, before you subject them to the general public, and that's what it is. I can't believe we're subjecting people to us. I mean it's just awful, it's criminal.

But people ought to know procedure, people ought to know resources that are available to the court. They ought to know what you have to do to get things done at the court. If nothing else, practical kinds of things they should know and they don't. We have to keep a worker under raps and close, not close, but keep your eye on them for six months after they get hired.

They don't know what they're doing. They can go through that training unit, volunteer training unit that we have, and that's good. I mean it's all right, but still it's not adequate, just not adequate at all. We have enough of a turnover in the court that when people are hired they should be put immediately into a training unit and just spend a week in detention, spend a week with the police, a week learning procedures, i.e., through courtrooms and clerical and computer and all that kind of crap. And let's really give them some kind of foundation and then they can use what they learned in school under the structure of the court. But we don't do that. It takes us six months. Okay, that's not fair to kids, that's not fair to the public, the parents. That's not fair to us because we're not getting our money's worth out of them.

PROBATION OFFICER

Because of the wide discretionary power inherent in the concepts of individualized justice and individualized social work, accountability within the juvenile court is minimal. It is extremely rare for a member of the court staff to be fired: Accordingly, the major point of control on the quality of personnel is at the hiring stage. But even there, with the exception of a basic educational requirement, the selection of new staff members is based upon the evaluation of unit supervisors with administrative review of recommendations. The criteria for assessing the success or effectiveness of a decision-maker are ill-defined. If the relationship between a decision-maker and client is strife-ridden or unfruitful, most commonly the failure is attributed to the client. Cases are rarely transferred because of a decision-maker's acknowledged inability to deal with a juvenile effectively. Complaints from juveniles and parents are easily discounted because of the latter's lack of credibility.

Even though the court has a formal structure to provide checks on the individual decision-maker, such mechanisms do not systematically challenge decision-makers. Supervisory personnel and presiding officers must demonstrate confidence in the integrity and skill of each decision-maker, for higher-echelon personnel base many of their individualized decisions on the input they receive from subordinate decision-makers. In essence, the philosophy of individualized justice necessitates that extreme confidence be placed in each staff member's ability to make decisions, but few consistent measures exist by which to evaluate these decisions.

Because each decision-maker is granted considerable latitude in the exercise of authority, the overall effectiveness of the court cannot be assessed by merely summing the strengths and weaknesses of all decision-makers. Individualized justice dictates that the strengths of one decision-maker will not compensate for the deficiencies of another. Accordingly, some juveniles benefit from the diligence and commitment of decision-makers, while some suffer from the lack of concern and inattention of others. To a great extent, a juvenile's fate is determined, not by the characteristics of that child, but by the characteristics and abilities of decision-makers who administer individualized justice.

The concept of individualized justice championed by traditional juvenile justice philosophy emphasizes the necessity of examining the behavior, attitudes, and propensities of juveniles. The present inquiry demonstrates that to truly understand the process of individualized justice as implemented within the modern juvenile court it is necessary to examine the behavior, attitudes, and propensities of those who administer juvenile justice. The philosophy of individualized justice stresses the characteristics of juveniles, but the implementation of that ideal focuses upon the characteristics of decision-makers. "Individualized" refers as much to the interpreter of juvenile characteristics as it does to the juvenile. The art of interpretation reveals more about the *artist* than the subject.

The Larger Context

Analysts too often succumb to the temptation of viewing an institution in isolation from the society which spawns it. We must recognize that, regardless of how benevolent or appealing it may be, the ideal of individualized justice has never been realized. Within the context of the vast bureaucracies which characterize modern day juvenile courts, decision-making is shaped by organizational demands and bureaucratic exigencies, not by the needs and potential of juveniles.

But the critique of individualized justice goes beyond mere problems of bureaucracy, for it extends to the biases of the larger society as well as those of individual decision-makers. The evidence clearly indicates that rather than viewing each child as an individual, the juvenile court often operates in such a manner that children are perceived and processed according to stereotypes. Individualized justice abdicates to assembly-line justice; the child is black or poor or female, not an individual. Visions of the unstable black family, the inadequate lower-class environment, or the troublesome female runaway supercede the needs of juveniles.

In the instances when decision-makers transcend these stereotypes, decisions are still more indicative of the individual decision-maker than the child. Perhaps these cases more closely approximate the model of individualized justice, but only a limited number of juveniles are able to benefit. When a juvenile's attitude or demeanor become crucial dimensions of the interactive process it appears to be individualized justice, but it must be acknowledged that middle-class, white juveniles are more likely to possess the social skills and abilities which enable them to impress decision-makers favorably. Being personable or "having potential" are social definitions and decision-makers who are predominately white and middle-class respond most to individuals of like background.

It is erroneous to suggest that decision-makers never give poor or black juveniles "a break." Decision-makers are touched or influenced by a particular tragedy, a particularly difficult family situation, or a child "who never got a chance." Such treatment does exist and to precisely that extent so does individualized justice. The dilemma is not that they never occur, but rather, that within the present context, they do not occur systematically; and furthermore, that such instances depend upon the idiosyncracies of decision-makers. The structure of the juvenile court permits vast discretion but too often it results not in individualized justice but in an inconsistency and arbitrariness which approach capriciousness.

The preceding analysis has emphasized the components of individualized justice as presently implemented. In an important sense, it is equally crucial to scrutinize those factors which the present system of juvenile justice *excludes*. Most notably, it precludes large-scale social analysis and criticism: In its concentration on and preoccupation with juvenile characteristics it fails to examine more encompassing issues. The focus is upon the malfunctioning of an individual or the instability of a particular family, not the deterioration of meaningful relationships within mass culture. It focuses upon the individual juvenile's failure within school, not the failure of schools as an institution. The spotlight is focused on the illegality and impropriety of juvenile acts without acknowledging the structural forces and social relations which generate such behavior. The juvenile court has been preoccupied with molding juveniles to fit existing economic, sexual, and social roles, rather than questioning the historical development and present efficacy of such roles.

Juvenile court personnel often ignore that they are attempting to "do justice" within an unequal and unjust context. It is this very lack of vision which condemns the juvenile court's efforts to limited and temporary solutions *at best*. Equally consequential, it is the court's reluctancy to develop a critical posture toward society that prevents it from recognizing the inadequacy of its efforts and the inevitability of its failure. There can be no such thing as individualized justice within a social context of injustice.

The Statistical Indicators: A Summary of Bivariate and Multivariate Analyses

Three samples have been used to explore the relationships between severity of disposition (the dependent variable) and legal and socioeconomic variables (the independent variables). The latter include legal variables such as number of referrals to court, the seriousness of the offense, legal representation for the juvenile and the detention decision, as well as socioeconomic variables such as gender, race, age, siblings' prior involvement with the court, and activity at the time of referral to court. The three samples provide information on diverse sectors of the delinquency referrals to court. They include a sample encompassing all of the year's delinquency referrals, a sample involving all those referrals processed formally by the court during the year's time, and the sample of 250 delinquency cases observed.

The Year's Referrals to Court

Of the 10,476 delinquency referrals during the year, 9,535 were afforded a final disposition by the court: 855 were either rejected due to improper handling or insufficient evidence or transferred to other jurisdictions; 86 were classified as "action pending" at the time of analysis. Thus, the analysis of a year's referrals is based on 9,535 referrals.

Initially, the severity of the disposition was divided into three classifications corresponding to the rankings provided by court personnel. Least Severe Dispositions included informal adjust-ment, dismissal, conditional dismissal, and taken under advise-ment. Moderately Severe Dispositions, included jurisdiction or supervision (probation). Finally, Most Severe Dispositions in-cluded the placement of the juvenile outside the home, but not in the Department of Corrections (D.O.C.), commitment to the D.O.C., with a stay of execution, commitment to D.O.C., and certification (transfer) to the adult criminal court. The percentage of referrals in each category, respectively, are 76.8 percent; 19.0 percent; and 4.2 percent.

The bivariate relationships between the severity of the dispo-sitions that were imposed and numerous predictor variables have been reported throughout the text. Table 1 provides a summary of the relative strength of association between independent var-iables and severity of disposition. Kendall's tau is used to assess the strength of bivariate relationships, and gamma scores are in-cluded for proportional reduction of error interpretations.

As indicated by Table 1, only three of the variables reached the established level of substantiality ($\pm.10$): the number of prior referrals, the detention decision, and the presiding officer. Ac-cordingly, the likelihood of receiving a severe disposition is greater with increased number of referrals and when a juvenile was detained at the time of apprehension. Also, those juveniles whose cases are heard by the juvenile judge and hearing officer #1 are likely to receive the more severe dispositions. The vari-ables of race, the involvement of his brothers or sisters with the

Table 1 The Relative Strength of Association between the Independent Variables and the Severity of Disposition for the Year's Delinquency Referrals.

Rank	Variable	Tau Value	Gamma Value
1	Number of prior referrals	.36	.76
2	Detention decision	.21	.67
3	Presiding officer	−.19	
4	Race	.06	.15
5	Prior sibling court involvement	.06	.14
6	Referral source	.05	.50
7	Seriousness of offense	−.02	−.05
8	Gender	.00	.00
9	Age	.00	−.01

court in the past, referral source, the seriousness of the offense, gender, and age failed to reach the level of substantiality at the bivariate level of analysis.

Multiple regression analysis was employed to analyze the direct effects of each independent variable while controlling for remaining known variables and their interrelationships. Because regression analysis requires that variables be interval scale, it was necessary to dichotomize the dependent variable (severity of disposition), as well as numerous independent variables. The dependent variable was dichotomized on the basis of whether or not the court disposition indicated further court involvement. It was divided into those cases in which there is no further (immediate) court involvement, including referrals which are adjusted informally, dismissed, or taken under advisement and those cases in which there is no further court intervention in the juvenile's activities, including probation, placement outside the home, commitment to D.O.C. with a stay, commitment to D.O.C., or certification to the adult court.

Table 2 indicates the manner in which independent variables were categorized,[1] as well as providing the bivariate correlations between severity of disposition and the independent variables when they are categorized thusly. The table also provides the following information derived from the multiple regression analysis. First, the standardized partial regression coefficients (beta weights) which assess the effect of an independent variable on the dependent variable while controlling for the effects of other known variables. Second, R Square Change scores which indicate the amount of variation in the dependent variable that can be statistically accounted for by the particular independent variable. Third, the multiple correlation coefficient (R) which provides a measure of the overall association between severity of disposition and all the predictor variables; and the square of the multiple correlation coefficient (R^2) which indicates the total amount of variation in the dependent variable which can be attributed to the variation in the best weighted combination of the independent variables.

As shown in Table 2, the relative importance of variables does not differ considerably from the findings provided by bivariate

1. The variable "presiding officer" was incorporated into the regression model through the use of dummy variables; this provides an estimate of the R Square change attributable to this variable, but does not yield a cumulative beta weight.

Table 2 Bivariate Correlations (r) and Beta Weights Representing the Direct Effects of the Independent Variables on the Severity of Disposition for Year's Delinquency Referrals.

Independent Variable	r	Beta	R Square Change
Number of prior referrals	.470	.318	.220
Presiding officer	.387	a	.133
Detention decision: not detained or detained	.315	.154	.051
Referral source: law enforcement or other	.133	.067	.012
Age	−.009	.029	.004
Seriousness of offense: status offenses and misdemeanors or felonies	.097	−.022	.003
Gender	−.003	.018	.001
Race	.053	−.002	.000
Number of siblings previously referred to court	.047	−.000	.000
$R = .65^b$ $R^2 = .42$			

[a] The use of dummy variables does not produce a cumulative beta weight for the variable, but does provide an estimate of the R Square Change.
[b] Multiple correlation coefficient.

analysis. Even when the effects of other known variables are controlled, the number of prior referrals, the presiding officer, and the detention decision account for the greatest amount of variation in the severity of the disposition. The relative influence of race, seriousness of offense, and involvement of brothers or sisters with the court decreases when other factors are controlled; conversely, the relative influence of age and gender increases. Nevertheless, none of these latter relationships meet the criterion for substantiality (beta = ±.10).

Referrals Processed Formally

Of 10,476 referrals made to the court during the year, 2551 were processed formally. A legal petition was filed; a formal hearing was held; and, if allegations were ruled true, the court was empowered to enter legally binding orders which would supersede juvenile or parental wishes. In approximately 40 percent of these cases the court did not exercise the option to become further involved in the juvenile's life, and accorded final dispositions of dismissal, conditional dismissal, or took the case under advisement. In 60 percent of the cases processed formally the court exercised the option to become involved in a juvenile's activities by according the more severe dispositions of probation, placement outside the home, commitment to D.O.C. with a stay, commitment to D.O.C., or certification to the adult court.

Bivariate and multivariate analysis of the cases reveals that independent variables exert divergent influences once the decision to formally process a referral has been made. As indicated in Table 3, the age of a juvenile has a substantial influence upon the severity of the disposition that is decided upon when a referral is processed formally. And, although the influence of the number of prior referrals and the detention decision maintain their influence on the final outcome of a case, the influence of the presiding officer diminishes. On the bivariate level, the serious-

Table 3 Bivariate Correlations (r) and Beta Weights Representing the Direct Effects of the Independent Variables on the Severity of Disposition for Referrals Processed Formally.

Independent Variable	r	Beta	R Square Change
Age	−.245	−.239	.046
Number of prior referrals	.290	.238	.050
Detention decision: not detained or detained	.274	.217	.080
Presiding officer	−.145	[a]	.010
Seriousness of offense: status offenses and misdemeanors or felonies	−.148	−.048	.008
Referral source: law enforcement or other	.091	.070	.006
Gender	.118	.042	.003
Race	.020	−.025	.001
Number of siblings previously referred to court	.009	−.030	.001

$R = .45^b$ $R^2 = .20$

[a] The use of dummy variables does not produce a cumulative beta weight for the variable, but does provide an estimate of the R Square Change.
[b] Multiple correlation coefficient.

ness of offense and the gender of the defendant reach the level of substantiality. However, the introduction of statistical controls for the effects of other known variables reduces the relative influence of these factors in the multivariate analysis.

The influence of the age of the defendant on those referrals processed formally may be attributed to the increased culpability of older juveniles due to their level of sophistication, the lack of community-based resources for older juveniles, and the statutory stipulation that only those over 14 years may be considered for transfer to the adult court.

The Sample of Observed Cases

Observations of delinquency hearings were conducted to provide insight into the overall workings of the court and to furnish the basis for the interpretive analysis. Accordingly, the observations were designed to permit participation in all four courtrooms and to provide exposure to cases involving a wide variety of offenses. Therefore, although the observations have been coded to facilitate statistical analysis, they do not represent a random sample, and therefore, the generalizability of the findings is limited.

Nevertheless, the sample of observed cases provides insight into the influence of a greater number of variables that were not available for the larger samples, in particular, it provides a measure of the effect of the *expressed* evaluations of decision-makers regarding the more subjective factors such as family stability and juvenile demeanor. In addition to the variables provided from the preceding analysis, observations included the juvenile's activity at the time of referral to court; information pertaining to previous placements outside the home; whether the juvenile participated in the alleged delinquency alone or in consort with others; whether or not the juvenile was represented by an attorney; whether or not the juvenile underwent a psychological evaluation; whether or not alcohol or drugs were associated with the referral; the marital status of the juvenile's biological parents; and evaluations of the family stability, parental concern, and juvenile demeanor as expressed by decision-makers during pretrial discussions and official hearings.

Table 4 provides a summary of the relative strength of association between predictor variables and the severity of disposition.

Table 4 The Relative Strength of Association Between Independent Variables and Severity of Disposition for Cases Observed.

Rank	Variable	Tau Value	Gamma Value	Level of Significance
1	Expressed evaluation of juvenile demeanor: positive or negative	.48	.79	.00
2	Expressed evaluation of family stability: positive or negative	.42	.72	.01
3	Expressed evaluation of parental action: negative, neutral, or positive	−.39	−.71	.00
4	Psychological evaluation: yes or no	−.34	−.72	.00
5	Detention decision: not detained or detained	.31	.67	.00
6	Referral source: law enforcement or other	.27	.57	.00
7	Number of prior referrals	.27	.33	.11
8	Presiding officer	−.24	−.33	.01
9	Marital status of biological parents: not together or together	−.22	−.43	.01
10	Previous placements outside the home: yes or no	−.21	−.58	.00
11	Race	.20	.45	.00
12	Alone or in consort with others	−.14	−.29	.06
13	Expressed evaluation of the juvenile's school performance: positive or negative	.18	.41	.05
14	Activity at time of referral to court: school, work, or other	.13	.36	.18
15	Age at the time of the hearing	−.13	−.40	.07
16	Legal representation: not represented or represented	.11	.22	.12
17	Number of siblings previously referred to court	−.09	−.27	.38
18	Gender	−.06	−.15	.42
19	Alcohol involvement: no or yes	.04	.17	.40
20	Drug involvement: yes or no	−.01	−.02	.99

Due to the smaller size of the sample, significance levels are reported for the relationships. Those relationships which are statistically significant (p ≥ .05) suggest that those referrals in which court personnel express a positive evaluation of a juvenile's demeanor, the family's stability, and the parents' level of concern are likely to receive less severe dispositions. They also suggest that those children who were not detained at the time of apprehension, those referred by sources other than law enforcement officials (by parents or community members), those who have not been placed outside their homes previously, and those who committed a crime alone receive less severe dispositions. Juveniles who are not requested to undergo psychological evalua-

Table 5 Bivariate Correlations and Beta Weights Representing the Direct Effects of the Independent Variables on the Severity of Disposition for Cases Observed.

Independent Variables	r	Beta	R Square Change
Expressed evaluation of juvenile demeanor	.48	.301	.142
Detention decision: not detained or detained	.31	.170	.063
Referral source: law enforcement or other	.27	.202	.012
Race	.20	.030	.010
Expressed evaluation of family stability	.42	.039	.008
Gender	−.06	.124	.006
Alcohol involvement: no or yes	.04	.100	.270
Previous placements outside the home	−.21	−.085	.008
Presiding officer	−.24	a	.049
Expressed evaluation of school performance	.18	.043	.001
Drug involvement: yes or no	−.01	.029	.001
Legal representation: not represented or represented	.11	−.046	.001
Seriousness of offense		.023	.000
Alone or in consort with others	−.14	−.01	.000

$R = .57$ $R^2 = .25$

[a] The use of dummy variables for the "presiding officer" provides an estimate of the R Square Change attributable to this variable but does not provide a cumulative beta weight.

Table 6 Comparison of the Relative Strength of Association between Independent Variables and Severity of Disposition for Three Samples.

	Tau Values		
Independent Variables	Year's Referrals[a]	Processed Formally[b]	Cases Observed[c]
Number of prior referrals	.47	.29	.27
Detention decision: not detained or detained	.32	.27	.31
Presiding officer	.39	−.15	−.24
Race	.05	.02	.20
Number of siblings previously referred to court	.05	.01	−.09
Referral source: law enforcement or other	.13	.09	.27
Seriousness of offense	.10	−.15	.15
Gender	−.00	.12	−.06
Age	−.01	−.25	−.28

[a] Year's delinquency referrals processed by court ($N = 9535$).
[b] Year's delinquency referrals processed formally ($N = 2551$).
[c] Cases observed ($N = 232$).

tions, those whose biological parents are living together, and those who are white are likely to receive less severe dispositions. As has been true in the other samples, these findings suggest that the disposition of a case is influenced substantially by the orientation of the presiding officer.

On the multivariate level it was possible to incorporate only fourteen of these variables and still maintain an acceptable sample size, due to the number of missing values within the variables. Table 5 provides a summary of the multivariate analysis for a subsample of 162 cases. It suggests that when other variables are controlled, the fact that the defendant was detained or released, the source of referral, gender, if the defendant was using alcohol, the decision-makers' expressed evaluation of the child's demeanor, and the presiding officer substantially influence the severity of disposition.

Those juveniles who are detained at the time of apprehension, those who are referred to court by law enforcement officials, those cases in which the juvenile is charged with having used

Table 7 Comparison of Beta Weights and R Square Change for Three
Samples.

	Beta Weights (R Square Change)		
Independent Variable	Year's Referrals[a]	Processed Formally[b]	Cases Observed[c]
Number of prior referrals	.318 (.220)	.238 (.050)	[e]
Detention decision: not detained or detained	.154 (.051)	.217 (.080)	.170 (.063)
Presiding officer	[d] (.133)	[d] (.010)	[d] (.049)
Race	−.002 (.000)	−.025 (.001)	.030 (.010)
Number of siblings previously referred to court	−.000 (.000)	−.030 (.001)	[e]
Referral source: law enforcement or other	.067 (.012)	.070 (.006)	.202 (.012)
Seriousness of offense	−.022 (.003)	−.048 (.008)	.023 (.000)
Gender	.018 (.001)	.042 (.003)	.124 (.006)
Age	.029 (.004)	−.239 (.046)	[e]

[a] Year's delinquency referrals processed by court. N = 9,535.
[b] Year's delinquency referrals processed formally. N = 2,551.
[c] Cases observed. N = 250.
[d] The use of dummy variables does not produce a cumulative beta weight for the variable, but does provide an estimate of the R Square Change.
[e] Variable not included in multivariate analysis of cases observed.

alcohol, and those juveniles whose demeanor is negatively evaluated by decision-makers are likely to receive more severe dispositions. Although the inferences which may be drawn from the sample of cases observed are limited, even such preliminary findings suggest that the more subjective aspects of decision-making, such as evaluation of demeanor and family stability, may contribute substantially to attempts to account for variation in severity of disposition. Accordingly, the design and execution of research which incorporates such factors and explores their impact upon decision-making is greatly needed.

Log-linear Analysis

Log-linear analysis was used to examine the three major junctures within the court process, that is, screening, detention,

Table 8 Likelihood Ratio Chi-square Values for Models of the Association between the Number of Referrals, Gender, Prior Sibling Involvement, Race, Offense Type, and Detention Decision.

Model	Degrees of Freedom	Likelihood Ratio Chi-square	P
1 Six-way interaction (saturated model)	0	0.0	1.00
2 All 5-way interactions	4	3.27	0.51
3 All 4-way interactions	24	21.10	0.63
4 All 3-way interactions	65	76.13	0.16
5 All 2-way interactions	109	184.79	0.0
6 All significant 2-way and 3-way interactions	100	117.13	0.12

and the final disposition. Tables 8 to 20 summarize the analysis discussed throughout the proceeding chapters. Variables were categorized as follows: Number of prior referrals (0, 1, 2+); Offense type (status, misdemeanor, felony); Prior sibling involvement with court (no, yes); Race (white, black); Gender (female, male); Detention decision (detained, not detained); Screening decision (informal processing; formal processing); Severity of disposition (least, moderate, severe).

Table 9 Tests of Net Contribution of Factors Affecting Detention Decision.

Factor	Degrees of Freedom	Net Contribution Likelihood Ratio Chi-square	P
Prior referrals	2	323.84	0.00
Offense type	1	283.61	0.00
Race	1	121.63	0.00
Gender	1	86.11	0.00
Offense/Gender	2	15.58	0.00
Offense/Number of prior referrals	4	12.12	0.016

Table 10 Effect Parameters For Detention Decision.

Main Effects	Detained	
	No	Yes
Race		
White	0.194	−0.194
Black	−0.194	0.194
Gender		
Male	0.096	−0.096
Female	−0.096	0.096
Number of prior referrals		
None	0.260	−0.260
One	0.092	−0.092
2+	−0.351	0.351
Offense type		
Status	−0.319	0.319
Misdemeanor	0.311	−0.311
Felony	0.008	−0.009

Table 11 Effect Parameters of Three-way Interactions with Detention Decision.

	Detained	
	No	Yes
Male, status offense	0.094	−0.094
Male, misdemeanor offense	0.030	−0.030
Male, felony offense	−0.124	0.125
Female, status offense	−0.094	0.094
Female, misdemeanor offense	−0.030	0.030
Female, felony offense	0.124	−0.124
No prior referrals, status offense	−0.079	0.079
No prior referrals, misdemeanor offense	0.086	−0.086
No prior referrals, felony offense	−0.010	0.010
One prior referral, status offense	0.012	−0.012
One prior referral, misdemeanor offense	−0.034	0.034
One prior referral, felony offense	0.022	−0.022
Two or more prior referrals, status offense	0.064	−0.064
Two or more prior referrals, misdemeanor offense	−0.052	0.052
Two or more prior referrals, felony offense	−0.012	0.012

Table 12 Likelihood Ratio Chi-square Values for Models of the Association between Number of Referrals (N), Detention Decision (D), Offense Type (O), Race (R), Gender (G), Sibling Involvement (Z), and Screening Decision (H).

Model	Fitted Marginals	Degrees of Freedom	Likelihood Ratio Chi-square	P
1	Saturated model	0	0.00	1.000
2	All 6-way interactions	4	4.93	0.294
3	All 5-way interactions	28	23.45	0.710
4	All 4-way interactions	89	83.58	0.642
5	All 3-way interactions	174	196.33	0.118
6	All 2-way interactions	244	483.64	0.000
7	(DRH) (DGH) (NRD) (NDG) (RGD) (NZH) (NGH) (NOH) (RGH) (NRG) (NRO) (NZO) (NGO) (RGO) (ZGO) (NOD)	208	241.38	0.056

Table 13 Tests of the Net Contribution of Factors Affecting the Screening Decision.

Factor	Degrees of Freedom	Likelihood Ratio Chi-square	P
Offense type	2	966.18	0.000
Prior referrals	2	564.67	0.000
Detention decision	1	199.80	0.000
Prior referrals and type of offense	4	118.17	0.000
Prior referrals based on sex	2	9.25	0.010
Detention decision based on race	1	8.46	0.004
Race and sex	1	7.65	0.006
Detention decision, based on sex	1	7.43	0.006
Prior referrals/siblings involvement with the court	2	5.79	0.055
Sibling involvement with the court	1	4.63	0.031
Race	1	1.82	0.177
Gender	1	0.11	0.740

Table 14 Effect Parameters for Screening Decision.

	Type of Processing	
Main Effects	Informal	Formal
Offense Type		
Status	0.164	−0.164
Misdemeanor	0.320	−0.320
Felony	−0.484	0.484
Detained		
No	0.223	−0.224
Yes	−0.224	0.223
Sibling involvement		
No	0.026	−0.026
Yes	−0.026	0.026
Race		
White	0.037	−0.038
Black	−0.038	0.037
Gender		
Male	0.031	−0.031
Female	−0.031	0.031
Number of prior referrals		
None	0.455	−0.455
One	0.036	−0.036
Two or more	−0.491	0.491

Table 16 Likelihood Ratio Chi-square for Models of the Association between Number of Referrals (N), Offense Type (O), Race (R), Gender (G), Detention Decision (D), Screening Decision (H), and Final Disposition (F).

Model	Fitted Marginals	Degrees of Freedom	Likelihood Ratio Chi-square	P
1	7-way interaction (saturated model)	0	0.0	1.0
2	All 6-way interactions	44	11.28	1.0
3	All 5-way interactions	102	48.76	1.0
4	All 4-way interactions	129	150.35	0.10
5	All 3-way interactions	96	674.93	0.0
6	All 2-way interactions	42	8795.05	0.0
7	(DON) (DOS) (FHO) (ON) (ORG) (FN) (DH) (DR) (NG) (DH)	367	401.81	0.10

Table 15 Effect Parameters of Three-way Interaction with the Screening Decision.

Interaction Effect	Type of Processing	
	Informal	Formal
White, not detained	0.049	−0.049
White, detained	−0.049	0.049
Black, not detained	−0.049	0.049
Black, detained	0.049	−0.049
Male, not detained	−0.045	0.045
Male, detained	0.045	−0.045
Female, not detained	0.045	−0.045
Female, detained	−0.045	0.045
No siblings involved, status offense	−0.016	−0.016
No siblings involved, misdemeanor	0.032	−0.032
No siblings involved, felony	−0.048	0.048
Siblings involved, status offense	−0.016	0.016
Siblings involved, misdemeanor	−0.032	0.032
Siblings involved, felony	0.048	−0.048
Male, status offense	0.073	−0.073
Male, misdemeanor	−0.019	0.019
Male, felony	−0.054	0.054
Female, status offense	−0.073	0.073
Female, misdemeanor	0.019	−0.019
Female, felony	0.054	−0.054
No prior referrals, status offense	0.094	−0.094
No prior referrals, misdemeanor	0.171	−0.171
No prior referrals, felony	−0.266	0.266
One prior referral, status offense	0.005	−0.005
One prior referral, misdemeanor	−0.034	0.034
One prior referral, felony	0.029	−0.028
Two or more prior referrals, status offense	−0.100	0.100
Two or more prior referrals, misdemeanor	−0.137	0.138
Two or more prior referrals, felony	0.237	−0.237
White male	−0.055	0.055
White female	0.055	−0.055
Black male	0.055	−0.055
Black female	−0.055	0.055

Table 17 Tests of the Net Contribution of Factors Affecting the Final Disposition.

Factor	Degrees of Freedom	Net Contribution Likelihood Ratio Chi-square	P
Screening decision	2	1136.70	0.00
Screening decision based on prior referrals	4	316.96	0.00
Detention decision	2	308.63	0.00
Offense type	4	87.02	0.00
Screening decision based on type of offense	4	27.63	0.00

Table 18 Effect Parameters for Severity of Final Disposition.

Main Effects	Severity of Final Disposition Least	Moderate	Severe
Detained			
No	0.486	−0.117	−0.369
Yes	−0.486	0.117	0.369
Offense Type			
Status	−0.017	0.312	−0.295
Misdemeanor	0.166	0.001	−0.167
Felony	−0.149	−0.314	0.462
Screening Decision			
Informal	0.945	−0.654	−0.291
Formal	−0.945	0.654	0.291
Number Prior Referrals			
None	0.685	−0.798	0.112
One	−0.012	−0.045	0.056
Two or more	−0.673	0.842	−0.164

Table 19 Effect Parameters of Three-way Interaction with Severity of Final Disposition

Interaction Effect	Severity of Final Disposition		
	Least	Moderate	Severe
Status offense, informal hearing	0.149	−0.073	−0.076
Status offense, formal hearing	−0.149	0.074	0.076
Misdemeanor, informal hearing	−0.030	0.016	0.013
Misdemeanor, formal hearing	0.030	−0.016	−0.013
Felony, informal hearing	−0.120	0.057	0.063
Felony, formal hearing	0.120	−0.057	−0.063
No prior referrals, informal hearing	0.248	−0.553	0.305
No prior referrals, formal hearing	−0.248	0.553	−0.305
One prior referral, informal hearing	−0.035	−0.165	0.200
One prior referral, formal hearing	0.035	0.165	−0.200
Two or more prior referrals, informal hearing	−0.213	0.719	−0.505
Two or more prior referrals, formal hearing	0.213	−0.719	0.505

Table 20 Test of the Net Contribution of Factors Affecting Final Disposition for the Model (RF) (ONF) (ORS) (SOF) (NRS)

Factor	Degrees of Freedom	Net Contribution	
		Likelihood Ratio Chi-square	P
Offense/Prior referrals	8	42.00	0.0
Race	2	28.82	0.0
Offense/Gender	4	11.86	0.0

Bibliography

Aries, Phillippe. 1962. *Centuries of Childhood: A Social History of Family Life* (translated by Robert Baldick). New York: Knopf.

Ariessohn, Richard M. 1972. "Offense vs. Offender in Juvenile Court," *Juvenile Justice,* 23:17–22.

Arnold, William R. 1971. "Race and Ethnicity Relative to Other Factors in Juvenile Court Dispositions," *American Journal of Sociology,* 77:211–227.

Barron, Milton L. 1954. *The Juvenile in Delinquent Society.* New York: Knopf.

Bartollas, Clemens, Stuart J. Miller and Simon Dinitz. 1976. *Juvenile Victimization: The Institutional Paradox.* Beverly Hills: Sage.

Barton, William H. 1976. "Discretionary Decision-Making in Juvenile Justice," *Crime and Delinquency,* 22:470–480.

Becker, Howard S. 1973. *Outsiders: Studies on the Sociology of Deviance.* New York: Free Press.

Besharov, Douglas J. 1974. *Juvenile Justice Advocacy: Practice in a Unique Court.* New York: Practicing Law Institute.

Black, Donald J. and Albert J. Reiss, Jr. 1970. "Police Control of Juveniles," *American Sociological Review,* 35:63–67.

Blumberg, Abraham S. 1967. *Criminal Justice.* Chicago: Quadrangle.

Bortner, M. A. 1980. "Due Process and Protection: The Juvenile Court's Response to Adolescent Needs and Rights," in Max Sugar (ed.), *Responding to Adolescent Needs.* New York: Spectrum Publications.

Bottomley, A. Keith. 1973. *Decisions in the Penal Process.* London: Martin Robinson.

Brigham Young University Law Review Staff. 1976. "Status Offenses and the Status of Children's Rights: Do Children Have the Right to Be Incorrigible?" *Brigham Young University Law Review,* 1976:659–691.

Caldwell, Robert G. 1976. "The Juvenile Court: Its Development and Some Major Problems," in Rose Giallombardo (ed.), *Juvenile Delinquency.* New York: Wiley.

Carter, Timothy and Donald Clelland. 1979. "A Neo-marxian Critique, Formulation and Test of Juvenile Disposition as a Function of Social Class," *Social Problems,* 27:197–207.

Carver, Lyell H. and Paul A. White. 1968. "Constitutional Safeguards for
the Juvenile Offender: Implications of Recent Supreme Court Decisions," *Crime and Delinquency,* 14:63–72.

Cassell, Russel N. 1973. *The Psychology of Decision Making.* North
Quincy, Mass.: Christopher Publishing House.

Cavan, Ruth S. (ed.). 1975. *Readings in Juvenile Delinquency,* 3rd ed.
Philadelphia: Lippincott.

Cavan, Ruth S. and Theodore N. Ferdinand. 1975. *Juvenile Delinquency,*
3rd ed. Philadelphia: Lippincott.

Chused, Richard H. 1973. "The Juvenile Court Process: A Study of Three
New Jersey Counties," *Rutgers Law Review,* 26:488–539.

Cicourel, Aaron V. 1968. *The Social Organization of Juvenile Justice.*
New York: Wiley.

Cicourel, Aaron V. and John I. Kitsuse. 1963. *The Educational Decision-
Makers.* Indianapolis: Bobbs-Merrill.

Cloward, Richard A. and Lloyd E. Ohlin. 1960. *Delinquency and Opportunity.* New York: Free Press.

Coffey, Alan R. 1974. *Juvenile Justice as a System: Law Enforcement to
Rehabilitation.* Englewood Cliffs, N.J.: Prentice-Hall.

———1975. *The Prevention of Crime and Delinquency.* Englewood Cliffs,
N.J.: Prentice-Hall.

Cohen, Albert K. 1955. *Delinquent Boys.* Glencoe, Ill.: Free Press.

Cohen, Lawrence E. 1975. *Delinquency Dispositions: An Empirical
Analysis of Processing Decisions in Three Juvenile Courts.* U. S. Department of Justice, National Criminal Justice Information and Statistics Service. Washington, D.C.: U. S. Government Printing Office.

Cohen, Lawrence E. and James R. Kluegel. 1978. "Determinants of Juvenile Court Dispositions: Ascriptive and Achieved Factors in Two
Metropolitan Courts," *American Sociological Review,* 43:162–176.

———1979. "The Detention Decision: A Study of the Impact of Social
Characteristics and Legal Factors in Two Metropolitan Juvenile
Courts," *Social Forces,* 58:146–61.

Cohn, Yona. 1963. "Criteria for the Probation Officer's Recommendations to the Juvenile Court Judge," *Crime and Delinquency,* 9:262–
275.

Columbia Human Rights Law Review Staff (eds.). 1973. *Legal Rights of
Children: Status, Progress, and Proposals.* Fair Lawn, N.J.: R. E. Bur-
dick.

Curtis, George B. 1976. "The Checkered Career of Parens Patriae: The
State as Parent or Tyrant?" *DePaul Law Review,* 25:895–915.

Dahl, Tove Stang. 1977. "State Intervention and Social Control in Nineteenth-Century Europe." *Contemporary Crises,* 1:163–187.

Datesman, Susan K. and Frank R. Scarpitti. 1977. "Unequal Protection for Males and Females in the Juvenile Court," *Juvenile Delinquency: Little Brother Grows Up,* 59–77.

Davis, Samuel M. 1976. "Juvenile Rights During the Pre-Judicial Process," *Practical Lawyer,* 21:23–42.

Davis, Samuel M. and Susan C. Chaires. 1973. "Equal Protection for Juveniles: The Present Status of Sex-Based Discrimination in Juvenile Court Laws," *Georgia Law Review,* 7:494–532.

deMause, Lloyd (ed.). 1974. *The History of Childhood.* New York: Psycho-history Press.

Dineen, John. 1974. *Juvenile Court Organization and Status Offenses: A Statutory Profile.* Pittsburgh: National Center of Juvenile Justice.

Duffee, David and Larry Siegel. 1971. "The Organizational Man: Legal Counsel in the Juvenile Court," *Criminal Law Bulletin,* 7:544–553.

Edwards, Leonard. 1973. "The Rights of Children," *Federal Probation,* 37:34–41.

Eldefonso, Edward. 1967. *Law Enforcement and the Youthful Offender: Juvenile Procedures.* New York: Wiley.

Eldefonso, Edward and Alan R. Coffey. 1976. *Process and Impact of the Juvenile Justice System.* Beverly Hills: Glencoe Press.

Ellis, Bobbe Jean. 1976. "Juvenile Court: The Legal Process as a Rehabilitative Tool," *Washington Law Review,* 51:697–732.

Emerson, Robert M. 1969. *Judging Delinquents: Context and Process in Juvenile Court.* Chicago: Aldine.

Empey, LaMar T. 1978. *American Delinquency: Its Meaning and Construction.* Homewood, Illinois: Dorsey.

Empey, LaMar T. and Maynard L. Erickson. 1966. "Hidden Delinquency and Social Status," *Social Forces,* 44:546–554.

Erickson, Patricia G. 1974. "The Defense Lawyer's Role in Juvenile Court: An Empirical Investigation Into Judges and Social Workers' Points of View," *University of Toronto Law Journal,* 24:126–148.

Faust, Frederic L. 1974. "A Perspective on the Dilemma of Free Will and Determinism in Juvenile Justice," *Juvenile Justice,* 25:54–60.

Faust, Frederic L. and Paul J. Brantingham. 1978. *Juvenile Justice Philosophy: Readings, Cases, Comments. Criminal Justice Series,* 2nd ed. St. Paul, Minn.: West Publishing.

Ferdinand, Theodore N. and Elmer G. Luchterhand. 1979. "Inner-City Youth, the Police, the Juvenile Court and Justice," *Social Problems,* 17:510–527.

Finestone, Harold. 1976. *Victims of Change: Juvenile Delinquents in American Society.* Westport, Conn.: Greenwood.

Fletcher, George P. 1974. "The Individualization of Excusing Conditions," *Southern California Law Review,* 47:1269–1309.

Flicker, Barbara Danzinger. 1977. *Standards for Juvenile Justice: A Sum-*

mary and Analysis. Institute of Judicial Administration and American
Bar Association Juvenile Justice Standards Project. Cambridge, Mass.:
Ballinger Publishing Company.

Fox, Sanford J. 1970. "Juvenile Justice Reform: An Historical Perspective," Stanford Law Review, 22:1187–1239.

————1974. "The Reform of Juvenile Justice: The Child's Right to Punishment," Juvenile Justice, 25:2–9.

————1975. "Juvenile Justice in America: Philosophical Reforms," Human Rights, 5:63–73.

Garfinkel, Harold. 1964. "Studies of the Routine Grounds of Everyday
Activities," Social Problems, 11:225–50.

In re Gault, 387 U. S. 1 (1967).

Gaylin, William. 1974. Partial Justice: A Study of Bias in Sentencing. New
York: Vintage.

Gerth, H. H. and C. Wright Mills (eds.). 1946. From Max Weber: Essays
in Sociology. New York: Oxford.

Gibbons, Don C. 1965. Changing the Lawbreaker: The Treatment of Delinquents and Criminals. Englewood Cliffs, N.J.: Prentice-Hall.

Gibson, James L. 1978. "Race as a Determinant of Criminal Sentences:
A Methodological Critique and a Case Study." Law and Society,
12:455–478.

Giller, Henry and Allison Morris. 1976. "Children who Offend: Care,
Control or Confusion?" Criminal Law Review, Nov: 656–665.

Goffman, Erving. 1961. Asylums: Essays on the Social Situation of Mental
Patients and Other Inmates. Garden City, N.Y.: Doubleday.

Gold, Martin. 1970. Delinquent Behavior in an American City. Belmont,
Cal.: Brooks/Cole.

Golde, Peggy. 1970. Women in the Field: Anthropological Experiences.
Chicago: Aldine.

Goldman, Nathan. 1963. The Differential Selection of Juvenile Offender
for Court Appearance. Washington, D.C.: National Council on Crime
and Delinquency.

Goldstein, Joseph. 1960. "Police Discretion Not to Invoke the Criminal
Process: Low Visibility Decisions in the Administration of Justice,"
Yale Law Journal, 69:543–594.

Goldstein, Joseph, Anna Freud, and Albert J. Solnit. 1973. Beyond the
Best Interests of the Child. New York: Free Press.

Gordon, Robert A. 1976. "Prevalence-The Rare Datum in Delinquency," in M. W. Klein (ed.), The Juvenile Justice System Beverly
Hills, Calif.: Sage.

Grant, John P. 1975. "The Legal Safeguards for the Rights of the Child
and Parents in the Children's Hearing System," Juridical Review,
20:209–232.

Gross, S. G. 1970. "The Prehearing Juvenile Report: Probation Officers'

Conceptions," in Peter G. Garabedian and Don C. Gibbons (eds.), *Becoming Delinquent: Young Offender and the Correctional Process.* Chicago: Aldine.

Guttmacher, Manfred S. 1968. *The Role of Psychiatry in Law.* Springfield, Ill.: Charles C. Thomas.

Hafen, Bruce C. 1977. "Puberty, Privacy, and Protection: The Risks of Children's 'Rights,'" *American Bar Association Journal,* 63:1383–1388.

Halleck, Seymour L. 1967. *Psychiatry and the Dilemmas of Crime: A Study of Causes, Punishment, and Treatment.* New York: Harper and Row.

Handler, Joel F. 1965. "The Juvenile Court and the Adversary System: Problems of Function and Form," *Wisconsin Law Review,* 7–51.

Hartjen, Clayton A. 1974. *Crime and Criminalization,* 2nd ed. New York: Praeger.

Haskell, Martin R. and Lewis Yablonski. 1978. *Juvenile Delinquency,* 2nd ed. Chicago, Ill.: Rand McNally.

Hawes, Joseph M. 1971. *Children in Urban Society: Juvenile Delinquency in Nineteenth-Century America.* New York: Oxford.

Hirschi, Travis. 1969. *Causes of Delinquency.* Berkeley: University of California Press.

Hogarth, John. 1971. *Sentencing as a Human Process.* Toronto: University of Toronto Press.

Horwitz, Allan and Michael Wasserman. 1980. "Formal Rationality, Substantive Justice, and Discrimination: A Study of a Juvenile Court," *Law and Human Behavior,* 4:103–115.

Hufnagel, L. and J. Davidson. 1974. "Children in Need: Observations of Practices of the Denver Juvenile Court," *Denver Law Journal,* 51:337–415.

Hyde, Margaret O. 1977. *Juvenile Justice and Injustice.* New York: Watts and Franklin.

Jeffrey, Clarence Ray. 1971. *Crime Prevention Through Environmental Design.* Beverly Hills, Calif.: Sage.

Johnson, Elmer H. 1974. *Crime, Correction, and Society,* 3rd ed. Homewood, Ill.: Dorsey.

Johnson, Thomas A. 1975. *Introduction to the Juvenile Justice System.* St. Paul, Minn.: West Publishing.

Kaufman, Irving R. 1976. "Of Juvenile Justice and Injustice," *American Bar Association Journal,* 62:730–734.

Keegan, W. J. 1977. "Jury Trials for Juveniles: Rhetoric and Reality," *Pacific Law Journal,* 8:811–839.

Keiter, Robert B. 1973. "Criminal or Delinquent? A Study of Juvenile Cases Transferred to the Criminal Court," *Crime and Delinquency,* 19:528–538.

Kent v. United States. 383 U.S. 541 (1966).

Kittrie, Nicholas N. 1971. *The Right to be Different: Deviance and Enforced Therapy.* Baltimore: Johns Hopkins University Press.

Klein, Malcolm W. (ed.), 1976. *The Juvenile Justice System.* Beverly Hills: Sage.

Kleinbaum, David G. and Lawrence L. Kupper. 1978. *Applied Regression Analysis and Other Multivariable Methods.* North Scituate, Mass.: Duxbury.

Kramer, John H. and Darrel J. Steffensmeier. 1978. "The Differential Detention/Jailing of Juveniles: A Comparison of Detention and Non-Detention Courts," *Pepperdine Law Review,* 5:796–807.

Krisberg, Barry and James Austin, (eds.). 1978. *The Children Ishmael: Critical Perspectives on Juvenile Justice.* Palo Alto, Calif.: Mayfield.

LaFave, Wayne. 1965. *Arrest: The Decision to Take into Custody.* Boston: Little, Brown.

Lefstein, Norman, Vaughan Stapleton, and Lee Teitelbaum. 1969. "In Search of Juvenile Justice: Gault and Its Implementation," *Law and Society Review,* 3:491–562.

Lemert, Edwin M. 1970. *Social Action and Legal Change: Revolution Within the Juvenile Court.* Chicago: Aldine.

Liska, Allen E. and Mark Tausig. 1979. "Theoretical Interpretations of Social Class and Racial Differentials in Legal Decision-Making for Juveniles," *Sociological Quarterly,* 20:197–209.

Mack, Julian W. 1909. "The Juvenile Court," *Harvard Law Review,* 23:104–122.

Mangrum, R. Collin. 1974. "Detours on the Road to Maturity: A View of the Legal Conception of Growing Up and Letting Go," *Law and Contemporary Problems,* 39:78–92.

Martin, John J. 1970. *Toward a Political Definition of Delinquency.* U.S. Department of Health, Education and Welfare. Washington, D.C.: Government Printing Office.

Matza, David. 1964. *Delinquency and Drift.* New York: Wiley.

McCall, George. 1978. *Observing The Law: Field Methods in the Study of Crime and the Criminal Justice System.* New York: Free Press.

McCleary, Richard. 1975. "How Structural Variables Constrain the Parole Officer's Use of Discretionary Powers," *Social Problems,* 23:209–225.

McDonough, J. Norman, Donald B. King and James E. Garrett. 1970. *Juvenile Court Handbook.* South Hackensack, N.J.: Rothman.

Meade, Anthony. 1974. "Seriousness of Delinquency, the Adjudication Decision and Recidivism: A Longitudinal Configurational Analysis," *Journal of Criminal Law and Criminology,* 64:478–86.

Mennel, Robert M. 1973. *Thorns and Thistles: Juvenile Delinquents in the United States.* New Hampshire: University Press of New England.

Miller, Frank W., Robert O. Dawson, George E. Dix, and Raymond I. Parnas. 1971. *The Juvenile Justice Process.* Mineola, N.Y.: Foundation Press.

Mills, C. Wright. 1942. "The Professional Ideology of Social Pathologists," *American Journal of Sociology,* 49:165–80.

Neigher, Alan. 1967. "The Gault Decision: Due Process and the Juvenile Courts," *Federal Probation,* 31:8–18.

Nyquist, Ola. 1975. *Juvenile Justice. Cambridge Studies in Criminality,* vol. 12. Westport, Conn.: Greenwood.

Paulsen, Monrad G. 1957. "Fairness to the Juvenile Offender," *Minnesota Law Review,* 41:547–576.

Piliavin, Irving and Scott Briar. 1964. "Police Encounters with Juveniles," *American Journal of Sociology,* 70:206–214.

Platt, Anthony. 1977. *The Child Savers: The Invention of Delinquency,* 2nd ed. Chicago: University of Chicago Press.

Polk, Kenneth, Dean Frease, and F. Lynn Richmond. 1974. "Social Class, School Experience and Delinquency," *Criminology,* 12:84–96.

Rainwater, Lee and David J. Pittman. 1967. "Ethical Problems in Studying Politically Sensitive and Deviant Communities," *Social Problems,* 14:357–366.

Reasons, Charles E. 1970. "Gault: Procedural Change and Substantive Effect," *Crime and Delinquency,* 16:163–171.

Reaves, Randolph P. 1976. "The Right to Treatment for Juvenile Offenders," *Cumberland Law Review,* 7:13–28.

Reckless, Walter C. 1961. "A New Theory of Delinquency and Crime," *Federal Probation,* 25:42–46.

Rodman, Hyman and Paul Grams. 1967. "Juvenile Delinquency in the Family," in *President's Commission on Law Enforcement and Administration of Justice, Juvenile Delinquency and Youth Crime.* Washington, D.C.: U.S. Government Printing Office.

Rosenheim, Margaret K. (ed.). 1962. *Justice For the Child: The Juvenile Court in Transition.* New York: Free Press.

Rosenheim, Margaret K. (ed.). 1976. *Pursuing Justice for the Child.* Chicago: University of Chicago Press.

Rothman, David J. 1980. *Conscience and Convenience: The Asylum and its Alternatives in Progressive America.* Boston: Little, Brown.

Ryerson, Ellen. 1978. *The Best-Laid Plans: America's Juvenile Court Experiment.* New York: Hill and Wang.

Sanders, William B. 1976. *Juvenile Delinquency.* New York: Praeger.

Scarpitti, Frank R. and Richard M. Stephenson. 1971. "Juvenile Court Dispositions: Factors in the Decision-Making Process," *Crime and Delinquency,* 17:142–151.

Schlossman, Steven L. 1977. *Love and the American Delinquent: The Theory and Practice of "Progressive" Juvenile Justice, 1825–1920.* Chicago: University of Chicago Press.

Schur, Edwin M. 1973. *Radical Nonintervention: Rethinking the Delinquency Problem.* Englewood Cliffs, N.J.: Prentice-Hall.

Sellin, Thorsten J. and Marvin E. Wolfgang. 1964. *The Measurement of Delinquency.* New York: Wiley.

Short, James F. and F. Ivan Nye. 1970. "Extent of Unrecorded Juvenile Delinquency: Tentative Conclusions," in P. G. Garabedian and D. C. Gibbons, (eds.), *Becoming Delinquent: Young Offenders and the Correctional Process.* Chicago: Aldine.

Shubow, Lawrence D. and Jeremy A. Stahlin. 1977. "Juvenile in Court: A Look at a System in Flux" *Massachusetts Law Quarterly,* 61:193–197.

Shullenberger, John D. and Patrick T. Murphy. 1973. "The Crisis in Juvenile Court—Is Bifurcation an Answer?" *Chicago Bar Record,* 55:117–128.

Shulman, Harry M. 1961. *Juvenile Delinquency in American Society.* New York: Harper and Row.

Siegel, Larry J., Joseph J. Senna, and Therese J. Libby. 1976. "Legal Aspects of the Juvenile Justice Process: An Overview of Current Practices and Law" *New England Law Review,* 12:223–264.

Simpson, Anna L. 1976. "Rehabilitation as the Justification of a Separate Juvenile Justice System," *California Law Review,* 64:984–1017.

Sjoberg, Gideon (ed.). 1967. *Ethics, Politics, and Social Research.* Cambridge, Mass.: Schenkman.

Smith, Kenneth C. 1974. "A Profile of Juvenile Court Judges in the United States," *Juvenile Justice,* 25:27–38.

Stern, David, Sandra Smith and Fred Doolittle. 1975. "How Children Used to Work," *Law and Contemporary Problems,* 39:93–117.

Sumner, Helen. 1970. "Locking Them Up," National Council on Crime and Delinquency: Western Region.

Susman, Jackwell. 1973. "Juvenile Justice: Even-Handed or Many-Handed?" *Crime and Delinquency,* 19:493–507.

Sussman, Alan N. 1977. *The Rights of Young People: The Basic American Civil Liberties Union Guide to a Young Person's Rights.* New York: Avon.

Sudnow, David. 1965. "Normal Crimes: Sociological Features of the Penal Code in a Public Defender Office," *Social Problems,* 12:255–276.

Sykes, Gresham. 1958. *The Society of Captives.* Princeton, N.J.: Princeton University Press.

Tappan, Paul W. 1946. "Treatment Without Trial," *Social Forces,* 24:306–320.

Tappan, Paul W. 1949. *Juvenile Delinquency.* New York: McGraw-Hill.

Teitelbaum, Lee E. and Aidan R. Gough (eds.). 1977. *Beyond Control: Status Offenders in the Juvenile Court.* Cambridge, Mass.: Ballinger.

Terry, Robert M. 1967. "The Screening of Juvenile Offenders," *Journal of Criminal Law, Criminology and Police Science,* 58:173–181.

Thomas, Charles W. 1976. "Are Status Offenders Really so Different?: A Comparative and Longitudinal Assessment," *Crime and Delinquency,* 22:438–455.

Thomas, Charles W. and Robin J. Cage. 1977. "The Effect of Social Characteristics on Juvenile Court Dispositions," *The Sociological Quarterly,* 18:237–252.

Thomas, Charles W. and Christopher M. Sieverdes. 1975. "Juvenile Court Intake: An Analysis of Discretionary Decision-Making," *Criminology,* 12:413–432.

Thornberry, Terrance P. 1973. "Race, Socioeconomic Status and Sentencing in the Juvenile Justice System," *Journal of Criminal Law and Criminology,* 64:90–98.

Von Pfeil, Helena P. 1974. *Juvenile Rights Since 1967: An Annotated Indexed Bibliography of Selected Articles and Books.* South Hackensack, N.J.: Rothman.

Voss, Harwin L. 1966. "Socio-economic Status and Reported Delinquent Behavior," *Social Problems,* 13:314–324.

Wales, Heathcote W. 1976. "An Analysis of the Proposal to "Abolish" the Insanity Defense in S. 1: Squeezing a Lemon," *University of Pennsylvania Law Review,* 124:687–712.

Wax, Rosalie. 1971. *Doing Fieldwork: Warnings and Advice.* Chicago: University of Chicago Press.

Weiner, Norman L. and Charles V. Willie. 1971. "Decisions by Juvenile Officers." *American Journal of Sociology,* 77:199–210.

Williams, Jay R. and Martin Gold. 1972. "From Delinquent Behavior to Official Delinquency," *Social Problems,* 20:209–229.

Wilkinson, Karen. 1974. "The Broken Family and Juvenile Delinquency: Scientific Explanation or Ideology?" *Social Problems,* 21:726–739.

In re Winship, 397 U.S. 358 (1970).

Wolfgang, Marvin E. and Franco Ferracuti. 1967. *The Subculture of Violence: Towards an Integrated Theory in Criminology.* New York: Tavistock.

Wolfgang, Marvin E., Robert M. Figlio, and Thorsten Sellin. 1972. *Delinquency in a Birth Cohort.* Chicago: University of Chicago Press.

Wooden, Kenneth. 1976. *Weeping in the Playtime of Others: America's Incarcerated Children.* New York: McGraw-Hill.

Index

Adjudication, 38-39, 44-46
  "fact finding" portion, 39
  level of proof necessary, 39
  pretrial conferences, 44-46
Adult court,
  transfer of juveniles to, 7, 60-61
  distinction between juvenile court
    and, 5
Aries, Phillippe, 14 n.3
Arnold, William R., 171
"Art of interpretation," 213, 215-223
  evaluation of juvenile's character,
    213-214
Attitude, court assessment of, 206-210,
  212-214
  negative characteristics, 212-213
  positive characteristics, 219-223
Attorneys,
  defense, 47-48, 52-56, 136-142
  prosecutors, 24, 45

Black, Donald J., 27, 92 n.1
Blumberg, Abraham S., 5, 8, 13 n.2
Bortner, M. A., 12
Briar, Scott, 27, 92 n.1, 150, 171
Brantingham, Paul J., 3, 4, 6, 47

Caldwell, Robert G., 5
Charres, Susan C., 10
Cicourel, Aaron V., 18, 36 n.5, 62 n.5,
  185 n.1, 197
Cohen, Albert K., 10
Cohen, Lawrence E., 11, 149, 171
Contested hearings, 44-46

Dahl, Tove Stang, 2
Davidson, J., 43, 62 n.5, 137
Davis, Samuel M., 10
Decision-makers,
  role descriptions, 23-26
  training of, 246-249
deMause, Lloyd, 14 n.3
Demeanor of juvenile, impact on deci-
  sions, 207-208, 212-223
Department of Corrections, 60
Depersonalization of clients, 11-12
  role of juveniles, 11-12
Detention decision, 28-33
Discrimination, charges of, 10-11
  racial, 148-151, 154-164
  sexual, 165-170
  social class, 170-174, 181-186
Disposition, 46-60
Doolittle, Fred, 14 n.3
Drug involvement, 125-126
Duffee, David, 14 n.4, 137, 147 n.3

Ellis, Bobbe Jean, 5, 12
Emerson, Robert M., 10, 12, 36 n.5, 47,
  62 n.5, 92 n.4, 137, 185 n.1, 197,
  207
Empey, LaMar T., 150
Erickson, Maynard L., 150

Family stability, court assessment of,
  187-188, 197-200, 203-206
  parental supervision, 188, 193, 197
  impact of social status, 197
Faust, Frederick L., 3, 4, 6, 47

Female delinquency, 165-170
  status offenses, 167-170
Ferdinand, Theodore N., 27
Fletcher, George P., 13 n.8
Flicker, Barbara Danzinger, 10, 170
Formal processing, 17, 36-60
  adjudication, 38-39, 44-46
  contested hearings, 44-46
  disposition, 46-60
  initial hearing, 39-44
  pretrial conferences, 44-46
Frease, Dean, 11, 149

Garfinkel, Harold, 18
Gerth, H. H., 8
Goffman, Erving, 11
Gold, Martin, 92 n.1, 150, 171
Goldman, Nathan, 27, 92 n.1
Goldstein, Joseph, 92 n.1
Gordon, Robert A., 11, 149
Grams, Paul, 187
"Great Synthesis," 224-227, 241-242
  role of intuition, 240-241

Haskell, Martin R., 12
Hawes, Joseph M., 5
Hearing officers, 23-24, 93-94, 143-147
Hirschi, Travis, 187
Hufnagel, L., 43, 62 n.5, 137

Individualized justice, 1-4, 8-9, 146-
  147, 243-251
  juvenile needs and characteristics, 1-2
  lack of criminal intent, 3-4
  lack of uniformity, 244-246
  larger context, 249-251
Informal processing, 35-36
Initial hearing, 39-44

Jeffrey, Charles Ray, 5
Johnson, Elmer H., 5, 37 n.6
Job opportunities, lack of, 23, 91
Johnson, Thomas A., 62 n.7
Juvenile court,
  criticisms of, 9-13, 15
  lack of commitment to adversary pro-
    cess, 142
  traditional philosophy, 1-8
Juvenile rights, 6-7, 12

Kluegel, James R., 11, 149, 171
Krisberg, Barry, 2

LaFave, Wayne, 92 n.1
Lefstein, Norman, 14 n.4
Lemert, Edwin M., 10, 12
Luchterhand, Elmer G., 27

Mack, Julian W., 13 n.1
Marks, F. Raymond, 14 n.3
Martin, John J., 10, 149, 170
Matza, David, 8, 206
McCall, George, 16
Mennel, Robert N., 2, 13 n.3
Mills, C. Wright, 8
"Moral character," court's assessment
  of, 207

Neigher, Alan, 39
Nye, F. Ivan, 150

Offense as factor in decisions, 102-105,
  117-118, 123-127
  definition of "seriousness," 103-105
  mitigating circumstances, 105, 117-
    118

Parens patriae, doctrine of, 1-4
Parental,
  referrals to court, 72-73, 150-151
  response to child's delinquency, 126,
    174, 192-197
Petition, delinquency, 17, 39
Paulsen, Monrad G., 13 n.1
Piliavin, Irving, 27, 92 n.1, 150, 171
Platt, Anthony, 2, 6, 10, 14 n.4, 137,
  149, 170
Plea bargaining, 46, 62
Police decisions, 28-29, 63-64, 66-68
  detention decision, 28, 66
  lack of uniformity, 64
  delay in referral, 67
Police brutality, allegations of, 67-68
Polk, Kenneth, 11, 149
Positivistic criminology, 4-5
Positive recidivism, 128
Presiding officer, impact on decisions,
  143-147

legalistic versus treatment orientation, 143-145
variation in dispositions, 146-147
Probation officer,
  role, 25-26
  recommendations of, 46
Pretrial conferences, 44-46
Protection of community, 5-6
Psychological services, 24-26

Racial identity, impact on decisions, 148-151, 154-164
Referral to court,
  number of prior referrals as factor in decision-making, 123-126, 128-132
  parental, 72-73
  school, 71-72
Referral process, 27-28
Reiss, Albert J., Jr., 27, 92 n.1
Research in juvenile court, 15-20
Retributionist argument, 5-6
Richmond, F. Lynn, 11, 149
Rodman, Hyman, 187
Rosenheim, Margaret K., 13
Rothman, David J., 2
Ryerson, Ellen, 2

Sanders, William B., 3
Scientific social work, 2-5, 240-241
Schlossman, Steven L., 2
School, involvement with courts, 71-72
Schur, Edwin M., 10, 149, 170
Screening decision, 33-34
  formal processing, 36-60
  informal processing, 35-36
  siblings of prior clients, 34

Sexual identity, impact on decisions, 165-170
Short, James F., 150
Smith, Sandra, 14 n.3
Social characteristics, influence in decision making, 148-149
Social class, impact on decisions, 170-174, 181-186
  private attorneys, 172-174
Social investigation and file, 97-101, 198-201, 203-206
Spiegel, Larry, 14 n.4, 137, 147 n.3
Stapleton, Vaughn, 14 n.4
Status offenses, 17, 103-104, 167-170
  sex bias in detention and treatment of, 20, 101-104
Statutes, juvenile, 26-27
Stern, David, 14 n.3
Stigmatization of juveniles, 9-10
Supreme court decisions, 6-7, 47
Sussman, Alan N., 37, 62 n.7

Tappan, Paul W., 13 n.1, 25
Teitelbaum, Lee E., 14 n.4
Terry, Robert M., 10, 149, 171
Thomas, Charles W. and Robin J. Cage, 170
Thornberry, Terrance P., 10, 149
Transfer to adult court (certification), 60-61
Treatment, agencies, 82, 244-245

Waite, Edward E., 13 n.1
Wales, Heathcote W., 3
Williams, Jay R., 92 n.1, 150, 171
Wilkinson, Karen, 187

Yablonski, Lewis, 12